CLEVELAND BROWNS

THE OFFICIAL ILLUSTRATED HISTORY

Writer, Editorial Director

RON SMITH

Design

MICHAEL NYERGES

Photographic Coordinator

ALBERT DICKSON

Prepress Project Coordinator

STEVE ROMER

Co-Writers

JOE HOPPEL

MARK CRAIG

DAVE SLOAN

"The signing of Paul Brown to coach and operate the Cleveland team in the new All-America Football Conference indicates that this organization will be a strong postwar factor in the anticipated mushrooming of professional football."

— THE SPORTING NEWS, February, 1945

The Sporting News books may be purchased for business or sales promotional use. For more information, you may write:

The Sporting News
10176 Corporate Square Dr., Suite 200
St. Louis, MO 63132

Published by The Sporting News
sportingnews.com

Distributed by NTC/Contemporary Publishing Inc.
4255 West Touhy Ave.
Lincolnwood, IL 60646-1975

ISBN: 0-89204-625-2

Printed in the United States of America

CONTENTS

Foreword

The 1999 Cleveland Browns may be an expansion team, but we are not an expansion franchise. We are attempting to design this organization to accommodate the space-age requirements that are anticipated in the next millennium. The structure of our metaphoric intergalactic vehicle is reinforced by the strength of our legendary past and it will be fueled by the unparalleled passion of a fan base that takes its commitment to the Browns to a level that simulates a religious experience.

I witnessed first-hand the effect of the former team's move to Baltimore, due to the fact I was a member of the NFL Finance Committee during the period surrounding the Cleveland saga. It became immediately apparent that the ramifications of that move would be extremely negative for the NFL in terms of fan reaction. I also felt that, notwithstanding the fan reaction, it would be impossible for the Cleveland community to effectively counteract this move by somehow retaining or obtaining a team that could continue the tradition of the Browns during the remainder of this generation.

Shortly after the initial shockwave of the news relating to the Baltimore relocation, I became acquainted with the efforts of the Cleveland leadership group relative to its crusade to keep the dream and reality of the Cleveland Browns alive. I gave these valiant community warriors a great deal of credit for their effort but little chance for success. However, the sheer force and intensity of the spirit of the legions from Cleveland came to a crescendo that resulted in the imposition of their will upon the decision-makers of the NFL. The "refusal to quit" caused everyone involved or related to this situation to view this phenomenon with a sense of awe and amazement. Several months later, Cleveland was promised a team that would bear the name Cleveland Browns and it became apparent to the entire sports world that the *fans* had won.

Fate and good fortune provided me with the occasion to meet Mr. Al Lerner in July 1998. A relationship developed that extended to me one of the greatest opportunities that was ever created in professional sport— the privilege of assembling an organization in one of the greatest sports cities in America. Al Lerner understood from the very beginning that the most valuable asset the Cleveland Browns would acquire would not be their new glistening stadium located on Lake Erie—it would be the depth and level of commitment from their fans.

The compact reached with the people of Cleveland is probably the greatest success story the NFL has experienced in the last 20 years in terms of its response to the voice of the fan. Although Al Lerner and I intend to be contributing partners to the NFL cause, our first priority will be to the people who support and cherish *their* Cleveland Browns. We are caretakers of the flame that burns very brightly here in Cleveland. Our goal is to help guide this organization to a level of accomplishment that generates trophies and civic pride.

Carmen A. Policy

A New Beginning

I t had been home for Otto, The Toe, Dante, Dub, J.B., Do It Pruitt, Big Daddy, Michael Dean, Bernie and Ernie, Ozzie and many other colorful characters. The Man in the Brown Suit was a regular there, as were Big Dawg, his barking buddies and the Muni parking lot chefs who spent fall Sunday mornings engulfed by delicious smokescreens. One Brown raised seven championship flags there, another raised eyebrows with his rushing exploits. Its fans will never forget the ice and snow, the rain and mud, the swirling winds, Red Right 88, The Drive and, of course, Stadium Dogs topped by Stadium Mustard.

Cleveland fans felt understandably violated on November 25, 1996, when a half-century of emotion was released into the winds of Lake Erie by a wrecking ball that pounded venerable Cleveland Municipal Stadium into submission. It was a passing of consequence, the last rites for a house of passion and tradition. Orange and Brown tears colored the landscape of Northeast Ohio. A city lost a piece of its soul—and it found a new beginning.

Call it a rebirth, a necessary cleansing, the tearing down of one Browns legacy so construction could begin on another. The seeds for that new legacy had been planted by National Football League officials with two promises—that a new Browns team, replacing the one that had been spirited off to Baltimore after the 1995 season, would begin play in 1999 and that the original Browns' history would remain property of Cleveland. New ownership, new stadium, new players. Old memories, old tradition, same old passion. Three painful seasons without football only heightened the fervor of bonding that would link player and team—the very essence of Cleveland Browns football.

"(Cleveland fans) know and support the game of football. They have the ability to

The 1996 demolition of Cleveland Stadium (above) cleared the way for constuction of a new legacy, which began with the purchase of the new Browns by Lerner (left, right photo) and the No. 1 selection of Couch in the draft.

accept you based on your talent," says Jim Brown, who spent nine incredible seasons bonding with fans and earning praise as the greatest running back in NFL history. "They have the ability to love you and when they grow up with you, they will express that.

"When I wrote my book *Out of Bounds*, I went into the Cleveland area for a signing session. And in those long lines were grandparents and great grandparents and they said to their offsprings, 'This is a great man.' It was the first time I recognized how football could play in the lives of fans. A lot of fathers and sons, fathers and daughters, mothers and daughters will grow up with you. And the attitude that you had on the field added to their family relationship. That's kind of deep."

It has been that way since 1946, when 60,135 fans piled into 15-year-old Cleveland Stadium to get their first look at the new All-America Football Conference creation of Ohio product Paul Brown, the man who would give life, vitality and his name to a baby-boomer franchise. The Browns became his family, the fans an extended family that always provided support. It was an alliance that would be passed from generation to generation.

"There's a loyalty there," explains former offensive tackle Doug Dieken. "You know, everybody talks about the traditions of the Motleys and the Grahams and the Kellys and the Kosars and the Sipes. But I hear so many people say, 'You know, my dad used to bring me down here and I'm bringing my son.' The real tradition is for the different generations bringing their kids down and now it's your turn to bring your young ones down."

That family passion was stoked by seven AAFC and NFL championships in the franchise's first 10 years and increased with every passing season, carrying the city through the dark times of burning rivers, "Mistake by the Lake" jokes and financial devastation to a metropolitan revival, featuring a cleaner, sleeker image and a growing civic pride. Such pride has

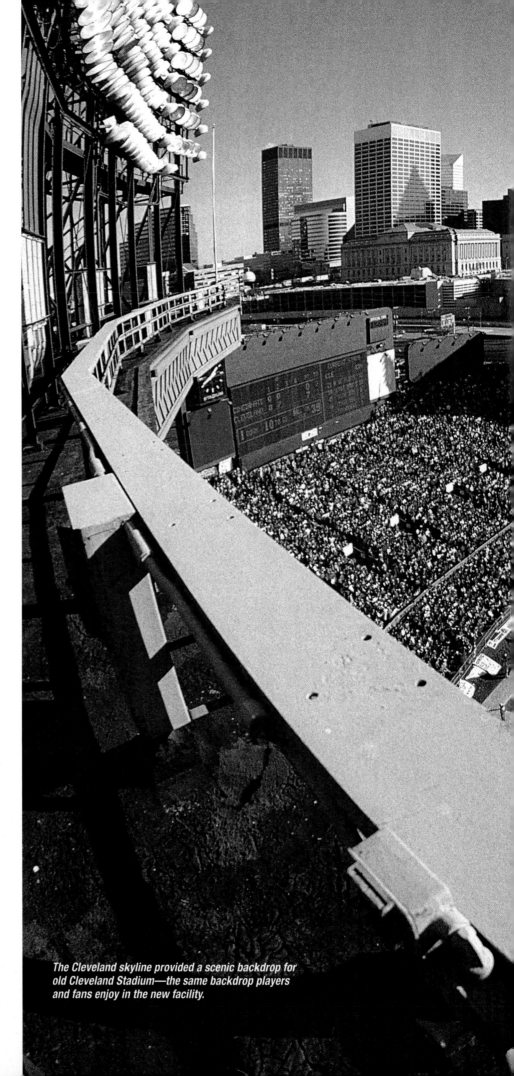

The Cleveland skyline provided a scenic backdrop for old Cleveland Stadium—the same backdrop players and fans enjoy in the new facility.

always been the driving force for Cleveland and football has often been the means to that end.

"The fans' commitment to the team has always been the thing that amazed me," says former defensive tackle Bob Golic. "At the time I was playing with the Browns, the Indians were absolutely horrible, the Cavaliers were only so-so. We were the only real successful show in town. The commitment to the team was incredible, and not just on Sundays or functions the players go to. The fans were always proud.

"The entire city, you couldn't talk to a person without them going, 'Go Browns, yeah!' It's like the whole city knows football and has committed itself to the Browns. It wasn't like they just fed off of us. We fed off of them, too, to see the kind of response we got no matter what we did. We as players, absolutely, felt there was nowhere else in the country we could get this kind of support."

And with such absolute, tunnel-vision commitment.

"Wherever you went, people knew about the Browns, at the market, the mall, the store, fast food, anyplace," says former linebacker Clay Matthews. "It was really important to them."

The fervor that fuels Cleveland football began regenerating on

John 'Big Dawg' Thompson and the team's mascot (left) were fitting symbols of the football fervor supplied in large doses by passionate Browns fans and responsive players like Sipe (right photo).

September 8, 1998, when the NFL awarded Al Lerner an expansion franchise and it took center stage in 1999 as Lerner's new Browns, constructed in the image of team president Carmen Policy much as the original team took on the identity of Paul Brown, prepared for their debut in the new Cleveland Browns Stadium. The link between old and new is not lost on even the casual observer. Paul Brown's first roster was filled with former players at Ohio State and Massillon High, schools where he had built his coaching legacy. Policy's first roster is dotted with former San Francisco 49ers, the organization he helped reach Super Bowl heights. The new stadium is built on the same ground as the old—with the same configuration and open East end. Former Browns are a welcome presence and part of the team's marketing strategy.

"I like the way we're building the foundation," says former quarterback and Youngstown, Ohio, product Bernie Kosar, a consultant with the new team and one of the most popular players in Browns history. "I think it's really important to lay your

foundation first, to gear toward being a good, consistent winning organization. I love the sense of family we're setting within the organization. And the commitment to the team. One of the nice things I see materializing is that team atmosphere."

That blueprint was provided by Brown more than 50 years ago and followed in successful construction by numerous professional franchises. Brown, always the innovator and stickler for detail, was an instant winner because he built around character players, stressed consistency and emphasized a "we are family," team-first dedication.

"Everybody was like a family," says Dante Lavelli, an outstanding wide receiver for Cleveland teams that dominated the AAFC from 1946-49 and the NFL from 1950-55. "The thing Brown used to say is, 'You're killing our team.' That was his favorite expression. You dropped a pass or missed a block or had a fumble, he said, 'You know, you're killing our team.' It was always team. Not you're hurting this, or Lavelli, you're doing this. It was always the team concept.

"Then, 25 or 30 players always stayed together and built like a family. Nobody had any money, so everybody pitched in and helped each other. I think that was the big development in the original Cleveland Browns."

Cleveland loves its heroes, as typified by the huge mural (above, left page) that once honored Lou Groza, Graham and Warfield in a parking lot on West 3rd Street. A faded 'Go Browns' mural still decorates the side of another downtown building (below left). Abe Abraham (above), a k a 'The Man in the Brown Suit,' was a sideline fixture during Browns games for many years—the kind of tradition the new Browns will develop. The player is former running back Calvin Hill.

they tabbed quarterback Tim Couch with the No. 1 overall pick in their first-ever draft—another link to the past. The first player Brown signed in 1946, quarterback Graham, was the cornerstone for his championship legacy and the standard by which all future Cleveland field generals would be judged.

Whether Couch possesses a Graham-like winning ability is unclear, but there's no doubt he will be accorded a hero status by fans starving for football. That became obvious during a post-draft minicamp when the Browns decided to move their 107 players outdoors after a closed indoor first day of practice. A group of about 200 fans, who stumbled onto the workout at Strongsville Center Junior High, stood and roared when Couch, working in shorts and helmet, fired a 55-yard touchdown pass to Leslie Shepherd during an 11-on-11 drill.

The red carpet also was being rolled out for old-Browns-new-Browns Antonio Langham and Orlando Brown and veteran linebacker Chris Spielman, a Canton-born former Cleveland fan who reached legendary status with his play at Massillon High and Ohio State before going on to professional success with the Lions and Bills. But special treatment was in store for all players on the first-year roster and rave reviews were being tossed about for management's approach to building a winning team.

"They're not only bringing in people of talent, but people of character," Dieken says. "In Chris Spielman, you're bringing in somebody who has leadership ability, somebody who has intensity, somebody who doesn't tolerate losing. It's that upper-third mentality. You always hear that teams have an upper third, a middle third and a lower third. When you're winning, it brings the lower third up. And when you're losing, it goes the other way.

"When you bring in people with character, I think Carmen likes

Couch and his No. 2 jersey could be Cleveland fixtures for many years, as could Cleveland Browns Stadium (top photo), which fittingly was built on the same location as the old stadium. The fervor gripping the new franchise was illustrated by countdown clocks (below, right page) located throughout the city in anticipation of the first 1999 kickoff.

to say 'heart,' you increase your chances."

Clark describes it more pragmatically.

"Our philosophy is to find players we think will still be here in three years," he says. "We are building for the future. We won't do anything to jeopardize our future. We aren't trying to impress anybody in 1999."

Cleveland fans don't care about being impressed. They just want football. The wide-eyed players, getting their first serious dose of the professional game, Cleveland-style, were being swallowed whole by the fan frenzy that already had gripped northeast Ohio by midsummer. All 1999 home games had been sold out by April. Luxury suites were added to the original stadium layout because the original ones were snapped up so quickly, creating a long waiting list. Digital clocks, broken down to one-hundredth of a second and located at shopping malls and bars throughout the city, were counting down to the kickoff at the August 21 preseason home opener. Hopeful fans were paying a yearly, non-refundable $20 fee just to get on the season-ticket waiting list. What had been billed as "The Summer of Love" was also the "Summer of Animosity," thanks to a trash-talking website battle that renewed the old rivalry with the Steelers and instigated a bitter new rivalry with the Ravens. Such craziness was not without precedent.

"You have 100 percent of the Cleveland people who breathe football," says former cornerback Frank Minnifield. "When we won the Central Division in

1987, they put helmets on the statues downtown. They put Orange and Brown helmets on the statues. It wasn't a prank, it wasn't a gimmick. It was Cleveland."

With a Hall of Fame game meeting with the Cowboys only six weeks away, thousands of Browns fans, decked out in Orange and Brown, Dawg uniforms and every other franchise affiliation tag imaginable, trekked to the Hiram College campus for a Browns reunion that featured more than 130 former players and coaches as well as new coach Chris Palmer. It was symbolic, an appropriate meeting of the old and the new, a mingling of tradition and hope. At least one northeast Ohio native wants to see that mingling process continue.

"Hopefully, with the new Browns the tradition will be bigger and better than it was in the past," says Hall of Fame wide receiver Paul Warfield. "The tradition is there and there's a lot to live up to, but hopefully the new organization and the players who wear those colors will wear them with the same pride and bring the performances to the people of Cleveland that have occurred in the past."

FRANCHISE
1946-1995
LEGENDS

Cleveland Stadium

From its 1931 grand opening to its 1996 demolition, Cleveland Stadium was a proud host to baseball, football and numerous other popular events ranging from tractor pulls to rock concerts. The venerable landmark on the shores of Lake Erie was a house of passion, the place where dreams lived and died. It was the only home the Browns ever knew, from their dominating opening game in 1946 to their emotional goodbye a half century later.

The Stadium meant a lot to Cleveland sports fans, but it also was important to the men who performed there. On the following pages, former players share their thoughts and memories on the

Doug Dieken, 1971-1984:

"The walk down the tunnel from the locker room. The locker room was never accused of being large. Once you got through the pep talk and prayer, you went down this set of steps and then, probably a good 40 or 50 yards, you got into the tunnel. With pads on you could only walk single file. And they had the wooden boards and you had on your cleats and you could just hear the cleats go, 'Click, click, click, click, click.' Otherwise it was pretty quiet in there. When you got to the bottom, which was where the dugout was, you started to come into the dugout and a helmet would come outside and all of a sudden you could hear the people. It was instant fans, like, 'Here's a switch, let's turn 'em on.' It kind of overwhelmed you."

Clay Matthews, 1978-1993:

"The way that you had to approach the field. You went down through this narrow tunnel that smelled like it was 100 years old and then you'd come up into a dugout that was always full of water and mud and right when you came out, the people were always so loud. You know, you would go down this tunnel and it wasn't the most impressive or clean thing in the world and you'd pop out and all those folks would cheer and yell and you'd realize that it was worth it."

Lou Groza, 1946-1959, 1961-1967:

"The first time through (the tunnel) was a sensation. You didn't know how long that thing was going to be. You go from the locker room, down the stairs and into the tunnel. The only thing I could think of, coming from Martins Ferry, was the sensation those guys had going into the coal mines."

Bob Golic, 1982-1988:

"I remember the layout of the locker room. It was amazing. About two-thirds of the lockers downstairs, about one-third of the lockers upstairs. It was just kind of cold and damp. And I remember the winds coming off the lake, just absolutely amazing. The way the Green Bay Packers felt about Lambeau was nothing to the way we felt about Cleveland Stadium. Ask any team that came to Cleveland to play from mid-November on, they'll tell you about the frozen tundra."

Farewell to a friend

It was appropriately dubbed "The Final Play," a nostalgic sendoff for Cleveland's oldest and grandest sports icon. When the city opened the Cleveland Municipal Stadium doors for a sendoff party on September 21 and 22, 1996, an estimated 100,000 fans trudged through to experience the aura one more time and say an emotional farewell.

The weekend was both festive and sad, an opportunity to revisit wonderful memories and mourn the passing of an era. Vendors booths ringed the playing field and colorful banners hung from the upper-deck facades. Activities (field-goal kicking, end zone diving) spiced up the action and a big-screen television, erected near the Dawg Pound, showed continuous highlights of Browns football.

Fans dressed in Cleveland sports-related attire braved harsh weather to roam the field, the concourse and the Dawg Pound for the last time.

Free tickets for the two-day event went quickly. So did the memorabilia— the scoreboard, bricks, the stadium flag, lockers and assorted other items— when it was auctioned on September 24 and 25. One month later, the facility, which played host to numerous events over its 66 years, was torn down, creating space for the new Cleveland Browns Stadium that would be erected for the 1999 football season.

These snapshots of Cleveland Stadium—its exterior in 1955 (top photo), players emerging from the tunnel before a game (above) and the wooden seats of the stadium concourse (left)—are reminders of a facility that began as just a building, but evolved into a second home for Browns fans.

Jim Brown, 1957-1965:

"I remember the size of it and the weather. It was cold, that wind coming off the lake. Unbelievable. I hated the baseball infield because I didn't want to run on that dirt. It was like an enemy. On the other hand, you knew the opposition wasn't going to be comfortable in that stadium because it was cold. But it was a place on the lake, baby, and if you couldn't stand cold weather, you couldn't come there."

Dub Jones, 1948-1955:

"I thought the stadium site was the most beautiful in the nation, right on the lake in downtown Cleveland. It wasn't all that great to play in sometimes. It could be tough. The wind was tricky. The turf was awful. We had a lot of games on frozen fields. But it was all part of football."

Frank Ryan, 1962-1968:

"It was just spectacular, immense. It was the biggest stadium and the grandstands just hung out over the top of you. You felt like you were in a great big, cavernous place. When the stadium was full, there was more noise than anyplace I ever played. The wind would come swirling in different directions at that one end of the field. It was tough."

Steve Everitt, 1993-1995:

"I remember the electricity before the game—I liked to go out on the field, tape my hands up and hang out for a couple of hours before the game even started. Once winter came, it was electricity combined with the cold and wind. If I wasn't totally in the mood for a game, I'd just go out and sit on the bench and watch the fans start coming in and you could hear the stuff going on in the parking lot, people partying, that's what I remember."

Bernie Kosar, 1985-1993:

"I loved the Stadium. I loved the turf. I loved the mud, the Dawg Pound, the winds coming off the lake. All that led to what I believe was a good homefield advantage. It was incredibly challenging to throw the ball in that stadium. But we did it week in and week out, so it was harder on the opposing team coming in that didn't get to deal with those swirling winds all the time."

Cody Risien, 1979-1983, 1985-1989:

"Probably the incredible sense of history and nostalgia, that old stadium right there on the lake, the architecture. You just knew there were a lot of great moments that had taken place in that stadium. You were linked to all those great teams—Jim Brown and Blanton Collier and Paul Brown, all those great teams. The setting down there on the lake, that was just beautiful."

Jim Kanicki, 1963-1969:

"It wasn't the best looking place I've ever seen, and other stadiums had better locations. But when those fans were in their brown and white, it was the most beautiful place in the world. The weather conditions were awful. Our turf was horrible. Other teams would come in and get upset about the conditions, but we never worried about it. It was always a big advantage to play at Cleveland Municipal Stadium.

Tommy James, 1948-1955:

"It was large, windy and cold—it was awful cold. I remember the championship game on the frozen turf. It was very hard. But I had lots of good memories there."

Brian Sipe, 1972-1983:

"I'll never forget the first time I walked into the Stadium. We came up that tunnel, near Art Modell's office, I don't remember the gate, and I looked out on that place. You know I was enough of a fan to know that Jim Brown had played there and Otto Graham—I mean I just got a chill thinking about the history. The overhangs, the open end, the immense feeling. It's unlike any other place I've ever played. I think when Jerry (Sherk) and I drove back for the last game (in 1995), more than anything else I just wanted to see the stadium."

Ozzie Newsome, 1978-1990:

"I remember that most of the time we played there it was dreary, rainy. The Stadium was all outdated, but it had so much character to it. I still feel that if I went out now to play a game, I would want to play in that stadium."

Paul Brown

Talented John Wooten served as one of Brown's messenger guards near the end of his Cleveland coaching regime.

From Day One of his coaching career, Paul Eugene Brown trusted only one man implicitly: Paul Eugene Brown.

And Paul Brown's faith in his ability to judge football talent was never more evident than in 1945 when he began to assemble players for the Cleveland team that would begin play in the fledgling All-America Football Conference the next year. If the Cleveland club were to succeed in the new professional league, it would do so largely on the shrewd decision-making of the man who had been named coach at famed Massillon (Ohio) High School at age 24 and was coaching the Ohio State Buckeyes by the time he was 33.

Serving as coach at Great Lakes Naval Training Station as World War II raged on, Brown somehow found time to put together a formidable team of sailors—Great Lakes embarrassed Notre Dame, a Top 10 team, 39-7, in '45—and also begin the process of molding a pro team that would be named in his honor, the Browns, a job to which he was entrusted by franchise owner Mickey McBride.

Not one to rely on a player's press clippings, coach/general manager Brown preferred to sign players who had shown him firsthand that they were a cut above—several cuts above, preferably. And he wanted to construct his Browns around a centerpiece talent on both sides of the ball. So Paul Brown reflected on the great players he had coached—and coached against— at Ohio State and then at Great Lakes.

Otto Graham, who as a single-wing tailback at Northwestern was largely responsible for dealing Brown's 1941 Ohio State team its only loss, was deemed the man to run the offense. Brown was confident that Graham, noted for his ball-handling wizardry, would adjust nicely—famously, even—as a T-formation passer in the pro ranks. With that decision made, the coach turned to the defense

first-rate organizational skills would be necessary.

His firm hand was evident when the Browns went to camp. In an annual speech lasting about three hours, the coach explained the physical, mental and moral demands that would be made of his players. "We intend to have good people," he said, "because that's the kind that win the big ones. If you're a drinker or a chaser (or a whiner, he would add), you'll weaken the team and we don't want you. We're just here for one thing, to win."

Brown also made intelligence a priority, handing out detailed tests involving reasoning and math skills. One year, Brown said, the test "showed one of our rookies would make a fine carpenter. And that's exactly what he became."

Brown's scrimmage-free practice sessions and minute-by-minute itineraries for road games became Browns trademarks, too.

"We don't scrimmage—not in training camp, not during the season," Brown said. "We work only four days a week during the season. I've always thought that a coach who has to scrimmage two or three times a week does it only because he doesn't know what else to do."

Brown's precise road routine was a way of keeping his troops focused on the game ahead, and his exacting practice regimen also allowed few minds to stray.

"It's like building a Cadillac," Brown said of dividing his squad into four units at practice, each working under an assistant coach. "You train the parts to perfection, put them together, and the engine runs."

Purr it did. With Brown introducing one innovation after another, the Browns became the scourge of the AAFC, winning 47 of 54 regular-season games (with only four losses) in the league's four-year existence and ruling as league champions each season. In 1948, Cleveland went 15-0 overall.

Brown turned the passing game into an art form in the pros, even having the audacity to let Graham cut loose deep in his own territory, a daring and heretofore no-man's-land tactic; he perfected game-breaking sideline and screen

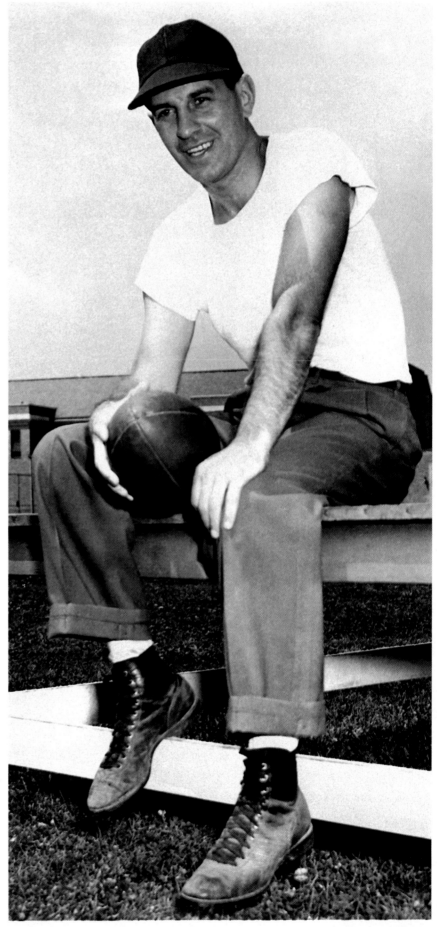

There were few idle moments in the long and successful football career of Brown, who brought new meaning to the term 'coaching.'

> **"He didn't want you in a T-shirt in a hotel lobby, smoking. If Otto Graham was sitting in a hotel bar, he didn't care that it was Otto Graham in the bar. It was that a *Cleveland Brown* was seen sitting in a bar."**
>
> — *Quarterback Otto Graham*

passes, with Speedie, Lavelli and Dub Jones proving elusive targets; he made scouting a year-round science and turned the dissection of game film into a Siskel and Ebert-like obsession; he developed the draw play; he conceived the system of sending in plays through messengers (usually guards), figuring he'd ease the mental load on his quarterback, prevent stereotypical play selection and let the player concentrate on execution; and, perhaps more than anyone else, he made the kicking game a critical part of his game plan, refusing to come up empty after a long drive (let's get at least three points, men) and never conceding field position, either (OK, let's pin 'em back with a punt).

Not only could Brown innovate, he could motivate, too. Before the Browns' 1947 AAFC championship game against the Buddy Young-led New York Yankees, the Cleveland coach went to Motley and asked his running back sensation what the Yankee Stadium throng most wanted to see that day. A great football game, Motley responded. No, Brown countered, the fans "want to know whether you or Buddy Young is the better man." Motley went out and rushed for 109 yards—he gained 8.4 yards per carry—and the Browns, also getting a big day from Graham (14-of-21 passing accuracy), salted away the title.

"Brown was the greatest coach in pro football history," Graham said earlier this year. "It was organization. He was so organized in everything he did—hired the right people, coaches and players. He was like a general in the Army, or an admiral in the Navy, or a CEO.

"(Vince) Lombardi would raise his voice. Paul Brown never would. But he would chew you out … and not gracefully. He'd just tell you that you were lousy. He didn't talk to you much when you played well.

"He didn't want you in a T-shirt in a hotel lobby, smoking. If Otto Graham was sitting in a hotel bar, he didn't care that it was Otto Graham in the bar. It was that a *Cleveland Brown* was seen sitting in a bar."

When the AAFC folded after the '49 season and the Browns, San Francisco 49ers and Baltimore Colts switched from the disbanded league to the NFL, most experts expected Brown and his Cleveland juggernaut to get their comeuppance. They should have known better.

Brown's team was introduced to the NFL in a season-opening matchup against the established league's reigning champions, the Philadelphia Eagles. The Browns' sophisticated passing game was too much for Greasy Neale's team, with Graham throwing for 346 yards in a 35-10 runaway. Cleveland went on to win the league title in its first NFL season, beating the Los Angeles Rams for the crown on a Groza field goal.

Cleveland was the NFL kingpin again in 1954 and 1955. Considering the Browns had lost in championship games in 1951, 1952 and 1953, the Ohioans had reached league title games in 10 consecutive seasons.

Receivers Lavelli and Dub Jones, who were integral parts of that

Brown, who changed the course of the professional game with his dedication to improvement in strategy and intelligent thinking, drilled his troops in a classroom atmosphere during the week and prowled the sideline during games on Sunday.

sustained success, have vivid memories of the man who made it all happen.

"Oh, I liked playing for him (Brown)," Lavelli said. "I knew he was a winner. I (was at) Ohio State with him, and finally the Browns. His main forte was organization and picking out talent. He could see down the road, maybe two or three years, that a guy was going to be pretty good. When we first started, the No. 1 team was hard to break into, but we still had some pretty good guys in back of us that ... down the road, they would fill in when the other guys left."

Jones called Brown "amazing," but he acknowledged that the man wasn't buddy-buddy with his players.

"By all means he was aloof," Jones said. "That doesn't mean a good coach can't be that way. He kept a distance. He was a person who told players what he expected and then he backed off and didn't get in the players' way. He didn't go around policing everything, but he could discipline when necessary."

Defensive back Tommy James remembers Brown's modus operandi. It

Paul Brown Innovations

■ **Intelligence testing.** He gave players detailed tests involving reasoning and math skills.

■ **Scouting.** He made it a full-time, year-round profession.

■ **Film study.** He turned it into a primary source for player evaluation.

■ **Player studies.** He mandated that all players carry notebooks, take notes, diagram plays and commit the contents to memory.

■ **The football facemask.**

■ **Taxi squads.** He kept "extra" players close at hand by securing jobs for them with team owner Mickey McBride's taxi company.

■ **The two-minute drill.**

■ **Messenger-guards system.** He shuttled hand-picked plays to the quarterback using offensive guards as alternate transports.

■ **Organizational skills and unprecedented attention to detail.**

■ **Practice without scrimmages.**

■ **Sideline and screen passes.**

■ **The draw play.**

■ **The kicking game.** Made it a critical part of every game plan.

Brown, always the innovator, equipped quarterback George Ratterman with a radio helmet in the 1956 preseason, a device that would allow him to call plays without use of his messenger guards. Ratterman had trouble hearing the plays and a storm of controversy finally led to a league-wide ban of the Citizens' Band system.

Larger-than-life Paul Brown was not the big man on campus when he stepped between fullback Jim Brown (32) and tackle Dick Schafrath.

was "practice—repeat, repeat, repeat," James said. "You had to know what all of your teammates were doing on every play."

Owning a considerable ego—one that by the mid-1950s seemed proportionate to his team's enormous success—even Brown acknowledged that the presence of what he called "phenomenal animals" went a long way toward establishing genius credentials for a coach. And no coach ever had more of a stud performer than Jim Brown, who came to Cleveland in 1957 out of Syracuse University as the sixth pick in the draft. But with Graham having retired after the '55 season, the Browns never won another NFL championship under Paul Brown—despite winning 18 of 24 regular-season games in Jim Brown's first two years with the club.

Paul Brown's critics began to surface—and one of them was Jim Brown, whose feelings spilled out when he said one of his Pro Bowl coaches, Allie Sherman, "praised us in a way Paul Brown never did." Others were taking aim on his inflexibility, poor trades and, ironically, what they perceived as a failure to keep up with the

game's ever-changing trends—a particularly cutting appraisal of a man so noted for always being several steps ahead of the other guy.

Maybe, by the time Paul Brown was dismissed as Cleveland coach after the 1962 season, the game was passing him by. Maybe, as some said, he failed to learn from the new breed of coaches as others had learned from him. Maybe he was just too set in his ways. Maybe, of all people, Paul Brown grew too predictable.

Graham, never comfortable with Brown's philosophy that play-calling ingenuity was best left to the coach, nevertheless believed Brown was "light years ahead of everybody" as a pro football coach and innovator. Still, in the years when Brown's dominance began to wane, Graham wondered if Brown "failed to realize that he himself could become stereotyped" in his overall approach to the game.

Perhaps. But only after Paul Eugene Brown had established the Cleveland Browns as one of the storied franchises in pro football history.

1946
HIGHLIGHTS

WEEK 1—In the first regular-season game in franchise history, the Browns rout the Miami Seahawks, 44-0, before 60,135 fans at Cleveland Stadium. Otto Graham, replacing starting quarterback Cliff Lewis, completes 6-of-13 passes for 109 yards, including a touchdown toss to Dante Lavelli.

WEEK 2—The Browns ruin the home debut of the Chicago Rockets with a 20-6 victory before 51,962 fans at Soldier Field. Marion Motley leads the way, rushing 12 times for 122 yards and a touchdown. The Browns hold Rockets rookie Elroy Hirsch to minus-1 net yards rushing and limit quarterback Bob Hoernschemeyer to 7-of-22 passing.

WEEK 4—The Browns become the last unbeaten, untied team with a 24-7 win over the New York Yankees at Cleveland Stadium. The Browns score two touchdowns in the first nine minutes and break the game open on a 43-yard TD run by Edgar "Special Delivery" Jones.

WEEK 7—A record Cleveland Stadium crowd of 71,134 watches the Browns improve to 7-0 with a 31-14 win over the Los Angeles Dons, who can't hold a 7-3 halftime lead. The victory is punctuated by Motley touchdown runs of 47 and 68 yards.

WEEK 10—The Browns snap a two-game losing streak and avenge a 34-20 loss to the 49ers two weeks earlier. The big play in Cleveland's 14-7 win at Kezar Stadium is a 64-yard Graham-to-Motley screen pass that sets up the second touchdown. The victory improves the Browns' record to 8-2 in the Western Division, two games ahead of the 49ers.

WEEK 12—The Browns defeat the Buffalo Bisons, 42-17, at Cleveland Stadium to clinch the Western Division title and earn the right to play host to the AAFC title game. The victory improves the Browns to 10-2 with two regular-season games remaining.

WEEK 14—The Browns conclude their first regular season with a 66-14 rout of the Brooklyn Dodgers at Ebbets Field. Nine different players score touchdowns as the Browns achieve their highest point total of the season.

CHAMPIONSHIP GAME—The Browns win the AAFC's first title by defeating the New York Yankees, 14-9, at Cleveland Stadium. It is Cleveland's third win over New York in as many games. The winning points come on a 16-yard fourth-quarter pass from Graham to Lavelli, who makes a diving TD catch.

THE SEASON AT A GLANCE

HEAD COACH
Paul Brown

REGULAR-SEASON RECORD
12-2 / 1st Western Division

SCHEDULE/RESULTS

Miami	W	44-0
at Chicago	W	20-6
at Buffalo	W	28-0
New York	W	24-7
Brooklyn	W	26-7
at New York	W	7-0
Los Angeles	W	31-14
San Francisco	L	20-34
at Los Angeles	L	16-17
at San Francisco	W	14-7
Chicago	W	51-14
Buffalo	W	42-17
at Miami	W	34-0
at Brooklyn	W	66-14
Championship Game		
New York	W	14-9

Motley (76), who doubled as a linebacker early in his career, was bad news for ballcarriers who ventured into his territory.

Motley (left, right photo) and Willis (right) had plenty of reason to celebrate after Cleveland's AAFC championship game victory over the New York Yankees. Another contributor to the Browns' first title run was Gaylon Smith, who got a piggy-back ride (below) from San Francisco's Earle Parsons while making a tackle in a Week 10 win over the 49ers.

In the Beginning

Call it a lovefest, the kind that would be replayed over and over through the next half century of Cleveland Browns football. The winter of '46 was a moment in time—a beginning and an end, a celebration and a social breakthrough all rolled into one incredible season. When 60,135 fans piled into Cleveland Stadium on September 6 to witness the unveiling of Paul Brown's AAFC masterpiece, a bond was formed that would permeate the very essence of the professional game.

It bears repeating—60,135. That's more fans than had attended an NFL game—ever. That's almost twice the number of fans who attended the 1945 NFL championship game that pitted the Cleveland Rams against the Washington Redskins at the same stadium. The Rams won, then closed their nine-year Cleveland era by high-tailing it for the sunnier skies of Los Angeles.

"There was a lot of hoopla, a lot of excitement," recalled offensive tackle and placekicker Lou Groza . "It was overwhelming, the noise and everything. The first pro game I saw was that one I played in. It was really a sensation playing in front of a crowd that large."

And play the Browns did. Starting quarterback Cliff Lewis opened the scoring with a 19-yard touchdown pass to Mac Speedie and the onslaught continued with an Otto Graham TD pass to Dante Lavelli, a 50-yard Tom Colella touchdown run and a 76-yard Ray Terrell interception return. The Browns' 44-0 victory over the Miami Seahawks served notice that the road to AAFC success would travel through Cleveland.

"I couldn't believe we beat a pro team 44-0," said Lavelli, who seemed less surprised by the first-game attendance than the score. "The Paul Brown name drew

Brown instructs the troops before a practice at Bowling Green State University, the site of Cleveland's early training camps (above).

most of the people. He had great backing in the state of Ohio."

Among the great players making their Cleveland debut that historic day were fullback Marion Motley and defensive guard Bill Willis, who had another reason to celebrate. Motley and Willis became the first blacks to play in a professional game since 1933, breaking the color barrier three weeks before Woody Strode and Kenny Washington made their NFL debuts with the Rams and almost eight months before Jackie Robinson would break baseball's color barrier with the Brooklyn Dodgers. There was no fanfare and little publicity surrounding the breakthrough in what would be a difficult, yet rewarding season.

"They (opponents) would throw fists to the jaw, they'd step on you, throw elbows instead of trying to block you, clip you when you weren't looking," Willis recalled more than three decades after the fact. "Lou Rymkus (offensive tackle) told me that if anyone fouled me, 'Don't get into a fight. We'll take care of it.' But I never went to Lou. I had a rather devastating forearm. When I proved to guys that I could take it, things got much better."

Football's quiet social experiment was choreographed by Brown, who searched through the AAFC's bylaws when he began constructing his team and found nothing about the exclusion of black players.

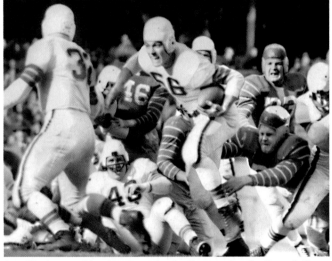

Lavelli, always a big-play threat for the Browns, breaks through the Buffalo Bisons defense for a big gain.

"I didn't care what color they were," said Brown, who did not take Motley and Willis to a late-season game at Miami because of a death threat. "I wanted men of character who could play ball. I knew I was rocking the boat with that decision to invite Motley and Willis to our first camp."

He also rocked the balance of power in the AAFC with Motley and Willis joining an all-everything cast that included Graham, Lavelli, Speedie, Rymkus, Groza, halfback Edgar "Special

SPOTLIGHT: MARION MOTLEY

Lou Groza still remembers his introduction to Marion Motley during Cleveland's 1946 training camp.

"I tackled Motley head on," Groza said. "I felt like I was being hit by a truck. He had huge thighs. From that point on, I tried to tackle him from the side, drag him down. He was a load."

That first impression became a universal nightmare during a 1946 season that introduced the bruising 6-1, 232-pound fullback to the new AAFC, where he quickly grabbed attention as a social pioneer who would help break professional football's color barrier and an unstoppable force for Paul Brown's powerful Cleveland offensive machine.

Motley was a human bulldozer, a quick-footed back who could kill you softly with nifty moves or blast you into submission with his powerful shoulders, tree-stump legs and intense desire to get from point A to point B. He also could pull in passes with his catcher's mitt-size hands and protect quarterback Otto Graham like an unscalable wall protects its castle. Early in his career, Motley doubled as a dominating linebacker.

"He was big, he had good speed, he had big, strong legs and he was a good blocker for Otto," recalled former Browns defensive back Tommy

James. "He was just a great football player."

And almost an afterthought when Brown was constructing his first Cleveland team in that inaugural camp. Brown, a former coach at Massillon High in Ohio, had seen Motley play for rival McKinley High of Canton and then coached him during World War II when he formed a team for Great Lakes Naval Station. Motley was invited to the Browns camp because Brown wanted a roommate for defensive guard Bill Willis, who was being groomed to break the color barrier.

Some roommate. Motley, at age 28, ran for 601 rookie yards and went on to lead Browns rushers in six of his eight Cleveland seasons. His final yards-per-rush average of 5.7 is phenomenal, as is his single-game NFL record of 17.09, which he recorded in a 188-yard, 11-carry effort against Pittsburgh. Most of Motley's early Browns teammates remember him as master of the draw—a play he first ran in an AAFC game by accident.

"Otto got such a hard rush that he handed the ball to Motley in desperation," Brown recalled. "The defense had overrun Motley in their desire to get to the quarterback, and Marion swept right through them for a big gain. We looked at the play again and decided it couldn't help but work. In a short time, it became Marion's most dangerous weapon."

Delivery" Jones and centers Frank Gatski and Mike Scarry. Motley became a bruising fullback who would dominate the AAFC for four seasons and Willis terrorized offensive linemen and quarterbacks with his lightning quickness and power rushes up the middle. A year later, Brown would add Horace Gillom, a black punter who put the phrase "hang time" into pro football vocabulary.

Not only did the integrated Browns thrive on the field, they became a close-knit unit off it. There was no tension—Paul

Brown wouldn't allow it.

"I've always said that the thread follows the needle," Willis said. "As Paul Brown reacted to myself, Motley and Gillom, the rest of the players had to follow. I was made to feel as important as Lou Groza and Otto Graham."

"Everybody was like a family," said Lavelli. "Brown used to say, 'You're killing our team.' That was his favorite expression. You dropped a pass or missed a block or had a fumble, he said, 'You know, you're killing our team.' It was always 'team.' Not,

'You're hurting this' or 'Lavelli, you're doing this.' It was always the team concept."

Family Brown rolled through its 1946 schedule with a 12-2 record, losing only to the San Francisco 49ers and Los Angeles Dons. Cleveland amassed 423 points, a professional football record, and 55 touchdowns, 17 on Graham passes. Groza led the league with 84 points, all produced by his accurate right foot. The Browns, known for a big-play explosiveness that produced victory margins of 42-17, 34-0, 51-14 and 66-14, also were explosive at the gate, where they averaged 57,136 for seven home dates.

"Cleveland, never a money-maker for the Rams, set all manner of crowd records," marveled league officials in their annual record book after the season. "And the operation was hailed as the finest all-around sports promotion of the year."

The Browns put the jewel on their first-year crown with a 14-9 championship game victory over the New York Yankees, the first of four straight AAFC titles they would claim. But this one would not come easily. The Yankees held a 9-7 lead with less than five minutes remaining in the fourth quarter, but Graham, who passed for 213 yards, threw a 16-yard title-securing scoring strike to Lavelli.

It was official. The Browns were king of the AAFC, a domain that would eventually spread to regions—and a league—beyond.

SPOTLIGHT: BILL WILLIS

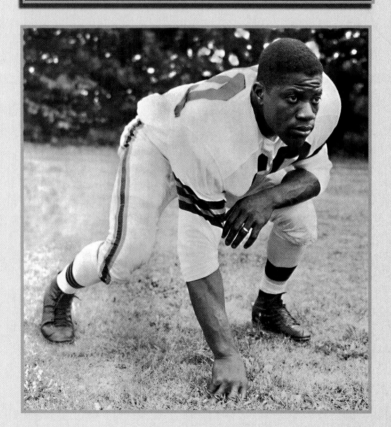

He was cat-quick, befitting the panther-like crouch from which he sprung at unfortunate centers who were assigned to block him. Bill Willis pounced on his prey, and those who didn't think fast paid a stiff price. He was a football pioneer, a devastating defender and a consummate team player tightly wrapped in a 6-2, 210-pound package. When Willis showed up at Paul Brown's 1946 training camp, he fit the coach's vision of a perfect football team, skin color be damned.

It didn't take Brown long to demonstrate his intention to cross the longtime professional football color barrier. He simply suited Willis up, positioned him as the middle guard in a five-man line and turned him loose on center Mike Scarry during a team scrimmage.

"I watched the ball intently, and as soon as Scarry tightened his grip, I charged," recalled Willis, who had played as a defensive tackle on Brown's 1942 Ohio State national championship team. "For four, five minutes, I charged over, under and through Mike Scarry. The offense couldn't get a play off. One time I landed on Otto Graham. Paul said, 'That's enough.' That night he signed me to a contract."

Scarry recalled the training camp episode as well. "That's enough," he said after Willis' final charge, throwing his arms up. "Willis has made the team as far as I'm concerned."

Not only did Willis make the team, he launched an eight-year career that would take him all the way to the Hall of Fame. He was small for the defensive line so Brown utilized his quickness by lining him up over center, where he could attack with his devastating forearm or zip past slower linemen who couldn't react. Occasionally he would drop behind the line and react to the play—football's pioneer middle linebacker. With Willis leading the charge, it's no coincidence the Browns dominated the AAFC in scoring defense and topped the NFL in four of their first six seasons.

Willis, whose ear-to-ear grin lit up the locker room and made him popular among Browns players until his 1953 retirement, will always be remembered for the game-saving tackle that lifted the Browns past the New York Giants in a 1950 American Conference playoff and set the stage for their first NFL championship.

The Browns held a precarious 3-0 fourth-quarter lead when Giants halfback Gene (Choo Choo) Roberts broke free, picked up a convoy of blockers and headed for an apparent 47-yard touchdown run. But Willis, in what appeared to be hopeless pursuit, fought through the blockers and caught Roberts from behind at the 3-yard line. The Browns held New York to a field goal in an eventual 8-3 victory.

The essence of Willis was captured by the words of former Chicago Bears center Clyde (Bulldog) Turner, a Hall of Famer. "The first guy that ever convinced me that I couldn't handle anybody I ever met was Bill Willis," Turner said. "They called him The Cat. He would jump right over you."

Brown enjoys a victorious moment (above) with Graham (left), Lavelli and Speedie (right) after watching his team capture its first AAFC championship. Cleveland fans also savored the moment (left), mobbing the Browns players and sharing their appreciation.

1947

HIGHLIGHTS

WEEK 1—The Browns roll over the Buffalo Bills, 30-14, before a season-opening crowd of 63,263 at Cleveland Stadium. Marion Motley scores two touchdowns, one as a running back and another on a 48-yard interception return.

WEEK 5—In a matchup of top teams in the Eastern and Western divisions, the Browns defeat New York, 26-17, before a record crowd of 80,067 at Cleveland Stadium. The Yankees become the first team to take a lead over the Browns, who secure victory in the fourth quarter on an Otto Graham TD pass to Mac Speedie and Lou Groza's second field goal.

WEEK 6—One week after winning their showdown against the Yankees, the Browns are upset, 13-10, by the Los Angeles Dons at Cleveland. L.A.'s Ben Agajanian misses his first attempt at the winning field goal, but a Cleveland penalty for 12 men on the field gives him a second chance. The loss snaps an 11-game Browns winning streak.

WEEK 8—In a battle of Western Division powers, the Browns beat the 49ers, 14-7, at Kezar Stadium. The game is played in heavy fog, but Graham completes 19-of-24 passes for 278 yards and TDs to Dante Lavelli and Speedie, who sets an AAFC single-game record with 10 receptions.

WEEK 10—In what should have been an easy game, the Browns struggle to beat the Brooklyn Dodgers, 13-12, at Cleveland Stadium. The Dodgers, who came to town with just two wins, miss two extra points and four field goals while outplaying the Browns. Graham's 72-yard TD pass to Lavelli is offset by a Brooklyn reverse that springs Monk Gafford for a 79-yard touchdown.

WEEK 12—The Browns rally for a 28-28 tie against the Yankees before a record football crowd of 70,060 at New York's Yankee Stadium. Down 28-0, the Browns score a touchdown just before halftime, add two touchdowns in the third quarter and tie the game in the final period.

CHAMPIONSHIP GAME—The Browns defeat the Yankees, 14-3, at New York to secure their second straight title. Playing a fourth straight road game does not faze the Browns, who score a first-quarter touchdown on Graham's 1-yard plunge and a late TD on a 4-yard Dub Jones run.

THE SEASON AT A GLANCE

HEAD COACH

Paul Brown

REGULAR-SEASON RECORD

12-1-1 / 1st Western Division

TOP DRAFT CHOICES

Dick Hoerner, HB, Iowa

Robert Rice, C, Tulane

SCHEDULE/RESULTS

Buffalo	W	30-14
at Brooklyn	W	55-7
Baltimore	W	28-0
at Chicago	W	41-21
New York	W	26-17
Los Angeles	L	10-13
Chicago	W	31-28
at San Francisco	W	14-7
at Buffalo	W	28-7
Brooklyn	W	13-12
San Francisco	W	37-14
at New York	T	28-28
at Los Angeles	W	27-17
at Baltimore	W	42-0
Championship Game		
at New York	W	14-3

Groza follows through and holder Graham watches the result of a field-goal attempt against the New York Yankees.

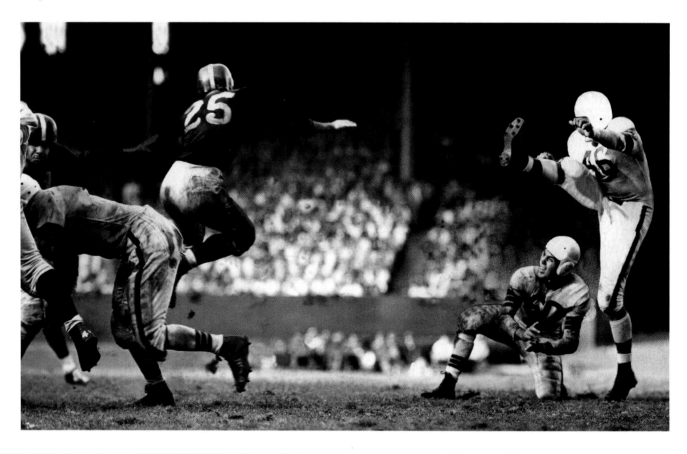

1948
HIGHLIGHTS

WEEK 2—The Browns roll up 508 total yards in whipping the Bills, 42-13, at Buffalo. Otto Graham throws for 197 yards, Mac Speedie catches 10 passes for 151 and Marion Motley rushes 17 times for 136. Cleveland blows the game open with second-half TDs by Graham, Tom Colella and Dean Sensanbaugher.

WEEK 5—The Browns run their unbeaten streak to 14 with a 14-10 victory in a windy downpour at Baltimore. The Colts strike quickly on a 74-yard Y.A. Tittle-to-Billy Hillenbrand pass, but the Browns come back on a pair of Edgar Jones TDs. Motley finishes with 130 rushing yards.

WEEK 6—Hours after the Indians lose Game 5 of the World Series to the Boston Braves, the Browns cap a big Cleveland sports day by defeating Brooklyn, 30-17, on the same field. The day is memorable for Lou Groza, who kicks a team-record 53-yard field goal. But the key play is turned in by George Young, who recovers a fumble by Ray Ramsey and returns it 12 yards for a TD.

WEEK 8—The Browns extend their unbeaten streak to 17 with a 35-7 win over New York at Cleveland Stadium. Dante Lavelli, in his first game back after

Halfback 'Special Delivery' Jones (90) and pass-catcher Speedie (below) were powerful weapons in the Browns' offensive arsenal.

breaking an ankle during preseason, catches two touchdown passes from Graham, who throws for 310 yards and four TDs. The turning point is a first-period goal-line stand sparked by Bill Willis and Tony Adamle.

WEEK 10—In a battle of unbeatens, the Browns hold San Francisco to 185 total yards and take a one-game Western Division lead over the 49ers with a 14-7 victory. The Browns draw first blood when Lou Saban recovers a fumble on the opening kickoff, setting up a 14-yard TD run by Graham.

WEEK 13—The Browns, playing their third game in eight days, record a 31-28 win at San Francisco. The victory comes three days after a 31-14 Thanksgiving Day win at Los Angeles. A banged-up Graham fires a 41-yard TD pass to Lavelli and a 33-yard game-winner to Edgar Jones.

CHAMPIONSHIP GAME—The Browns crush the Bills, 49-7, to win their third straight championship. Motley rushes for 133 yards and two TDs and the final score comes on a 39-yard interception return by Saban. The Browns finish with an 18-game winning streak and 24-game unbeaten streak.

THE SEASON AT A GLANCE

HEAD COACH
Paul Brown

REGULAR-SEASON RECORD
14-0 / 1st Western Division

TOP DRAFT CHOICE (Rd.)
Jeff Durkota, HB, Penn State (1)

SCHEDULE/RESULTS

Los Angeles	W	19-14
at Buffalo	W	42-13
at Chicago	W	28-7
Chicago	W	21-10
at Baltimore	W	14-10
Brooklyn	W	30-17
Buffalo	W	31-14
New York	W	35-7
Baltimore	W	28-7
San Francisco	W	14-7
at New York	W	34-21
at Los Angeles	W	31-14
at San Francisco	W	31-28
at Brooklyn	W	31-21
Championship Game		
Buffalo	W	49-7

1949
HIGHLIGHTS

WEEK 1—The Browns open the season with a 28-28 tie at Buffalo, extending their unbeaten streak to 25. The Bills lead, 28-7, in the fourth quarter before Otto Graham gets hot, completing 14-of-16 passes, two for touchdowns, to salvage the tie. Mac Speedie catches 10 passes, including a spectacular grab of Graham's game-tying throw.

WEEK 5—The Browns pile up 550 yards total offense in a 42-7 rout of the Los Angeles Dons. Fullback Marion Motley leads the way with 139 rushing yards and Graham throws a spectacular 79-yard TD bomb to Bill Boedeker.

WEEK 6—The Browns' 29-game unbeaten streak ends in a 56-28 thrashing at San Francisco. The AAFC's highest-scoring team rolls up 511 yards against the Browns, who had outscored the 49ers 110-63 in their five previous meetings. Two Frankie Albert TD passes and a Johnny Strzykalski run puts the 49ers ahead 21-0 and Cleveland never gets within seven points in their worst—and last—AAFC loss.

WEEK 7—A week after being blown out at San Francisco and receiving a public tongue-lashing from coach Paul Brown, the Browns crush the Dons, 61-14, at Los Angeles. Graham sets a conference record with six

Receiver Lavelli was a big play waiting to happen.

touchdown passes, a club-record five to Dante Lavelli. Edgar Jones suffers a broken collarbone, an injury that would hasten the end of his Cleveland career after four seasons.

WEEK 11—In the final game between the AAFC's fiercest rivals, the Browns crush the Yankees, 31-0, at New York. The game is a mismatch with Graham throwing for 382 yards and Speedie catching 11 passes for 228. Dub Jones scores two Cleveland TDs, Motley and Boedeker one each.

PLAYOFF GAME— After two regular-season ties against Buffalo, the Browns pound out a 31-21 victory over the Bills in a playoff battle at Cleveland Stadium. The key, as usual, is the arm of Graham, who throws TD passes to Lavelli and Dub Jones.

CHAMPIONSHIP GAME—Two days after NFL commissioner Bert Bell had announced that the Browns, San Francisco 49ers and Baltimore Colts would be absorbed into the NFL for the 1950 season, the Browns defeat the 49ers, 21-7, holding AAFC rushing leader Joe Perry to 36 yards. All three Browns TDs come on the ground, courtesy of Edgar Jones, Marion Motley and Dub Jones.

THE SEASON AT A GLANCE

HEAD COACH

Paul Brown

REGULAR-SEASON RECORD

9-1-2 / 1st Western Division

TOP DRAFT CHOICE (Rd.)

Jack Mitchell, QB, Oklahoma (1)

SCHEDULE/RESULTS

at Buffalo	T	28-28
Baltimore	W	21-0
New York	W	14-3
at Baltimore	W	28-20
Los Angeles	W	42-7
at San Francisco	L	28-56
at Los Angeles	W	61-14
San Francisco	W	30-28
Chicago	W	35-2
Buffalo	T	7-7
at New York	W	31-0
at Chicago	W	14-6
Playoff Game		
Buffalo	W	31-21
Championship Game		
San Francisco	W	21-7

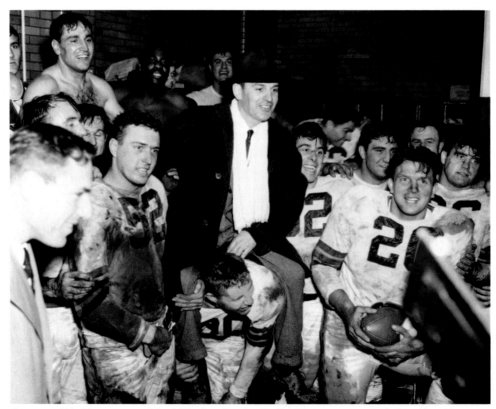

Brown and his Browns were riding high after Cleveland's fourth consecutive AAFC championship.

Motley, wearing high-top sneakers for better traction on an icy field, turns the corner on a first-quarter run in the Browns' conference playoff victory over the New York Giants.

David Slays the NFL Goliaths

They had quietly endured the arrows of disrespect. As four-time champions of the "Humpty Dumpty" All-America Football Conference, the Cleveland Browns were like an angry fly buzzing the NFL establishment, a wanna-be professional football power that wouldn't go away. The fly would land in 1950, and nobody in the "smug, superior" NFL would be quick enough to swat it away. The first opportunity to squash the Browns went to Bert Bell, the NFL commissioner who had uttered the infamous "come back when you get a football" line to AAFC owners in 1946.

When the AAFC folded after the 1949 season and three teams were absorbed by the NFL, Bell took special delight in scheduling the Browns for a season-opening game at Philadelphia, home of the two-time defending NFL-champion Eagles. It was lesson time, put up or shut up for the new kids on the NFL block.

"For that game, we were the most rehearsed team in the history of sports," Otto Graham said. "No team was ever more ready, physically and mentally.

Pass-catcher Speedie and his fired-up Cleveland teammates soared past the stunned Eagles in a season-opening battle that introduced the Browns to the NFL.

We had something to prove to the world. We had waited four years for this. Paul Brown didn't have to do one thing to get us up—he had to get us to keep it down."

Tommy James, a defensive back and longtime holder for kicker Lou Groza,

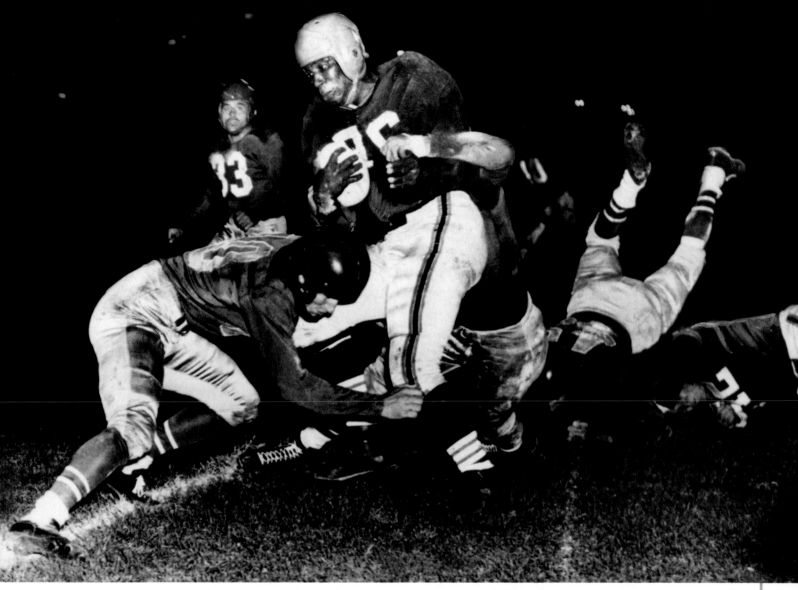

The Eagles were soft up the middle in the season opener, a vulnerability the Browns exploited with the power running of Motley.

remembered the intensity. "Our feelings coming into that game were intense," he said. "If they (the coaches) had told us to run through the end of the stadium, we probably would have done it."

What the Browns did stunned the crowd of 71,237 fans who crowded into Philadelphia's Municipal Stadium to witness a good, old-fashioned whipping. They gave one to the Eagles—with shocking ease.

"That probably was the top shelf of the Browns' early existence," said Dub Jones, who caught a 59-yard touchdown pass, one of three bombs Graham dropped on the Eagles in a 35-10 victory. "It was the biggest game any of us had ever been in. They had the great defense that nobody in the NFL had penetrated in two years. It was a great coaching game. What a game plan Paul Brown put together. It worked to perfection."

What Brown did was widen the gaps between his offensive linemen, attack the Eagles' spread-out 5-4 defense by running Marion Motley on draw plays up the suddenly-soft middle and

unveil an impressive Graham aerial show. Graham riddled the Eagles in a 21-of-38, 346-yard performance that included touchdown passes of 26 yards to Dante Lavelli and 13 yards to Mac Speedie. The 487-yard offensive blitz provided an in-your-face warning that the NFL's balance of power was about to change.

"This was the highest emotional game I ever coached," Brown said. "We had four years of constant ridicule to get us ready."

And it didn't stop there. After watching his team get blown away, Eagles coach Greasy Neale called the Browns a basketball team, a reference to their dependence on the forward pass. So when Cleveland met the Eagles in a December rematch, Brown refused to throw a pass—and his Browns still prevailed, 13-7.

The Eagles weren't the only team to feel the wrath of the Browns, who rolled through their first NFL season with a 10-2 record and tied New York for the American Conference crown. An 8-3 playoff victory over the Giants put the Browns into a championship game matchup against the Los Angeles Rams on the frozen turf of bitterly-cold Cleveland Stadium.

It was a classic.

On the game's first play, Rams quarterback Bob Waterfield connected with Glenn Davis on an 82-yard touchdown bomb. The Browns' first possession ended with Graham's game-tying 32-yard TD pass to Jones. And so it went. The Rams added another first-quarter touchdown on Dick Hoerner's 3-yard run, but the Browns struck back before halftime on Graham's 35-yard strike to Lavelli, setting up a key play in the game—a missed conversion opportunity.

"We were up at the open end and it was awful breezy," James said. "A gust of wind pulled me off my knee as I tried to get a high snap and I jumped up and caught the ball. I saw Tony Adamle open in the end zone and threw the ball to him, but he dropped it. I guess I hit Tony in a bad spot—right in the hands."

"Yeah," Adamle said, "I could have been the goat. But that made the game exciting, didn't it?"

That missed point loomed large in the third quarter when Los Angeles' Larry Brink returned a Motley fumble 6 yards for a touchdown and early in the fourth when Graham threw a 14-yard TD pass to Rex Bumgardner, cutting the Rams' lead to 28-27. When a late drive ended at the Rams' 20-yard line on a Graham fumble, it appeared there might be two goats.

"When they recovered, Motley and

Graham (60) finds running room in the title game against the Rams, thanks to the in-your-face block of receiver Lavelli on Los Angeles defender Bob Boyd.

Cleveland players and coaches (below, left to right) Warren Lahr, Weeb Ewbank, Brown and Adamle watch closely as Groza's championship-securing field goal sails over the crossbar (right). The Browns had plenty of reason to celebrate after rising to the top of the NFL and silencing critics who had predicted they wouldn't be able to compete in the tougher league.

THE SEASON AT A GLANCE

HEAD COACH

Paul Brown

REGULAR-SEASON RECORD

11-1 / 1st
American Conference

TOP DRAFT CHOICE (Rd.)

Kenny Konz, HB, LSU (1)

SCHEDULE/RESULTS

at San Francisco	L	10-24
at Los Angeles	W	38-23
Washington	W	45-0
Pittsburgh	W	17-0
N.Y. Giants	W	14-13
at Chi. Cardinals	W	34-17
Philadelphia	W	20-17
at N.Y. Giants	W	10-0
Chicago Bears	W	42-21
Chi. Cardinals	W	49-28
at Pittsburgh	W	28-0
at Philadelphia	W	24-9
Championship Game		
at Los Angeles	L	17-24

Dub Jones breaks free for a 20-yard gain against the Giants at New York's Polo Grounds.

WEEK 2—A rematch of the 1950 title game is played at a different venue with the same result: The Browns beat the Rams, 38-23, at Los Angeles. Before a crowd of 67,186, the Rams lead early before the Browns come back to take the lead on a third-quarter TD run by Ken Carpenter and put it away on Warren Lahr's touchdown interception of a Bob Waterfield pass.

WEEK 4—The Browns record back-to-back shutouts for the first time in franchise history, beating Pittsburgh 17-0 at Cleveland Stadium a week after a 45-0 romp past Washington. Emerson Cole rushes for 126 yards in place of Marion Motley, but Horace Gillom's TD return of a botched punt and Lahr's touchdown interception of a Joe Geri pass are the big plays.

WEEK 7—Paul Brown wins his 200th game (high school, college, professional) as the Browns beat the Eagles, 20-17, at Cleveland. The Browns wipe out an early 10-0 deficit and do not take their first lead until Lou Groza kicks the game-winning field goal following Lahr's interception.

WEEK 9—In the first regular-season meeting between the Browns and George Halas' Chicago Bears, the Browns win easily, 42-21, at Cleveland. The game belongs to Dub Jones, who ties Ernie Nevers' 22-year-old NFL record by scoring all six Cleveland touchdowns. The finale comes in the fourth quarter on a 43-yard pass from Otto Graham.

WEEK 11—The Browns clinch their sixth straight division title with their 10th straight victory, a 28-0 decision at Pittsburgh. The Browns' second shutout of the Steelers and their team-record fourth of the season is secured on touchdown runs by Carpenter, Motley and Carl Taseff and a Graham TD pass to Dante Lavelli.

CHAMPIONSHIP GAME—Before 57,540 fans at the Los Angeles Coliseum, the Browns suffer their first loss in a league title game, falling 24-17 to the Rams. The Rams broke a 17-17 tie late in the final quarter on Norm Van Brocklin's 73-yard touchdown bomb to Tom Fears after the Browns had tied on Carpenter's 2-yard run minutes earlier. Three of Cleveland's points were provided by Groza's 52-yard field goal. Fears' TD gave the Rams their first championship since leaving Cleveland in 1946.

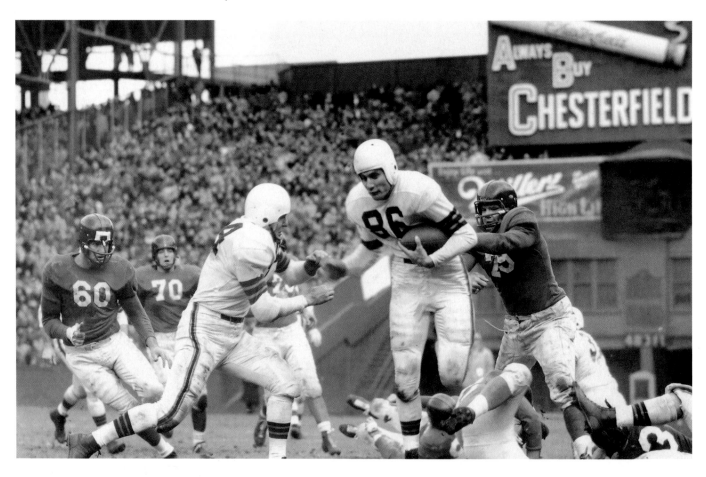

THE SEASON AT A GLANCE

HEAD COACH

Paul Brown

REGULAR-SEASON RECORD

11-1 / 1st
Eastern Conference

TOP DRAFT CHOICE (Rd.)

Doug Atkins, DT,
Tennessee (1)

SCHEDULE/RESULTS

at Green Bay	W	27-0
at Chi. Cardinals	W	27-7
Philadelphia	W	37-13
at Washington	W	30-14
at N.Y. Giants	W	7-0
Washington	W	27-3
Pittsburgh	W	34-16
San Francisco	W	23-21
at Pittsburgh	W	20-16
Chi. Cardinals	W	27-16
N.Y. Giants	W	62-14
at Philadelphia	L	27-42
Championship Game		
at Detroit	L	16-17

Chick Jagade runs nine yards for a TD (below) in another title-game loss to the Lions.

WEEK 1—In the first meeting between Cleveland and Green Bay, the Browns roll up 376 yards and Otto Graham completes 18-of-24 passes to highlight a 27-0 season-opening win at Milwaukee. The Browns yield 159 yards and allow the Packers to penetrate Cleveland territory just four times.

WEEK 5—Graham scores the game's only touchdown on a 4-yard run in the second period as the Browns beat the Giants, 7-0, on a muddy Polo Grounds field. Graham, who attempts only five passes in the inclement conditions, scores after an offsides penalty on Lou Groza's missed field-goal attempt gives the Browns a critical first down.

WEEK 6—The undefeated Browns make life miserable for Redskins quarterback Eddie LeBaron by intercepting four passes in a 27-3 win at Cleveland Stadium. Tommy James ties his own Browns record with three as Cleveland scores 24 points off turnovers.

WEEK 8—A Cleveland Stadium crowd of 80,698

watches the Browns dispatch longtime rival San Francisco, 23-21. With the Browns leading 10-0, Graham is knocked out of bounds by defensive back Fred Bruney and elbowed in the face by linebacker Art Michalik, who opens a gash that requires 15 stitches and nearly incites a riot. Graham returns for the third quarter wearing a clear plastic protective bar in front of his face, a device that will evolve into today's face mask. Showing little effect from his injury, Graham leads the Browns to 13 second-half points and the victory.

WEEK 11—The Browns improve to 11-0 by winning a 62-14 laugher over the Giants at Cleveland Stadium. George Ratterman starts in place of Graham and completes 15-of-27 passes for 235 yards and four TDs. Graham plays briefly and completes 3-of-4 passes, two for touchdowns. Pete Brewster catches seven passes for 182 yards and three scores in the most productive game of his career.

CHAMPIONSHIP GAME—Two weeks after their dream of an undefeated season ended in a 42-27 loss at Philadelphia, the Browns lose their third straight title game and second in a row to Detroit, 17-16. Graham plays the worst game of his career, completing 2-of-15 passes with two interceptions. A Graham fumble sets up the Lions' first touchdown, and their other 10 points come after interceptions.

Lavelli, the master of catching passes in traffic, goes up and over Steelers defender Art DeCarlo to pull in a throw from Graham.

THE SEASON AT A GLANCE

HEAD COACH

Paul Brown

REGULAR-SEASON RECORD

9-3 / 1st
Eastern Conference

TOP DRAFT CHOICE (Rd.)

Bobby Garrett, QB,
Stanford (1)

John Bauer, OG,
Illinois (1)

SCHEDULE/RESULTS

at Philadelphia	L	10-28
Chi. Cardinals	W	31-7
at Pittsburgh	L	27-55
at Chi. Cardinals	W	35-3
N.Y. Giants	W	24-14
Washington	W	62-3
at Chicago Bears	W	39-10
Philadelphia	W	6-0
at N.Y. Giants	W	16-7
at Washington	W	34-14
Pittsburgh	W	42-7
Detroit	L	10-14
Championship Game		
Detroit	W	56-10

WEEK 1—The Browns are no match for the Eagles in a 28-10 season-opening loss at Philadelphia. Otto Graham completes just nine passes while Adrian Burk and Bobby Thomason both throw two TD passes for the Eagles. It is the Browns' third consecutive loss dating back to 1953 and their third in four games against the Eagles.

WEEK 2—Graham follows one of his worst career performances with one of his best, throwing for 228 yards and three TDs while leading the Browns to a 31-7 rout of the Chicago Cardinals. Graham plays only a half as coach Paul Brown empties the bench with a 31-0 lead. The win is Cleveland's 23rd without a loss against Chicago-based pro football teams (the Rockets, Bears and Cardinals).

WEEK 3—After eight consecutive wins, the Browns suffer their first-ever loss to the Steelers, a 55-27 humiliation at Pittsburgh. Graham completes 22 passes, twice as many as Pittsburgh quarterback Jim Finks. But four of Finks' throws result in touchdowns, twice as many as Graham,

who also throws five interceptions—two of which are returned for scores.

WEEK 6—The Browns rout the Redskins, 62-3, in the most lopsided victory in franchise history. Most of the offensive damage is inflicted by backup quarterback George Ratterman, who completes 11-of-12 passes for 208 yards and three touchdowns (to Dub Jones, Pete Brewster and Dante Lavelli) in just 17 minutes after Graham injures his arm.

WEEK 9—The Browns' sixth straight win comes at the expense of the injury-depleted Giants, 16-7, at New York. The Giants start the game without halfback Frank Gifford and lose quarterback Charlie Conerly in the first period. With rookie Bobby Clatterbuck at the controls, the Giants mount just 68 yards of offense and score one TD—on a punt return. Graham throws for 278 yards and Pete Brewster catches eight passes for 126.

WEEK 11—The Browns avenge their earlier loss at Pittsburgh with a 42-7 victory that is never in doubt. Chet Hanulak scores Cleveland's first touchdown on a 13-yard run, and Ken Konz gets the second on a 54-yard interception return, the first of his two thefts. The win lifts Cleveland to 9-2 and sets the stage for another championship game battle against Detroit.

Tackle Mike McCormack (left) watches the progress of halfback Fred Morrison (32) during Cleveland's 62-3 pounding of Washington.

Browns offensive linemen Frank Gatski (52, above photo) and Abe Gibron (64) and defensive end Len Ford (80, left) were key figures in the 1954 Cleveland championship run, which paired Brown and Lions coach Buddy Parker (left, left photo) in the title game.

The first of three Graham touchdown runs in the 1954 championship game (right) was made possible by the gaping hole his blockers created in the Detroit front wall. But the going was not so clear for kick returner Billy Reynolds (46), who was penned in by the swarming Lions.

Taming of the Lions

It was the perfect way to say goodbye, a career-closing performance made in heaven. From the moment Otto Graham set foot on the frozen Cleveland Stadium turf before his last game as Browns quarterback, the Detroit Lions were in deep trouble. The old man was throwing a party and 43,827 guests were there to catch his final act.

"He was amazing," recalled Dub Jones, who had been on the receiving end of Graham passes since 1948, the team's third season in the AAFC. "He could make a mediocre ballplayer great, a mediocre team great. When you have a quarterback you know can make the big play, it makes all the difference in the world. You never break."

Graham (right) and Otto Graham Sr. share a moment after the title-game victory.

Mediocrity was the crisis a 33-year-old Graham faced when the Browns opened the 1954 season without many of the familiar faces from eight straight division championship teams. Tony Adamle, Lou Rymkus and Cliff Lewis were gone. So was Mac Speedie and four key performers—Marion Motley, Bill Willis, Lin Houston and George Young—who had retired after Cleveland's loss to the Lions in the 1953 title game. A 1-2 start in 1954 didn't bode well for continued success.

But with Graham pushing all the right buttons and Paul Brown setting his usual clear course, the "old" Browns regrouped to win eight consecutive games and powered their way to a 9-3 record, a ninth straight division crown and a third consecutive date with the Lions in the NFL championship game. The game, Graham announced, would be his last.

"I thought it was smart to finish on top," Graham recalled more than four decades later. And Graham's decision provided the perfect motivation for a team that had

Fred Morrison (above) broke through for a third-period championship game touchdown, but the day still belonged to Graham (14, right), who either passed or ran for an amazing six TDs.

never beaten the Lions in a regular-season or postseason game and had lost to them in the 1952 and 1953 title games. A week before the '54 title game, the Browns had closed the regular season with a 14-10 loss to Detroit.

"The Lions probably were one of our biggest rivals at that time," recalled wide receiver Dante Lavelli. "They had Bobby Layne and a lot of other great players."

Graham, who completed 2-of-14 passes in a dismal 1953 championship game performance, threw an interception on his first pass in the 1954 title game and a field goal by Detroit's Doak Walker set an uneasy tone. But Brown, the master strategist who turned film study into an artform, had picked up on a Detroit tendency that would prove fatal to the Lions' hopes for a third straight championship. Brown noticed that every time his team ran from a tight T-formation without a wideout, Lions cornerback Billy Stits would come up close to guard against a wide running play. Graham called for the formation, sent speedy Ray Renfro deep and hit him with a 35-yard touchdown pass. That opened the flood gates.

Before he was through, Automatic Otto had fired an 8-yard scoring strike to Pete Brewster and a 31-yarder to Renfro, who caught five of Graham's nine completions. Graham, who threw only 12 passes, also ran for three touchdowns and directed drives that ended with 12-yard TD runs by Fred Morrison and Chet Hanulak. The eight-touchdown, 56-10 blitz of the stunned Lions ranked only behind Chicago's 73-0 victory over Washington as the most lopsided victories in championship game history.

"What can you say?" said Lions coach

SPOTLIGHT: OTTO GRAHAM

The first thing you noticed about Otto Graham was his poise, the cool efficiency with which he guided the Browns to the top of the professional football world. He was the perfect quarterback for the near-perfect franchise, the on-field extension of Paul Brown's winning legacy. Graham was Brown's executioner, the man who could cut out an opponent's heart with a feathery pass, a scramble to daylight or a defense-confusing audible.

"Oh they were soft," said former Browns wide receiver Dante Lavelli of Graham's passes. "I used to catch a lot of them one-handed. He had great touch in his hands."

And competitive fire throughout his body. Graham was the consummate athlete, a single-wing tailback and All-American basketball player at Northwestern. Brown's Ohio State teams had lost twice to the Graham-led Wildcats and Brown was impressed enough to peg him as the centerpiece for his new T-formation Cleveland offense. Graham was the first player Brown signed, but not before he had played the 1945-46 season with the Rochester Royals of the National Basketball League.

The Brown-Graham pairing was choreographed in football heaven. Graham was a relentlessly accurate passer who could go deep or drop soft throws into the arms of Lavelli, Mac Speedie or Dub Jones. He was a master tactician who could scramble for the unexpected yards, pick apart defenses with unerring decisions and make big plays at crucial moments.

"He was great, one of the great football players of all time," former Browns linebacker Tony Adamle said. "He could have played today for any team out there. He was one of the greatest quarterbacks ever."

Ara Parseghian, another teammate, seconded that notion. "I view Otto Graham as the absolute complete player," Parseghian said in a late-1980s interview. "I'd match him with any quarterback today for touch and timing on the ball. They say that Joe Montana doesn't have the strongest arm, but he gets the ball into the end zone. Graham

was the same way."

Brown turned Graham loose on the AAFC in 1946 and he directed the Browns to the league's first championship. Three more years in the AAFC yielded three more titles and six years in the NFL produced three championships and three losses in the championship game. Over 10 professional seasons, Graham's Browns never failed to win a division title and play for the championship.

"The test of a quarterback is where his team finishes," said Brown, who used Graham to introduce such innovations as the timing pass, the face mask and the draw play. Graham also was the first NFL quarterback to throw consistently from deep in his own territory.

The bottom line is the Browns were the monster of professional football through 1955, the year Graham retired. In 1956, the franchise dropped to 5-7, its first losing season. Graham, who finished his career with an impressive .557 completion percentage, actually retired two times—the first after Cleveland's victory over Detroit in the 1954 championship game. But Brown talked him into returning for one final season and he responded by leading the Browns to a 38-14 championship game win over the Los Angeles Rams.

Chet Hanulak got in on the fun when he sliced across the goal line for Cleveland's eighth touchdown against the helpless Detroit defense.

Buddy Parker when asked to explain how his team could beat the Browns one week and get dominated the next. "No one quit. Overconfident? I don't think I would say that. The Browns were up. Maybe next week it would be different. I don't know."

Neither did Layne, who said "they just outplayed us. That's the same team we beat one week ago, too."

When Graham left the game with just over two minutes remaining, the crowd, his teammates and even Brown joined in a long standing ovation. "That almost made me change my mind (about retiring)," Graham said after the game, "but I've got to quit sometime. And I always said I'd like to go out on top."

As ecstatic fans jammed up tight against the outside of the Browns' dressing room chanting, "We want the Browns, we want the Browns," players inside celebrated the team's sixth

championship in nine Cleveland seasons.

Nobody said much about the prospect of a 1955 season without Graham, but everybody in the room was thinking about it. "I hated to see Otto go because I thought he could still play," offensive tackle/kicker Lou Groza recalled. And, indeed, a funny thing happened to Graham on his way to retirement.

He relented to Brown's plea for one more season and returned to lead Cleveland to one final championship in 1955—incredibly, his seventh in 10 professional seasons. Then, without a second thought, he did retire. For good.

"I always thought of Joe Louis and how he had to go back and fight (because of financial needs)," Graham said. "The luster was removed. That was never going to happen to me."

And it didn't.

Graham got a warm sideline greeting from coach Paul Brown (above) when he left the field for the final time in 1954 and he was the center of attention (left) when well-wishers engulfed him after the game.

1955

WEEK 1—The Browns start the season with a 27-17 loss to Washington, the first opening home loss in franchise history. Otto Graham, who had missed training camp before deciding to come out of retirement, starts at quarterback but struggles badly, drawing boos from his hometown fans. Graham is replaced by George Ratterman after Cleveland falls behind, 13-3.

WEEK 3—The Browns overcome deficits of 10-0 and 17-14 to defeat the Eagles, 21-17, at Cleveland. Graham directs an 87-yard drive over the final three minutes and throws a game-winning TD to Dante Lavelli. Halfbacks Fred Morrison and Ed Modzelewski, who was acquired from Pittsburgh in an offseason trade for Marion Motley, combine for 107 yards on 27 attempts.

THE SEASON AT A GLANCE

HEAD COACH

Paul Brown

REGULAR-SEASON RECORD

**9-2-1 / 1st
Eastern Conference**

TOP DRAFT CHOICE (Rd.)

Kurt Burris, C, Oklahoma (1)

SCHEDULE/RESULTS

Washington	L	17-27
at San Francisco	W	38-3
Philadelphia	W	21-17
at Washington	W	24-14
Green Bay	W	41-10
at Chi. Cardinals	W	26-20
N.Y. Giants	W	24-14
at Philadelphia	L	17-33
Pittsburgh	W	41-14
at N.Y. Giants	T	35-35
at Pittsburgh	W	30-7
Chi. Cardinals	W	35-24
Championship Game		
at Los Angeles	W	38-14

WEEK 7—The Browns defeat the Giants, 24-14, for their sixth straight victory. Graham is knocked out of the game on a blitz with the Browns trailing 14-3, but backup George Ratterman throws a 30-yard TD pass to Ray Renfro and a 14-yarder to Pete Brewster and the Browns ice the game with a late TD run by Modzelewski.

WEEK 10—Graham throws three touchdown passes but the Browns and Giants play to a 35-35 tie at New York. Trailing 28-21, the Browns tie it on a Modzelewski TD run and take the lead on linebacker Chuck Noll's 14-yard interception return. Charlie Conerly's 23-yard TD pass to Frank Gifford forces the tie and Cleveland misses a chance to win when New York's Ray Krouse blocks a Lou Groza field-goal attempt with 30 seconds left.

WEEK 12—In the final regular-season game of his career, Graham throws three touchdown passes to lead the Browns to a 35-24 win over the Chicago Cardinals. The Browns, who scored three TDs in the final five minutes, improve to 9-2-1, good enough for a return to the NFL title game.

CHAMPIONSHIP GAME—A title game-record crowd of 87,695 at Los Angeles watches the Browns win their second straight NFL crown with a 38-14 victory over the Rams. Graham caps his splendid career by throwing for two touchdowns and running for two more. When Paul Brown takes him out after his final pass—a 35-yard TD to Renfro, making the the score 38-7—the L.A. fans give the future Hall of Famer a long ovation.

Graham penetrates the Rams defense for the final touchdown of his storied career—a one-yard championship-securing run.

1956 HIGHLIGHTS

WEEK 1—The post-Otto Graham era begins with a 9-7 loss to the Cardinals at Chicago. Cleveland's only score comes on a 46-yard touchdown pass from George Ratterman to Ray Renfro in the first quarter. But Pat Summerall's third field goal, a 9-yarder with 29 seconds remaining, wins it for Chicago. The Cardinals' victory snaps a string of 12 straight losses to the Browns.

WEEK 4—Not only do the Browns drop to 1-3—the worst start in franchise history—with a 20-9 loss at Washington, they lose Ratterman to a career-ending knee injury. Cleveland fails to score after backup quarterback Babe Parilli enters the game.

WEEK 5—Parilli, making his first Cleveland start, completes only 7-of-16 passes for 126 yards and three interceptions in a 24-16 loss to Pittsburgh. After the Browns build a 13-0 lead on a 68-yard Parilli-to-Dante Lavelli TD pass and a Don Paul interception return, the Steelers score three unanswered TDs and pull away.

WEEK 7—The Browns fall to Baltimore, 21-7, at Cleveland Stadium and set a team record with their fifth loss. The Browns had lost four games in 1952, but they went on to lose to Detroit in that season's NFL championship game. There would be no such resurgence in '56, a fact that is painfully clear by midseason.

WEEK 10—The Browns edge the Eagles, 17-14, on a 37-yard Lou Groza field goal with 29 seconds remaining. But the game becomes memorable because of a small, but vocal crowd (20,654) that pelts the officials with snowballs when no pass interference is called on a controversial final-quarter play. The assault continues despite pleas from coach Paul Brown to stop.

WEEK 11—The Browns record their most satisfying win—a 24-7 victory at New York. The Giants, on the verge of clinching the Eastern Conference title, are denied by the defending-champion Browns. Preston Carpenter and Fred Morrison lead a ground assault that rolls up 193 yards.

WEEK 12—Needing a final-game win to avoid their first losing season, the Browns come up short, dropping a 24-7 decision to the visiting Cardinals. The victory gives the Cardinals a season sweep over their former nemesis. Browns quarterback Tommy O'Connell throws four interceptions in defeat.

THE SEASON AT A GLANCE

HEAD COACH

Paul Brown

REGULAR-SEASON RECORD

5-7 / T 4th
Eastern Conference

TOP DRAFT CHOICE (Rd.)

Preston Carpenter, HB, Arkansas (1)

SCHEDULE/RESULTS

at Chi. Cardinals	L	7-9
at Pittsburgh	W	23-12
N.Y. Giants	L	9-21
at Washington	L	9-20
Pittsburgh	L	16-24
at Green Bay	W	24-7
Baltimore	L	7-21
at Philadelphia	W	16-0
Washington	L	17-20
Philadelphia	W	17-14
at N.Y. Giants	W	24-7
Chi. Cardinals	L	7-24

Lavelli can't pull in this pass, thanks to the work of Eagles defenders Eddie Bell (81) and Lee Riley (22). The Week 10 victory over Philadelphia was the third-to-last game in Lavelli's outstanding career.

THE SEASON AT A GLANCE

HEAD COACH

Paul Brown

REGULAR-SEASON RECORD

9-2-1 / 1st
Eastern Conference

TOP DRAFT CHOICE (Rd.)

Jim Brown, FB, Syracuse (1)

SCHEDULE/RESULTS

N.Y. Giants	W	6-3
at Pittsburgh	W	23-12
Philadelphia	W	24-7
at Philadelphia	L	7-17
at Chi. Cardinals	W	17-7
Washington	W	21-17
Pittsburgh	W	24-0
at Washington	T	30-30
Los Angeles	W	45-31
Chi. Cardinals	W	31-0
at Detroit	L	7-20
at N.Y. Giants	W	34-28
Championship Game		
at Detroit	L	14-59

Brown found plenty of room to rumble in a 237-yard explosion against the Los Angeles Rams in Week 9.

1957
HIGHLIGHTS

WEEK 1—The Browns beat the Giants, 6-3, at Cleveland Stadium in the NFL debut of former Syracuse fullback Jim Brown, who carries 21 times for 89 yards. One of Brown's runs is a 15-yarder that sets up Lou Groza's game-winning 47-yard field goal.

WEEK 4—After opening the season with three wins, the Browns fall, 17-7, at Philadelphia. The loss comes seven days after a victory over the Eagles at Cleveland—an unusual back-to-back scheduling quirk. The difference is Eagles rookie Sonny Jurgensen, who plays well in place of starting quarterback Bobby Thomason. Milt Plum leads the Browns to their only touchdown after starting quarterback Tommy O'Connell is knocked out of the game.

WEEK 6—Brown records the first 100-yard game of his career as the Browns defeat the Washington Redskins, 21-17, at Cleveland. Brown finishes with 109 yards on 15 carries and scores two TDs as Cleveland improves to 5-1.

WEEK 9—In his ninth NFL game, Brown sets a team record that still stands—237 yards on 31 carries in a 45-31 win over the Los Angeles Rams at Cleveland Stadium. Brown scores four touchdowns, one on a 69-yard run.

WEEK 10—One week after running roughshod over the Rams, Brown is held to 57 yards by the lowly Chicago Cardinals. But the Browns win easily, 31-0, behind two O'Connell-to-Ray Renfro TD passes.

WEEK 12—Having already clinched the Eastern Conference crown and assured of a spot in the NFL title game against Detroit, the Browns close out the regular season on a winning note, 34-28 over the Giants at New York. The Browns roll up 488 yards to finish at 9-2-1, a stark improvement over the 5-7 mark of 1956. Brown rushes for 78 yards to conclude his rookie season with a league-leading 942.

CHAMPIONSHIP GAME—The Lions, seeking revenge for the 56-10 drubbing they took from the Browns in the 1954 championship game, crush Cleveland, 59-14, at Briggs Stadium. The game is never in doubt as the Lions race to a 17-0 lead and a 31-7 halftime margin. The only bright spot for Cleveland is a 29-yard touchdown run by Brown.

1958
HIGHLIGHTS

THE SEASON AT A GLANCE

HEAD COACH

Paul Brown

REGULAR-SEASON RECORD

9-3 / T 1st
Eastern Conference

TOP DRAFT CHOICE (Rd.)

Jim Shofner, DB, TCU (1)

SCHEDULE/RESULTS

at Los Angeles	W	30-27
at Pittsburgh	W	45-12
Chi. Cardinals	W	35-28
Pittsburgh	W	27-10
at Chi. Cardinals	W	38-24
N.Y. Giants	L	17-21
Detroit	L	10-30
at Washington	W	20-10
Philadelphia	W	28-14
Washington	W	21-14
at Philadelphia	W	21-14
at N.Y. Giants	L	10-13
Playoff Game		
at N.Y. Giants	L	0-10

The power running of Brown (right) keyed a Week 3 victory over the Chicago Cardinals, but a field goal by Groza (above) was too little, too late in a 30-10 Week 7 loss to Detroit. Cleveland's Pete Brewster lost control of a Plum pass (below right) thanks to Pittsburgh defender Jack Butler, but the Browns still beat the Steelers, 27-10, in Week 4.

WEEK 1—Jim Brown picks up his rookie pace, rushing for 171 yards and two touchdowns in a 30-27 season-opening win at Los Angeles. Brown's first TD comes on a 38-yard third-quarter run, the second on a 6-yard run in the fourth. Cleveland's winning points come on a 9-yard field goal by Lou Groza with 23 seconds remaining.

WEEK 2—Brown comes back with a 129-yard, three-touchdown effort in a 45-12 rout of the Steelers at Pittsburgh. The game matches Brown with rookie Bobby Mitchell in a potentially lethal backfield. Mitchell rushes for 65 yards and takes a Milt Plum screen pass 21 yards for a TD. The Steelers commit nine turnovers in the first pro game at Pitt Stadium.

WEEK 3—The Browns go to 3-0 with a 35-28 win

over the Chicago Cardinals at Cleveland Stadium. The score is surprisingly close considering Brown rushes for 182 yards and three touchdowns and Mitchell rumbles 63 yards for another TD.

WEEK 6—The Browns' first loss is a 21-17 clunker against the Giants at Cleveland. The Giants shut off Plum's passing and an offense that had been averaging 35 points per game. Mitchell fumbles three times and his performance so dismays coach Paul Brown that it costs him his starting job.

WEEK 8—Brown breaks the NFL single-season rushing record as the Browns post a 20-10 win at Washington. Brown rushes for 152 yards to improve his season total to 1,163, eclipsing the record of 1,146 set by Philadelphia's Steve Van Buren in 1949. Brown, who also scores two TDs, needs only eight

games to break a record Van Buren set in 12.

WEEK 9—Mitchell almost single-handedly beats Philadelphia as the Browns record a 28-14 win at Cleveland Stadium. Mitchell returns the opening kickoff 98 yards and a punt 68 yards for first-quarter TDs. The performance is sweet for Mitchell, who had been stripped of his starting halfback job three weeks earlier because he fumbled too much.

EASTERN CONFERENCE PLAYOFF—A week after beating Cleveland, 13-10, in the season finale at New York, the Giants prove the result is no fluke by beating the Browns again, 10-0. The Giants' defense harasses quarterback Plum and Giants linebacker Sam Huff shadows Brown, holding him to 18 rushing yards.

1959

WEEK 2—Jim Brown rushes 37 times for 147 yards on a slushy Soldier Field to lead the Browns to a 34-7 win over the Chicago Cardinals. Milt Plum throws two touchdown passes and Junior Wren returns a fumble 44 yards in helping Cleveland to its 17th win in 19 games against the Cardinals.

WEEK 5—The Browns improve to 3-2 with an easy 34-7 win over visiting Washington. Plum throws for 253 yards and four touchdowns—two, including a 76-yarder, to Bobby Mitchell. Brown rushes for 122 yards and one TD.

WEEK 6—In their first NFL meeting, Brown and Colts quarterback Johnny Unitas stage memorable performances in a 38-31 Browns victory at Baltimore. Brown opens the scoring on a 70-yard run, courtesy of great blocks by tackle Mike McCormack and Mitchell. Unitas counters with a TD pass to Lenny Moore. When the game ends, Brown has 178 rushing yards and five TDs; Unitas is 23-of-41 for 397 yards and four TDs.

THE SEASON AT A GLANCE

HEAD COACH

Paul Brown

REGULAR-SEASON RECORD

**7-5 / T 2nd
Eastern Conference**

TOP DRAFT CHOICE (Rd.)

Rich Kreitling, DE, Illinois (1)

SCHEDULE/RESULTS

at Pittsburgh	L	7-17
at Chi. Cardinals	W	34-7
N.Y. Giants	L	6-10
Chi. Cardinals	W	17-7
Washington	W	34-7
at Baltimore	W	38-31
Philadelphia	W	28-7
at Washington	W	31-17
Pittsburgh	L	20-21
San Francisco	L	20-21
at N.Y Giants	L	7-48
at Philadelphia	W	28-21

WEEK 8—Mitchell rushes for 232 yards on 14 carries—an incredible 16.6-yard average—in leading the Browns to a 31-17 win at Washington. Mitchell's rushing total, which falls five yards shy of Brown's team record, is only 42 yards more than Washington's John Olszewski, who finishes with 190 in a losing cause.

WEEK 9—Needing a win to keep pace with the Giants in the Eastern Conference, the Browns lose to the Steelers, 21-20, at Cleveland Stadium. Quarterback Bobby Layne hits Gern Nagler for 17 yards and the tying touchdown, then kicks the extra point for the win. Ray Renfro drops a potential TD pass on a last-ditch drive and Lou Groza misses a game-winning 42-yard field goal as time runs out.

WEEK 11—Everything that can go wrong does for the Browns, who are throttled, 48-7, by the Giants at New York. The game is over early as the Giants bolt to a 24-0 halftime lead and quarterback Charlie Conerly torches the Browns for 271 passing yards and three TDs. With two minutes remaining, thousands of fans rush the field in an attempt to get to Cleveland coach Paul Brown. The game is stopped for nearly 20 minutes under threat of forfeit before order is restored. Eventually it resumes without further incident.

Mitchell breaks free en route to a 65-yard touchdown run in Cleveland's 28-7 Week 7 victory over the Philadelphia Eagles.

WEEK 1—The Browns get the season off to a roaring start as Bobby Mitchell and Jim Brown combine for 309 rushing yards in a 41-24 win at Philadelphia. The Eagles, who would lose only one more game en route to an NFL championship, are no match for Mitchell, who gains 156 yards on 14 carries and scores three touchdowns, and Brown, who rumbles for 153 yards and one TD.

WEEK 2—The Browns bolt to a 21-0 halftime lead and hold off Pittsburgh, 28-20, at Cleveland Stadium. Milt Plum enjoys a big first half that includes a 69-yard touchdown bomb to Rich Kreitling and a 54-yard pass to Kreitling that sets up a short Jim Brown TD run.

THE SEASON AT A GLANCE

HEAD COACH
Paul Brown

REGULAR-SEASON RECORD
8-3-1 / 2nd Eastern Conference

TOP DRAFT CHOICE (Rd.)
Jim Houston, DE, Ohio State (1)

SCHEDULE/RESULTS

at Philadelphia	W	41-24
Pittsburgh	W	28-20
at Dallas	W	48-7
Philadelphia	L	29-31
at Washington	W	31-10
N.Y. Giants	L	13-17
St. Louis	W	28-27
at Pittsburgh	L	10-14
at St. Louis	T	17-17
Washington	W	27-16
Chicago	W	42-0
at N.Y. Giants	W	48-34

WEEK 3—The inaugural meeting between the Browns and expansion Cowboys is a mismatch as Cleveland rolls to a 48-7 victory at Dallas. Mitchell scores three touchdowns, one on a 46-yard screen pass, another on a 30-yard run and the third on a 30-yard punt return. The Browns intercept four passes.

WEEK 4—The Browns suffer their first loss, 31-29, in a rematch with the Eagles at Cleveland. The game is filled with big plays, including a 71-yard touchdown run by Brown, an 86-yard TD pass by Plum and TD passes of 49 and 57 yards by Philadelphia quarterback Norm Van Brocklin. The game is decided with 15 seconds remaining on a 38-yard field goal by the Eagles' Bobby Walston.

WEEK 6—With first place on the line and a record Cleveland Stadium crowd of 82,872 in the stands, the Browns lose to the Giants, 17-13—the Browns' sixth straight loss to New York since 1958. The Cleveland offense never gets going as Brown is held to 29 yards and Plum throws for just 89 yards.

WEEK 10—Brown becomes the first runner to reach 1,000 yards in three straight seasons with a 135-yard effort in a 27-16 win over Washington. Brown, who increases his season total to 1,047 yards, scores his only touchdown on a pass reception.

WEEK 11—The Browns intercept seven passes, return three for touchdowns and pound the Bears, 42-0, at Cleveland. Bernie Parrish returns one interception 92 yards, but Bobby Franklin becomes only the third NFL player to return two for touchdowns in the same game. The Browns gain 213 yards on interception returns.

Mitchell, half of Cleveland's big-play backfield tandem, bursts through the Philadelphia defense for one of his patented long-gainers in 1960.

A Rushing Odyssey

Brown (above) was always in a class by himself, although many of his record-setting rushing yards were piled up behind the power blocks of guard Wooten (60, right photo).

In their first decade, the Browns elevated the pro passing game to an art form. Having mastered—some say perfected—the passing attack in the All-America Football Conference and then the National Football League, the Browns proceeded to set the NFL on its ear with a thunderous running game. The poor opposition. Not long after heaving a sigh of relief when Otto Graham rode off into retirement, Cleveland opponents had to turn around and adjust their defenses when bruising fullback Jim Brown rode in. Truth be told, they never did adjust.

Brown arrived in 1957, one year after Cleveland had endured a thoroughly disconcerting transition from a Graham-led passing machine to Brown-oriented smashmouth football. With Graham in his first year of retirement and Brown still lugging the ball for Syracuse University as a man among boys, the 1956 Browns stumbled to a 5-7 record.

But when Brown—picked after Paul Hornung, Jon Arnett, John Brodie, Ron Kramer and Len Dawson in the NFL draft—settled into the Cleveland backfield, the Browns were off and ... steamrolling. In his pro debut—at Cleveland Stadium on September 29, 1957—Brown rushed for 89 yards against the New York Giants. Five weeks later, against the Washington Redskins, he recorded his first 100-yard day. And on November 24, Brown became a full-fledged NFL force when, using his uncommon blend of raw power and scintillating speed to maximum efficiency, he shredded the Los Angeles Rams for an NFL-record 237 yards. This breakthrough came in his ninth pro game.

By season's end, Brown had 942 yards—in a 12-game schedule— enough to lead the league in rushing, and enough to lead the Browns back to what almost seemed their rightful place—the NFL championship game. Not even a 45-point title-game loss to the Detroit Lions was cause for great angst. Brown was just embarking on what surely would be a long and glorious career, in which he would power Cleveland to god-knows-how-many championships.

Kelly was a special-teams force (above against the Steelers) early in his career before following in Brown's sizeable footsteps.

had been fooled before—by what they perceived as countless carries and hits finally taking a toll on Brown, evidenced by his slow, slower and slower-yet habit of getting up after being tackled.

"I (was) just saving my energy for the next play," Brown explained. "I learned this from (Olympian) Bob Mathias. Once I entered the national decathlon trials, and I saw how Bob seemed to flop down completely after each event. We talked about it and he said it was his method of total relaxation and helped him come back fresh for the next event. (I used) the Mathias formula."

And, no, Brown wasn't wearing down. Reinvigorated by Collier's appointment as coach after the 1962 season, he experienced an extraordinary year in 1963: 1,863 yards rushing and 6.4 yards per

carry. He followed up with 1,446 yards in 1964 and 1,544 in 1965.

"What acceleration he had," marveled longtime Browns guard Gene Hickerson.

"Jim Brown was the greatest ever," said John Wooten, another of his blockers.

Brown is quick to point out the importance of Hickerson, Wooten and company.

"I wouldn't have been successful without the offensive line," he said. "I had Dick Schafrath and Gene Hickerson, who should be in the Hall of Fame. We had the best downfield blockers in the history of professional football—Schafrath, Hickerson, John Wooten, Monte Clark.

"These guys were dedicated individuals who would listen, take direction and execute to the best of their ability. They worked to the maximum of their ability, which made me into a successful running back. …"

The long and glorious career envisioned for Brown in '57 had now covered nine seasons and brought glory on individual and team fronts—Brown was the NFL's all-time rushing leader with 12,312 yards and Cleveland, after an eight-year drought, had recaptured the league championship in '64.

But the Browns and their fans wanted more. A return to the title game in '65 (a loss to Green Bay) only whetted everyone's appetite for a return to the franchise's true glory days. And with Brown only 29 years old, the bevy of titles expected after his arrival still seemed possible. But he had more on his mind than football.

Deeply committed to blacks' economic and social advancement at the height of the civil-rights movement, Brown said he wanted to be at the forefront of "the struggle that is going on in our country." He also had begun an acting career. So he did what he felt he had to do: He walked away from the game. And no one could believe it.

Collier didn't want to believe it. But he took some solace when he received a letter from Brown saying that Leroy Kelly, who had been limited to 43 carries in his first two seasons with Cleveland, had the ability to become one of the NFL's best backs.

"I told Blanton he wouldn't miss me," Brown recalled.

That, of course, was an overstatement. But Kelly, an eighth-round draft choice out of Morgan State, had showed breakaway capability on special teams and apparently needed only more playing time. Crucial, perhaps, was that he already had won the respect of his teammates.

Reflecting on the Browns' 1964 NFL title, linebacker Jim Houston said: "One key element was Leroy Kelly, who was our return guy. It was his first year. He had an explosive start and he always gave us positive field position. (That's) the key to everything."

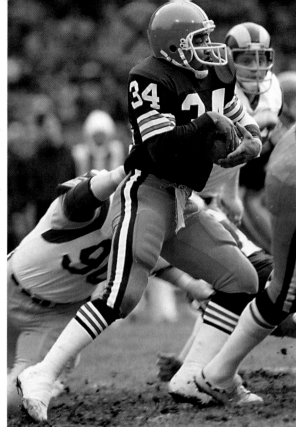

Kelly (44, right) did most of the legwork in the years following Brown, and the Pruitts, speedy Greg (above) and hard-charging Mike (left), kept the running back lineage alive in the 1970s and early '80s. Mack (below left) and Byner both topped 1,000 yards in 1985—the first and only Browns teammates to accomplish that feat in the same season.

Teammate Paul Warfield said Kelly was a kick-return innovator.

"All the NFL teams generally formed a wall for the kick receiver, who would then make a break for the sidelines," he explained. "That's the way the defense usually adjusted. But Leroy would take a lightning step to the left or right and break clear up the middle of the field. Coach Collier would say, 'For us, it's just like a draw play.'"

With Brown gone, Kelly's responsibilities grew. Immediately. After carrying the ball 37 times in the previous season, Kelly toted it 209 times in 1966 and put up Brown-like numbers (1,141 yards and 5.5 yards per attempt).

"I never tried to copy his style," Kelly said of Brown, "but I learned so much just watching him run, especially the way he got out quick for a pitchout, snapped his head, made his move and was under control after a few steps."

Kelly quickly won plaudits for his own elusive moves. He ran for 1,205 and 1,239 yards in his second and third seasons as the go-to guy in the Cleveland backfield, and from '66 through 1968 he rushed for 42 touchdowns.

"I can feel it in my legs, on Saturday or Sunday, if I'm going to have a good day," he said. "When we loosen up before the game, if the legs really feel good and strong, then I know. ...

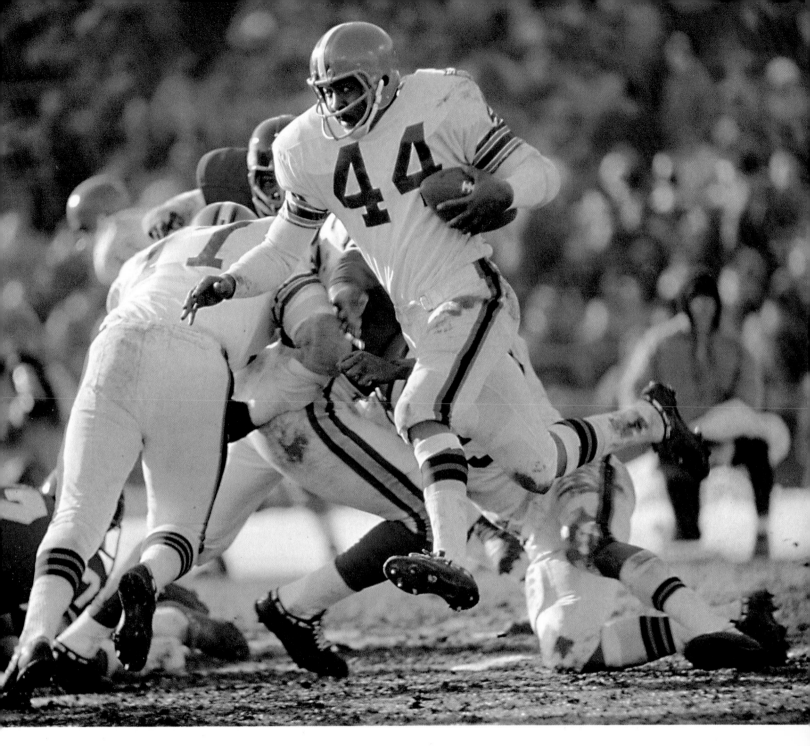

"Actually, I know it's up to the blocking."

Or just maybe it depended on the field conditions. *Bad conditions*, that is.

"Leroy was a guy who was kind of flat-footed," said teammate Doug Dieken, an offensive lineman. "He had the ability to stop and go. He was one of those guys ~~~~~~~ rainy day, you said, 'Oh, man, Leroy's going to have a big day.'"

Kelly had a decade's worth of big days, winding up with 7,274 rushing yards when he called it a career after the 1973 season.

Fortunate to have Kelly waiting in the wings when Jim Brown retired, Cleveland kept the running-back lineage going. Fleet Greg

Pruitt stepped in for Kelly, and when Greg began wearing down in the late '70s, muscular Mike Pruitt (no relation) was there to take over.

Greg Pruitt had three consecutive ~~~~~rd seasons and just missed a fourth. Mike reeled ~~~~~~~~ 0-yard totals in a ~~~~~~~~ ing in 1983.

~~~~~~~~ 40 yards," Greg Pruitt said. And, time and again, he proved it with long bursts from the line of scrimmage.

"God gave (Mike Pruitt) a tremendous body and talent," former Cleveland backfield coach Jim Garrett said. And, time and again, Mike Pruitt proved it with high-yield production despite taking a relentless pounding.

Although Cleveland's tradition of great running backs suffered a bit in the final 10 seasons of the original team's existence, there was one last hurrah: In 1985, two Browns players rushed for 1,000 yards in the same season, a franchise first. Second-year man Earnest Byner gained 1,002 and Kevin Mack, playing his first NFL season after spending one year in the United States Football League, netted 1,104, accounting for the 18th and 19th 1,000-yard seasons in Browns history.

That one of those seasons was not recorded by Marion Motley seems odd. Motley, a 235-pounder (by conservative estimates), was the Browns' first great runner and one of pro football's first truly effective big backs.

Truly effective? How about season rushing averages of 8.2 and 6.1 (twice) in the AAFC? How about a 5.8 mark in his first NFL season?

Motley's brute strength served him well.

"Just run right at them and over them," coach Paul Brown once suggested. And Motley did just that.

No, Motley never gained 1,000—he came closest in 1948, when he got to 964—but high season yardage totals were rare in those days. The man is best judged by his gain-per-carry figures—in a 1950 game against the Steelers, he averaged 17.1 yards on 11 rushes.

"He had speed for the size of man that he was," longtime teammate Dante Lavelli said. "(And) he was a great blocker."

Bobby Mitchell never ran for 1,000, either, but he was a remarkable complement to Brown in a short-lived Cleveland career.

Motley, whose style was power and strength, set a fast pace for Cleveland's running tradition.

He was at his best in 1959 when he rushed for 743 yards (232 in one game) and set a franchise record with a 90-yard run from scrimmage. But, after four years with the Browns, the speedy Mitchell was traded to Washington for the draft rights to Ernie Davis.

Speed, size, strength. Those words come up a lot when discussing the rich history of Browns running backs, a history that includes Hall of Famers Jim Brown (judged the No. 1 player in pro football history by The Sporting News), Leroy Kelly, Marion Motley and many others who displayed uncommon skill while building upon a remarkable ballcarrying tradition.

Jim Brown by the numbers

How good was Jim Brown? Consider this: When he retired he owned at least a dozen major NFL records for scoring and rushing (right). Only three of Brown's records remain intact (■), but remember: He didn't play a game after age 29. The chart below compares Brown to the men who have passed him on the all-time rushing list.

- ■ Consecutive seasons rushing leader (5)
- ■ Seasons leading league in rushing (8)
- ■ 100-yard rushing games, career (58)
- ■ Highest average gain, career (5.22)
- ■ Rushing touchdowns, career (106)
- ■ Rushing attempts, career (2,359)
- ■ Yards gained, game (237, twice)
- ■ Rushing attempts, season (305)
- ■ 1,000-yard rushing seasons (7)
- ■ Yards gained, career (12,312)
- ■ Yards gained, season (1,863)
- ■ Touchdowns, career (126)

PLAYER (SEASONS)	RUSHING YARDS	GAMES PLAYED	YARDS PER CARRY
Walter Payton (13)	16,726	190	4.4
Barry Sanders (10)*	15,269	153	5.0
Eric Dickerson (11)	13,259	146	4.4
Tony Dorsett (12)	12,739	173	4.3
Emmitt Smith (9)*	12,566	140	4.3
JIM BROWN (9)	12,312	118	5.2

*Through the 1998 season.

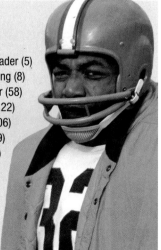

1961
HIGHLIGHTS

WEEK 1—Lou Groza, returning from a one-year retirement, watches Timmy Brown return the opening kickoff 105 yards and the defending-champion Eagles go on to post a 27-20 win at Philadelphia. The kick return is the longest ever against the Browns, who later botch a punt, throw an interception and fumble at the Eagles' 1.

WEEK 2—The Browns bounce back from the Philadelphia loss with a 20-17 comeback win over St. Louis. The turnover-prone Browns fall behind 14-0, but Milt Plum throws touchdown passes to halfback Tom Watkins and receiver Leon Clarke and Groza wins the game with a field goal in the final minute.

WEEK 5—In the first meeting between coaching legends Paul Brown and Vince Lombardi, the Packers rout the Browns, 49-17, at Cleveland Stadium. Green Bay's Jim Taylor rushes for 158 yards, Bart Starr throws for 266 and Paul Hornung scores one touchdown and kicks seven extra points. The Packers hold Jim Brown to 72 yards.

WEEK 9—Brown rushes for 133 yards, but his first career touchdown pass proves decisive in a 17-6 win over

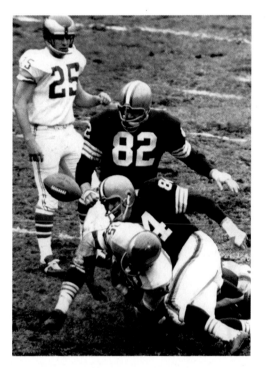

Washington. With the Browns leading 3-0, Brown pulls up on a sweep and throws a perfect 37-yard scoring pass to Ray Renfro—the first pass attempt of his career. Cleveland's only other points come on a Plum-to-Rich Kreitling TD pass.

WEEK 10—Needing a win to keep pace with the Eagles, the Browns defeat Philadelphia, 45-24, at Cleveland. Brown ties his own team rushing record with 237 yards on 34 attempts. He also scores four touchdowns, his best single-game total since a five-TD effort against Baltimore in 1959.

WEEK 11—The Browns lose a critical game to the Giants, 37-21, at Cleveland. Plum throws a 43-yard TD pass to Renfro on the Browns' first possession, but backup Len Dawson comes in later and throws a key interception. The Browns fall two games behind the Giants in the Eastern Conference race.

WEEK 13—The Browns blow a 14-0 lead and watch their playoff hopes officially end in a 17-14 loss at Chicago. One bright spot is Groza, who kicks two extra points and passes Don Hutson for the No. 1 spot on the NFL's career scoring list.

Everybody was optimistic in 1961 when Art Modell (left) bought the team and posed with Jim Brown and Paul Brown. The season did not produce a conference title or playoff berth, but the Browns did have their moments—including a double-team tackle (top photo) by ends Jim Houston (82) and Paul Wiggin (84) that forced a fumble by Philadelphia's Clarence Peaks.

THE SEASON AT A GLANCE

HEAD COACH

Paul Brown

REGULAR-SEASON RECORD

**8-5-1 / 3rd
Eastern Conference**

TOP DRAFT CHOICE (Rd.)

**Bobby Crespino, TE,
Mississippi (1)**

SCHEDULE/RESULTS

at Philadelphia	L	20-27
St. Louis	W	20-17
Dallas	W	25-7
Washington	W	31-7
Green Bay	L	17-49
at Pittsburgh	W	30-28
at St. Louis	W	21-10
Pittsburgh	L	13-17
at Washington	W	17-6
Philadelphia	W	45-24
N.Y. Giants	L	21-37
at Dallas	W	38-17
at Chicago	L	14-17
at N.Y. Giants	T	7-7

1962
HIGHLIGHTS

THE SEASON AT A GLANCE

HEAD COACH

Paul Brown

REGULAR-SEASON RECORD

7-6-1 / 3rd
Eastern Conference

TOP DRAFT CHOICE (Rd.)

Gary Collins, E, Maryland (1)

Leroy Jackson, RB,
Western Illinois (1)

WEEK 1—The Browns give a record opening-day crowd of 81,115 at Cleveland Stadium something to remember in a 17-7 victory over the Giants. The game's most memorable play is a flea-flicker that sets up a 29-yard Lou Groza field goal. Quarterback Jim Ninowski hands the ball to Jim Brown, who hands to receiver Ray Renfro, who hands the ball back to Ninowski, who completes a 53-yard pass to Rich Kreitling.

WEEK 2—Bobby Mitchell, traded by coach Paul Brown to Washington during the offseason, haunts his old team by scoring the winning touchdown in

a 17-16 Redskins victory at Cleveland. With the Browns leading 16-10 late in the fourth quarter and trying to run out the clock, Brown fumbles, giving the Redskins possession near midfield. Norm Snead throws a short pass to Mitchell, who races for the go-ahead touchdown. The Browns get two shots at a final-minute game-winning field goal, but both of Groza's attempts are blocked.

WEEK 5—The Browns are beaten decisively by the Colts, 36-14, at Cleveland Stadium. The Browns do not get a first down until Baltimore has a 23-0 lead. Brown is held to his lowest rushing total ever:

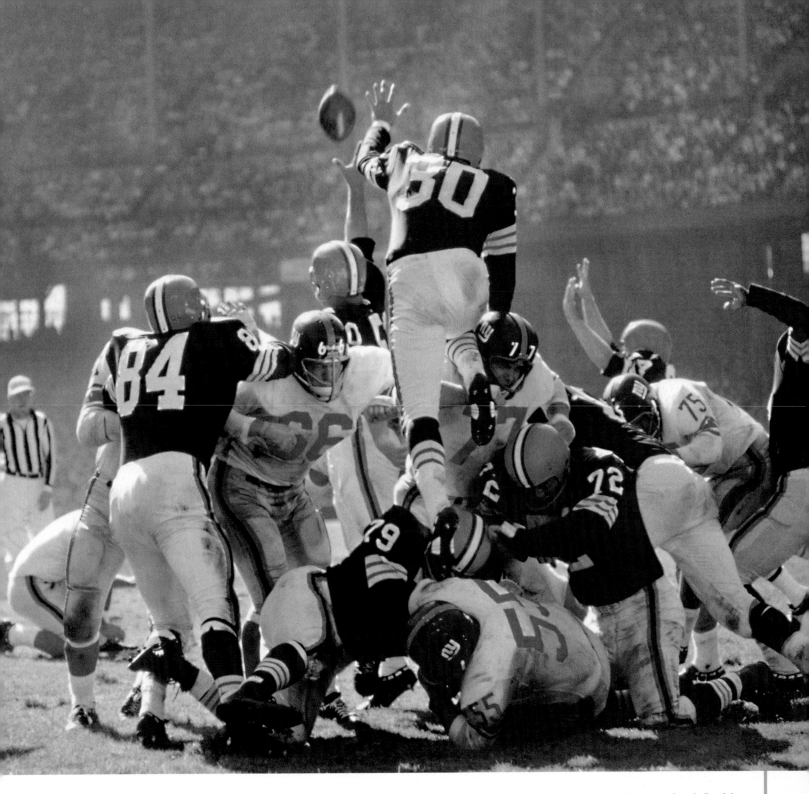

11 yards on 14 attempts, with seven of those yards coming on one carry.

WEEK 8—In one of the uglier games played at Cleveland Stadium, the Browns and Eagles combine for eight turnovers and five missed field goals in a 14-14 tie. Brown finishes with 69 rushing yards on 20 carries, his seventh consecutive game with fewer than 100 yards.

WEEK 11—Brown, ending the longest 100-yard drought of his career at nine games, pounds for 110 in a 35-14 win at Cleveland Stadium. Frank Ryan complements Brown by throwing for 284 yards and three touchdowns.

WEEK 14—In what would be the final game of Paul Brown's Cleveland coaching career, the Browns beat the 49ers, 13-10, at Kezar Stadium. The Browns avoid their second losing season but cannot save their coach's job. Needing 139 yards for another 1,000-yard campaign, Jim Brown falls just short, ending the year at 996. Although Brown fails to win a rushing title for the first time in his career, he does lead the team in receiving for the first time, catching 47 passes for 517 yards and five touchdowns.

Defensive back Bernie Parrish climbs the mountain of bodies (above) while trying to block an extra-point attempt by the New York Giants. Center John Morrow (left, above left photo) and guard John Wooten get advice from above while quarterback Ninowski (below left) takes his instruction from the sideline.

The Awful Truth

The player whose uniform number eventually would be retired by the Cleveland Browns received a thunderous ovation when he was first introduced to the home crowd—and the man had yet to play a single down for the Browns.

It was the night of August 18, 1962, and a crowd of 77,000-plus at Cleveland Stadium, on hand for an NFL exhibition doubleheader, rose to applaud the player. The fans were cheering his remarkable accomplishments as a collegian and his vast potential as a pro—and showing they were with him as he dealt with an illness, shrouded in mystery, that so far had kept him from suiting up for the Browns.

It was an emotional moment for the gifted player and the fans honoring him—neither of whom had any real sense of the awful truth: Ernie Davis would never play a single down for the Browns.

What might have been—what should have been—would not be. Davis, the 1961

Brown (left) poses in a happy moment with No. 45-to-be Davis.

Heisman Trophy winner out of Syracuse, was to be paired in the same backfield with former Orangemen star Jim Brown, already considered among the greatest runners in football history after only five NFL seasons. Syracuse's fabled No. 44s would be united—the seasoned pro wearing No. 32, the rookie sporting No. 45, together in one hellacious backfield, the likes of which the game had never seen and likely would never see again.

When the Browns opened their preliminary training camp in early August of '62, the intrigue was enormous. Brown was coming off a 1,408-yard season and Davis, the first African-American to win the Heisman, had completed a college career in which he had averaged 6.6 yards per carry. The thought of what the double-blockbuster backfield might mean to Cleveland's championship aspirations was heady stuff.

"I made the deal that brought Ernie Davis to Cleveland," said coach/general manager Paul Brown, alluding to the trade that sent standout runner/receiver Bobby Mitchell to the Redskins for the draft rights to Davis. "We wanted him to join Jim Brown in giving us two big backs. The Packers had been very successful with big runners. ..." (Using Jim Taylor and Paul Hornung as heavy-duty ballcarriers, Vince Lombardi had coached Green Bay to the '61 NFL championship.)

Davis was in the Cleveland camp only briefly before heading to Evanston, Ill., to join the College All-Stars in preparation for their game against the Packers. While in Evanston, Davis woke up with a badly swollen face after having two teeth extracted and also developed a mouth infection. Plus, he was slowed by a muscle pull in his leg.

Davis wound up in the hospital and missed the game against Green Bay. Though disappointed, Davis rarely complained. About anything. An All-American player on the field, he was an all-American kid off it—unfailingly modest, polite, kind and happy.

"He radiated pleasantness and had the highest ideals," said

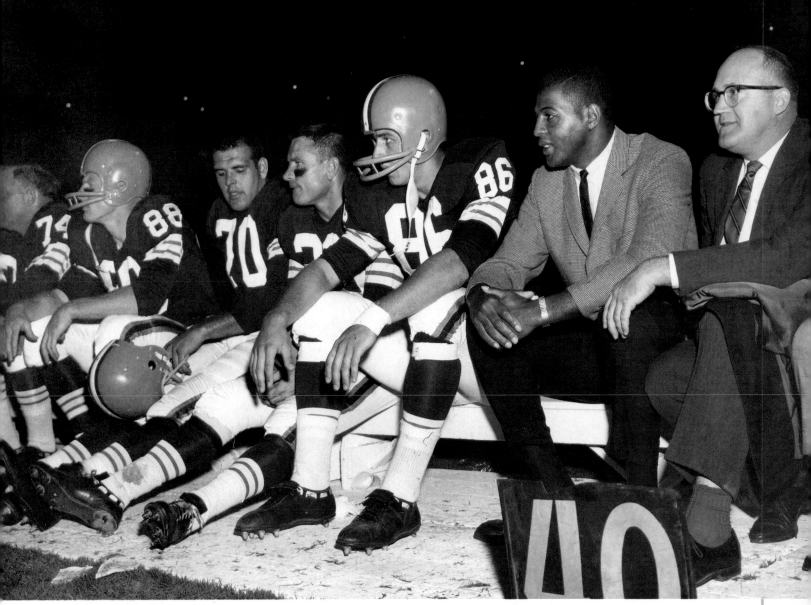

Davis had an emotional moment in the spotlight: a 1962 preseason game in which he was honored at midfield before sitting on the Browns' bench.

Ben Schwartzwalder, his college coach. "He just couldn't do enough for people, and he did it all with a smile. He even thanked folks who asked for his autograph."

Davis' personality didn't change—not when ensuing hospital tests revealed he had a blood disorder (the specifics of which weren't divulged at the time), and not even when he was told in early October that he had leukemia.

As the 1962 season wore on, Davis' leukemia went into remission and he looked ahead with steely resolve: "Starting next year, I expect to play 10 or 11 years and then go into business. I'd like to get into purchasing or marketing."

Early in 1963, Davis wrote a national magazine story—it was titled "I'm Not Unlucky"— in which he further vowed to beat his illness and return to the sport he loved so much. "The big thing to me in football has always been the competitiveness," he said. "Sometimes, when the game is close and the play is roughest, you forget the crowd and the noise, and it is just you against somebody else to see who is the better man. This is what I liked and took pride in ... and, after all the waiting, I want a chance to do (it) again."

Davis never got that chance. The leukemia turned virulent, and he re-entered a Cleveland hospital in May 1963—but not before visiting Browns owner Art Modell, a get-together in which Ernie discussed the team's outlook and apologized for the mounting medical bills his illness was costing the franchise.

On May 18, 1963, the player who so fervently yearned to compete—to find out who was the better man—died at age 23.

The Browns, convinced there hardly could have been a better man, have made Ernie Davis' number one of only five they have retired in franchise history. Though Davis surely would have appreciated the retiring of No. 45, just imagine how thrilled he would have been to have worn it. Even once.

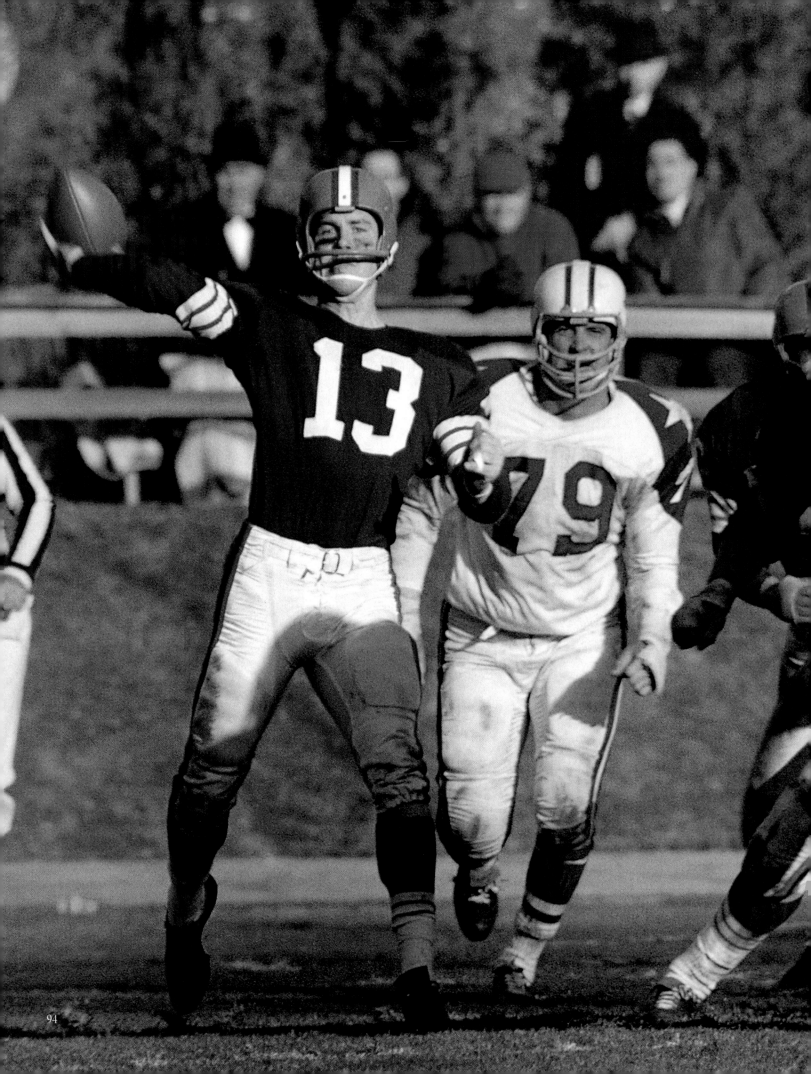

Ryan (13) passed the Browns to a 27-17 Week 11 win over the Cowboys, two days after President John F. Kennedy had been assassinated in Dallas. The somber game was played amid a storm of controversy created by NFL commissioner Pete Rozelle's decision to play the Sunday schedule in the wake of a national tragedy.

1963
HIGHLIGHTS

WEEK 1—Blanton Collier, making his coaching debut, watches his Browns pound Washington, 37-14, at Cleveland Stadium. Frank Ryan, after winning the starting job from Jim Ninowski, completes 21-of-31 passes for 334 yards while helping the Browns roll up 543 total yards. Jim Brown rushes for 162 yards and catches three passes for 100 more. Former Brown Bobby Mitchell makes a 99-yard touchdown reception for the Redskins.

WEEK 2—Brown rushes for 232 yards on 20 carries and leads Cleveland to a 41-24 win at Dallas. Brown's rushing total, which includes touchdown runs of 71 and 62 yards, overshadows a fine effort by Ryan, who runs for one TD and completes 11-of-18 passes for 188 yards and two TDs, both to second-year receiver Gary Collins.

WEEK 4—In an early-season showdown of unbeaten Eastern Conference teams, the Browns defeat the Steelers, 35-23, before a record Cleveland Stadium crowd of 84,684. Brown rips the Steelers for 175 yards and Cleveland rolls up 357, but Pittsburgh wins the yardage battle with 400. The Steelers settle for field goals twice after

having the ball at the 1-yard line.

WEEK 6—The Browns defeat the Eagles, 37-7, for their sixth straight win, but the spotlight focuses on Brown, who becomes the NFL's all-time leading rusher. Brown's 144-yard effort increases his career total to 8,385, bettering the 8,378 yards compiled by former 49ers star Joe Perry. Brown breaks Perry's record in his 82nd game, barely more than half the 155 games Perry played.

WEEK 7—One week after a crushing 33-6 loss at home to the Giants, the Browns post an ugly 23-17 win over the Eagles at Philadelphia. The 2-4-1 Eagles outgain the Browns, who get a 223-yard effort and 62-yard touchdown gallop from the relentless Brown.

WEEK 9—The Browns' hopes of winning the Eastern Conference title are dealt a severe blow in a 9-7 loss at Pittsburgh. The Browns don't get inside the Steelers' 18-yard line after scoring their only touchdown on a 4-yard Ryan pass to Collins.

WEEK 12—The Browns avenge a 20-14 loss at home two weeks earlier with a 24-10 win over the Cardinals at Busch Stadium in St. Louis. Brown, who ran for 154 yards in the first meeting between the teams, scorches the St. Louis defense for 179 in the rematch, increasing his season total to 1,677, bettering his previous career high of 1,527 set in 1958.

Collier's first crack at an NFL head coaching job produced a 10-4 record—an impressive first season while replacing a legend.

THE SEASON AT A GLANCE

HEAD COACH
Blanton Collier

REGULAR-SEASON RECORD
**10-4 / 2nd
Eastern Conference**

TOP DRAFT CHOICE (Rd.)
Tom Hutchinson, E, Kentucky (1)

SCHEDULE/RESULTS

Washington	W	37-14
at Dallas	W	41-24
Los Angeles	W	20-6
Pittsburgh	W	35-23
at N.Y. Giants	W	35-24
Philadelphia	W	37-7
N.Y. Giants	L	6-33
at Philadelphia	W	23-17
at Pittsburgh	L	7-9
St. Louis	L	14-20
Dallas	W	27-17
at St. Louis	W	24-10
at Detroit	L	10-38
at Washington	W	27-20

1964

HIGHLIGHTS

WEEK 2—Quarterbacks Frank Ryan and Charley Johnson each throw for three touchdowns and kickers Lou Groza and Jim Bakken each kick four field goals as the Browns and Cardinals battle to a 33-33 tie. The game is decided in the final 90 seconds on clutch efforts by both teams. Ryan, facing fourth-and-19 at the St. Louis 45, throws deep to Gary Collins, who makes a diving catch to set up Jim Brown's 2-yard TD run and give the Browns a 33-30 lead. But Johnson answers with a desperation drive that sets up Bakken's game-tying field goal.

THE SEASON AT A GLANCE

HEAD COACH

Blanton Collier

REGULAR-SEASON RECORD

**10-3-1 / 1st
Eastern Conference**

TOP DRAFT CHOICE (Rd.)

**Paul Warfield, WR,
Ohio State (1)**

SCHEDULE/RESULTS

at Washington	W	27-13
St. Louis	T	33-33
at Philadelphia	W	28-20
Dallas	W	27-6
Pittsburgh	L	7-23
at Dallas	W	20-16
N.Y. Giants	W	42-20
at Pittsburgh	W	30-17
Washington	W	34-24
Detroit	W	37-21
at Green Bay	L	21-28
Philadelphia	W	38-24
at St. Louis	L	19-28
at N.Y. Giants	W	52-20
Championship Game		
Baltimore	W	27-0

WEEK 4—Ryan completes 15-of-26 passes for 256 yards and three touchdowns to lead the Browns to a 27-6 win over Dallas, but the victory is costly. Defensive tackle Bob Gain suffers a season-ending broken leg and defensive back Ross Fichtner sustains a concussion that will sideline him for most of the regular season. Collins catches a TD pass in his sixth straight game, breaking a team record shared by Dante Lavelli and Ray Renfro.

WEEK 5—Pittsburgh pounds out a 23-7 victory at Cleveland, thanks to a 200-yard effort by John Henry Johnson—the most rushing yards ever yielded by a Browns defense. Johnson scores on runs of 33, 45 and 5 yards as the Steelers hand the Browns their first loss. The Steelers, using five linemen, five defensive backs and one linebacker, hold Brown to 59 yards.

WEEK 9—The Browns take a two-game Eastern Conference lead over the Cardinals by beating the Redskins, 34-24, at Cleveland. The Browns, leading 13-3 at the half, score twice in the third quarter—on Brown's 13-yard halfback pass to Collins and a 62-yard bomb from Ryan to rookie Paul Warfield.

WEEK 10—The Browns defeat the Lions, 37-21, before 83,064 fans at Cleveland Stadium. Brown gains 147 yards and scores twice, putting him over the 1,000-yard mark for the sixth time. The game ends with Walter Beach returning an interception of former Browns quarterback Milt Plum 65 yards for a touchdown.

WEEK 14—Needing a season-closing victory to clinch the Eastern Conference crown, the Browns pound out a 52-20 win over the Giants at Yankee Stadium. Ryan completes 12-of-13 passes for 202 yards and five touchdowns and runs 13 yards for a sixth TD. Warfield catches five passes for 103 yards and Brown rushes for 99 yards.

Ernie Green (48) slices through the Pittsburgh defense as quarterback Ryan (13) watches the result of his handoff.

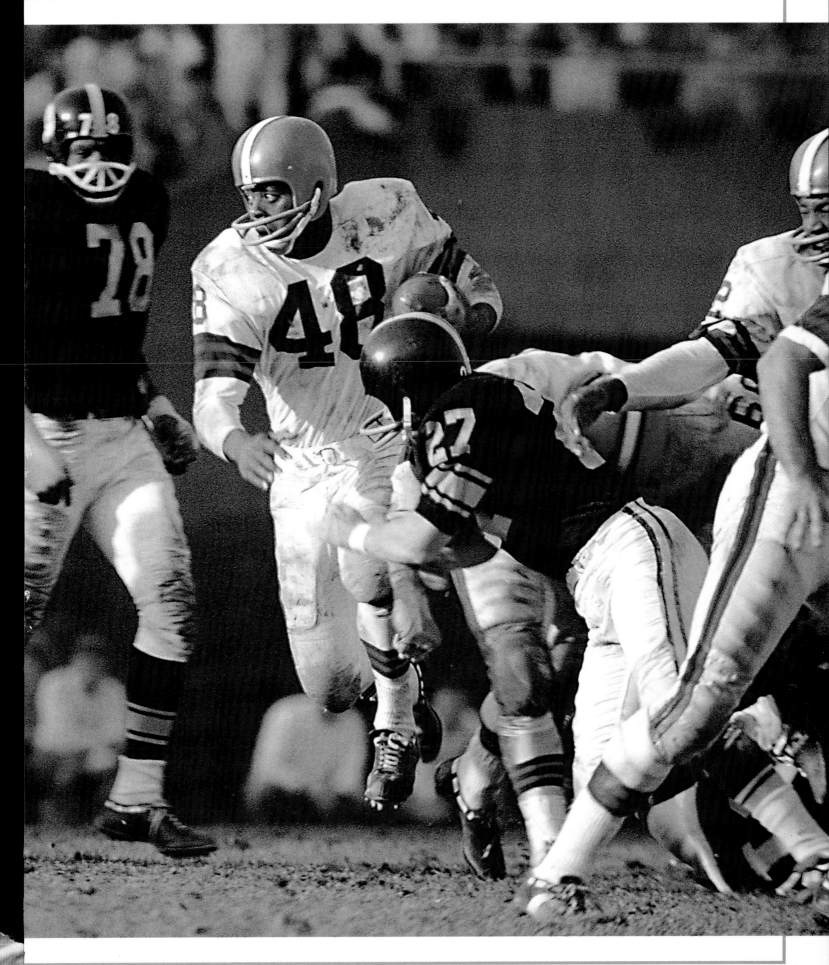

Champions Again

Frank Ryan. Gary Collins. Jim Brown. Lou Groza. Their names dominate the statistical summaries of Cleveland's 1964 championship game victory over the heavily-favored Baltimore Colts. But Browns linebacker Jim Houston, with all due respect, thinks the most important name is missing.

"Galen Fiss breaking through and nailing Lenny Moore was the key play," Houston recalled. "Galen diagnosed the play very well, and when Moore caught that pass, whack, he was down. It set the tone. I think it was the most important play of the game."

The play, which occurred in the first quarter of a game the Browns would win 27-0, did not decide the outcome, prevent a touchdown, force a turnover or even merit a mention in the game story that graced the front page of the New York Times the next day. But years later, it remains a highlight-film staple that never fails to trip the emotional switch inside Cleveland fans.

It was a simple screen pass and Fiss, the right linebacker, moved up quickly, shot past a blocker and executed a roll-block just as Moore turned upfield after catching the Johnny Unitas toss. Moore went down hard and fast, triggering a mighty roar that shook Cleveland Stadium and sent the 79,544 fans into a frenzy.

"I caught the pass, looked upfield and wondered where everybody was," Moore remembered. "Nothing but daylight. I turned my head and here he comes and trips me up.

"I should still be running with that ball. Yeah, that play really inspired them."

Browns defenders Jim Kanicki (69), Dick Modzelewski and Bill Glass (80) kept Colts quarterback Johnny Unitas (19) under wraps. Baltimore kept Brown out of the end zone (32, right photo), but he still ran for 114 yards.

And it delivered a message that the Browns' rubber-band defense would neither bend nor break on this cold, blustery afternoon. Defense had not been the staple throughout a 10-3-1 season powered by a high-scoring offense.

"We had Jimmy Brown, Frank Ryan, a good line—Gene Hickerson, Monte Clark,

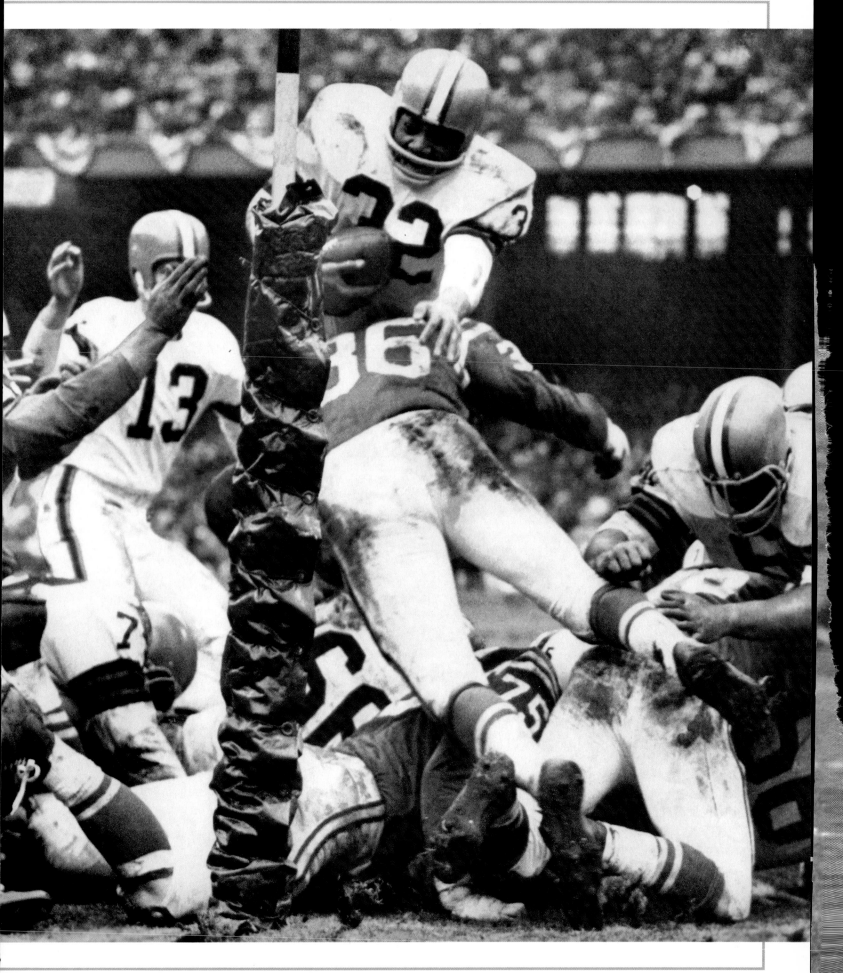

John Morrow, John Wooten, Dick Schafrath—Paul Warfield, as much offense as we needed," Houston said. "We had plenty of reason to be confident."

The key, of course, was Brown, who posted 1,446 yards during the season as the centerpiece of the Cleveland attack. Quarterback Ryan, with Brown attracting defenders like a magnet, enjoyed the luxury of throwing to veteran Gary Collins and rookie Warfield, the graceful receiver by way of Warren, Ohio, and Ohio State University.

But the defense?

"We had given up a lot of passing yards all year, but part of it was that we'd always get ahead and play that bend-but-don't-break defense," said tackle Jim Kanicki, who replaced injured veteran Bob Gain as a starter early in the season. "We gave up a lot underneath that we didn't give the Colts."

Baltimore, 12-2 during the regular season, entered the championship game on a roll, thanks to a powerful defense and an offense that featured Unitas, Moore, Raymond Berry, John Mackey and Jimmy Orr. But the Colts appeared ill prepared for a well-conceived Browns defensive strategy and the ill winds that blew in off Lake Erie.

"It was overcast, windy, cold, blustery, damp—it was perfect," Kanicki said with a smile. "I just think we had enough pressure on Unitas that he didn't have a chance to set up. For some reason, their offense wasn't ready for our defense. We had a good rush and he just never got into his good rhythm.

"We were rolling up on the corners against Berry and Orr, something we hadn't been doing all year. We had let teams have the outs and slants all year, but we took those quick passes away from Unitas. That seemed to confuse him."

Coach Blanton Collier's defensive strategy was aided by a conservative Baltimore approach that failed to generate much first-half offense. But the Browns were equally laid back and satisfied to go into the intermission with a scoreless tie—something of a moral victory.

"We had not been terribly successful moving the ball, but neither had they," recalled Ryan. "There was a lot of wind, tough conditions. There was a lot of optimism that we were in the game, not in a hole."

There was nothing conservative about the Browns in the second half. Cleveland, with the wind at its back, broke through early in the third quarter when a wind-blown punt by Tom Gilburg set up Lou Groza's 42-yard field goal. On the Browns' next possession, Brown took a Ryan pitch and raced for 46 of his game-high 114 yards to the Baltimore 18, setting up the first of three Ryan-to-Collins touchdown passes.

Collins' first touchdown catch, much to the dismay of Colts defender Jim Welch (46), jump-started the Browns after a scoreless first half.

SPOTLIGHT: PAUL WARFIELD

Paul Warfield considers himself a lucky man. But opponents who tried to slow him down insist luck had nothing to do with it. In Warfield's case, luck was in the eye of the beholder: Browns and Dolphins fans who watched him work his graceful, prancing magic over 13 seasons as a wide receiver.

"Paul had incredible moves," recalled former Browns quarterback Frank Ryan. "He was so quick, so fast—with Paul, there was never traffic. It was fun to throw to him. Invariably, he was open whenever you wanted him."

Warfield was the classic big-play receiver, the man who could break open a game or keep defenses honest. He was an important factor in the success of running backs Jim Brown and Leroy Kelly in Cleveland and the trio of Jim Kiick, Larry Csonka and Mercury Morris in Miami. He drew constant double-team attention, keeping defenses from keying too heavily on those runners.

Warfield's graceful style looked more like ballet than football and his white-collar image seemed to contradict the blue-collar style that suited Cleveland, but he was a dangerous weapon who could strike deep with his speed, turn around defenders with his elusiveness and throw efficient blocks with his 188-pound frame. He was a natural for the City by the Lake.

"I am a native of Northeast Ohio," Warfield said. "My hometown (Warren) is 50 miles east of Cleveland. I grew up as a follower of the Indians and Browns. I played against Cleveland scholastic football teams in high school and I moved on to Ohio State University. There's a special bond between myself and the fans because I'm one of them."

The bond was sealed when rookie Warfield played on the Browns' 1964 NFL championship team. He helped the Browns post a six-year mark of 59-23-2 and reach the title game in 1965, 1968 and 1969 before a shocking trade sent him to Miami on January 27, 1970.

"I'm playing with one of the best organizations, one of the the best teams, in my own backyard, in the area I grew up in, I have a tremendous relationship with the fans, my life professionally at that point is pretty darn good—and I get the blow of my life," Warfield said. "I get a telephone call telling me I'm not only going to what was then an inferior league (the AFL), but to one of the worst teams in pro football."

But not for long. The expansion Dolphins, with new coach Don Shula calling the shots, quickly developed into a winner and posted a 57-12-1 record over Warfield's five Miami seasons, winning three AFC championships and consecutive Super Bowls ('72 and '73 seasons). But, like his early years with the Browns, a run-oriented attack kept him from displaying his full array of talents.

Still, when he retired in 1977 after two career-ending seasons in Cleveland, the numbers were impressive: 427 receptions for 8,565 yards. Warfield's 20.1-yard per catch average ranks among the best all time. His one-touchdown-per-five-receptions ratio ranks second to Don Hutson.

"I accomplished everything I needed to accomplish," said Warfield when asked if he regretted not having the opportunity to play in a pass-oriented offense. "I played with great teams, I played with great players, I experienced some of the greatest moments in winning at the highest level. People recognize what I brought to the table individually so that now I'm in the highest place of honor, the Hall of Fame."

"The first touchdown was a broken play," Ryan said. "Gary was supposed to run a corner route, but he was covered and went to the middle. I was under pressure, and there he was. Gary was behind Bobby Boyd when he caught the ball. Boyd was a tenacious defensive back, and he probably overcommitted."

The 6-4 Collins vs. the 5-11 Boyd was a mismatch Ryan would exploit the rest of the afternoon. Just before the end of the quarter, the Browns struck again.

"On the second touchdown, Boyd obviously overplayed the hook-and-go," Ryan said. "Collins was wide open. I thought I completely underthrew him, but that huge wind picked the ball up and it hit him right in stride."

The 42-yard bomb gave Cleveland a 17-0 lead, but the best was yet to come.

"The third touchdown (51 yards) was a miraculous catch and throw," Ryan

WEEK 1—Frank Ryan throws two touchdown passes, an 80-yarder to Walter Roberts and a 35-yarder to Gary Collins, as the Browns open defense of their 1964 championship with a 17-7 win at Washington. Cleveland's defense does not allow a point until the final minutes of a game played in near 100-degree heat. Linebacker Galen Fiss pulls a calf muscle, an injury that will sideline him five weeks.

WEEK 2—A crowd of 80,161 watches St. Louis pick off six passes and crush the Browns, 49-13, in the home opener. The Cardinals score four touchdowns in the second quarter to erase an early 10-7 deficit and St. Louis quarterback Charley Johnson finishes the day with six TD passes. The only bright spot is Lou Groza's 200th career field goal.

WEEK 3—Two Browns achieve notable career milestones in a 35-17 win at Philadelphia. Jim Brown scores three touchdowns to increase his total to 108, bettering Don Hutson's NFL record of 105. And Groza plays his 177th NFL game, surpassing the 176 of recently retired quarterback Y.A. Tittle. Two Jim Brown TDs come after Philadelphia turnovers, and defensive back Ross Fichtner returns an interception 32 yards for another.

WEEK 8—One week after losing to Minnesota for the first time ever, the Browns win a shootout against the Eagles at Cleveland Stadium, 38-34. Brown rushes for 131 yards and two touchdowns and Collins grabs eight receptions for 128 yards and two TDs. The Eagles waste a 186-yard rushing effort by Timmy Brown.

WEEK 11—The Browns jump out to a 21-0 lead and hold on to clinch their second straight Eastern Conference title with a 42-21 victory at Pittsburgh. Brown rushes for 146 yards and scores four touchdowns.

WEEK 12—In what would be his final game at Cleveland Stadium, Brown rushes for 141 yards and leads the Browns to a 24-16 win over Washington. Brown's only touchdown is his 20th of the season and ties the NFL record set by Baltimore's Lenny Moore in 1964.

CHAMPIONSHIP GAME—The Browns' dream of a second straight title is doused by the Packers, who win their third championship of the Vince Lombardi era with a 23-12 win at slushy Lambeau Field. The Packers dominate the clock behind the running of Jim Taylor and Paul Hornung while holding Brown to 50 rushing yards and Cleveland to 26 second-half yards.

THE SEASON AT A GLANCE

HEAD COACH
Blanton Collier

REGULAR-SEASON RECORD
**11-3 / 1st
Eastern Conference**

TOP DRAFT CHOICE (Rd.)
Jim Garcia, T, Purdue (2)

SCHEDULE/RESULTS

at Washington	W	17-7
St. Louis	L	13-49
at Philadelphia	W	35-17
Pittsburgh	W	24-19
Dallas	W	23-17
at N.Y. Giants	W	38-14
Minnesota	L	17-27
Philadelphia	W	38-34
N.Y. Giants	W	34-21
at Dallas	W	24-17
at Pittsburgh	W	42-21
Washington	W	24-16
at Los Angeles	L	7-42
at St. Louis	W	27-24
Championship Game		
at Green Bay	L	12-23

Jim Brown's final game

Although nobody knew it at the time, January 2, 1966, would carry a special significance in Cleveland Browns history—a significance beyond the team's championship game loss to the Green Bay Packers at Lambeau Field.

The game was the last in the amazing career of fullback Jim Brown, who stunned the football world by retiring rather than leave the set of the movie he was filming to report to the Browns' 1966 training camp. Brown, who had just turned 30, was coming off a 1,544-yard rushing season, the seventh 1,000-yard effort in his nine-year career.

Brown's final performance was not as dazzling as the 12,312 yards he posted in becoming the most prolific ground gainer in NFL history. The powerful Packers, who recorded a 23-12 victory, held Brown to 50 yards on 12 carries and 44 yards on three receptions. He did not score a touchdown, a feat he had accomplished a then-record 126 times during the regular season.

Brown made his shocking announcement from Elstree, England, where he was completing work on the movie *The Dirty Dozen*.

Quarterback Frank Ryan (13) was pressured all day by a relentless Green Bay rush and Brown (32, right photo) was shadowed by the ever-present Ray Nitschke (66)—a big reason why the Packers were able to shut Brown down in his final professional game.

"It wasn't the weather, it was the Green Bay defense. Willie Davis is their leader in the line and they've got two great defensive backs in Herb Adderley and Willie Wood. As for Ray Nitschke at middle linebacker, well, he seems to know where I'm going before I know myself."

— Fullback Jim Brown

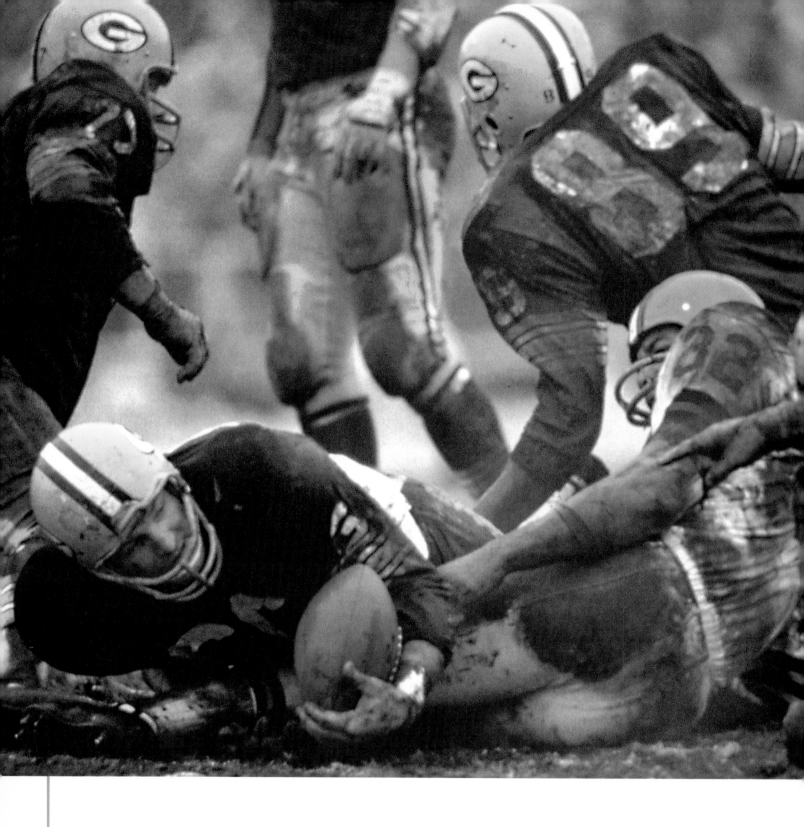

"What it amounted to was that they made the big plays and we couldn't.
We stopped ourselves with mistakes and they didn't make any mistakes.
When they needed the big play on third down, they got it, we didn't."

— *Coach Blanton Collier*

The swarming Packers, featuring such stars as Nitschke (with ball, above left photo) and Dave Robinson (89), stopped Brown and held Cleveland to 26 second-half yards in a muddy, but impressive, title-game victory. The Browns did get two field goals from Lou Groza (top) and a touchdown pass from Ryan, who exchanged pleasantries with Green Bay quarterback Bart Starr (left, left photo) after the game.

1966
HIGHLIGHTS

WEEK 1—In their first regular-season game after Jim Brown's retirement, the Browns roll to a 38-14 win at Washington, spoiling former quarterback Otto Graham's NFL coaching debut. Frank Ryan throws three touchdown passes and Walter Beach, Ross Fichtner and Erich Barnes intercept second-half passes that result in Cleveland TDs.

WEEK 2—Playing before a record home-opener crowd of 83,943 (the third largest ever at Cleveland), the Browns lose to the Green Bay Packers, 21-20, on a Bart Starr-to-Jim Taylor touchdown pass with $2^{1}/_{2}$ minutes to play. Ryan throws two TD passes to Gary Collins and Lou Groza boots two field goals for the Browns.

WEEK 4—After losing back-to-back games for the first time since 1963, the Browns regain their footing on a trip to New York, defeating the Giants, 28-7. The game is never in doubt as the Browns engineer four long scoring drives and pile up 418 total yards. Leroy Kelly rushes for 138 yards and scores a touchdown.

WEEK 7—The Browns make their first trip to Atlanta and hand the expansion Falcons their eighth straight defeat, 49-17. Kelly breaks a 70-yard run on the fifth play from scrimmage and Ryan and Jim Ninowski combine for six touchdown passes. Six different Browns score.

WEEK 10—The Browns defeat Washington, 14-3, as Graham returns to Cleveland Stadium as coach of the Redskins. Graham, who experienced few defeats in the Browns' glory years, suffers his sixth as an NFL coach. Kelly takes over the league lead in rushing with his fourth 100-yard game and interceptions by Ernie Kellerman and Vince Costello trigger both Cleveland scoring drives.

WEEK 12—Defenses take the day off as the Browns outlast the Giants, 49-40, at Cleveland. Kelly rushes for three touchdowns, but the offensive hero is Ryan, who throws for 317 yards and three TDs while guiding the Browns to 35 second-half points. The Browns' last two scores come on a 31-yard run by Ernie Green and a 13-yard fumble return by Bill Glass.

WEEK 14—Ryan has the biggest passing day of his Cleveland career, completing 17-of-30 for 367 yards and four touchdowns in a season-closing 38-10 victory at St. Louis. Ryan hits Collins with scoring passes of 42 and 44 yards, Green for 19 yards and Clifton McNeil for 50.

THE SEASON AT A GLANCE

HEAD COACH

Blanton Collier

REGULAR-SEASON RECORD

**9-5 / T 2nd
Eastern Conference**

TOP DRAFT CHOICE (Rd.)

**Milt Morin, TE,
Massachusetts (1)**

SCHEDULE/RESULTS

at Washington	W	38-14
Green Bay	L	20-21
St. Louis	L	28-34
at N.Y. Giants	W	28-7
Pittsburgh	W	41-10
Dallas	W	30-21
at Atlanta	W	49-17
at Pittsburgh	L	6-16
Philadelphia	W	27-7
Washington	W	14-3
at Dallas	L	14-26
N.Y. Giants	W	49-40
at Philadelphia	L	21-33
at St. Louis	W	38-10

While defensive tackle Dick Modzelewski (74, below) and linebacker Jim Houston (82) tried to slow the opposition, Kelly (above), Jim Brown's replacement, and Paul Warfield (left photo), who averaged 20.6 yards on 36 receptions, stoked the offensive fires.

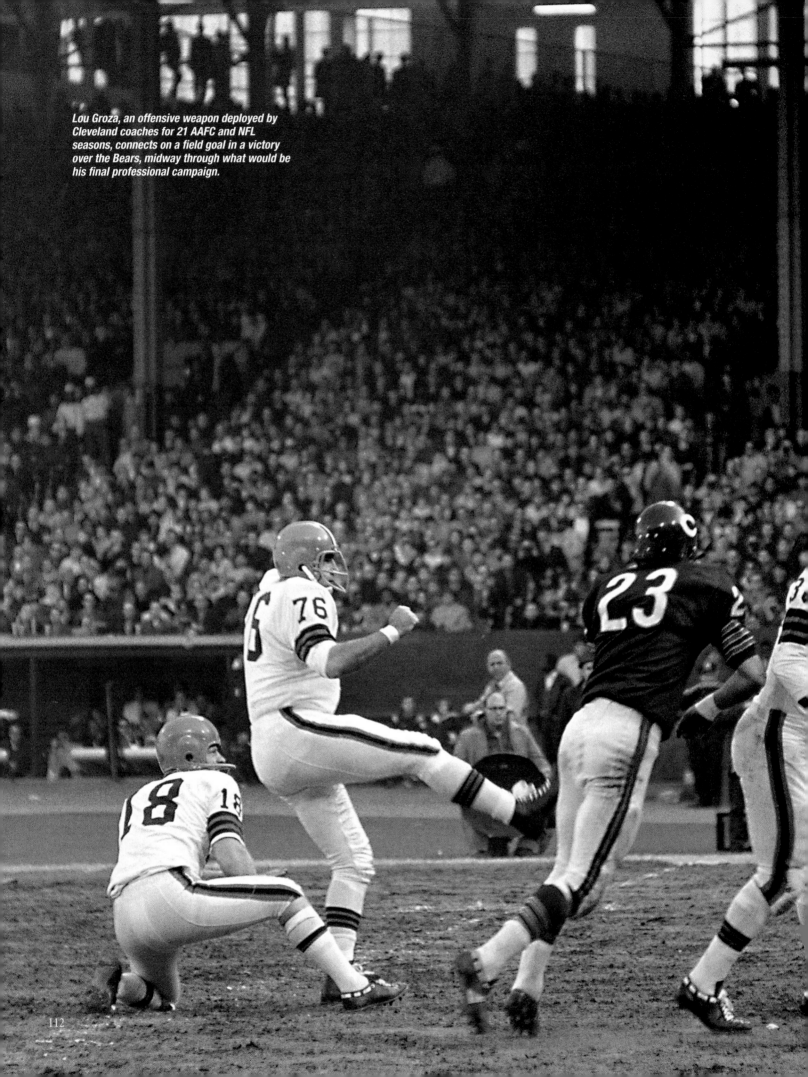

Lou Groza, an offensive weapon deployed by Cleveland coaches for 21 AAFC and NFL seasons, connects on a field goal in a victory over the Bears, midway through what would be his final professional campaign.

WEEK 3—After opening 0-2 for the first time ever, the Browns make the NFL's newest team—the New Orleans Saints—pay with a 42-7 pounding at Tulane Stadium. Quarterback Frank Ryan keys the victory with scoring throws of 41 yards to Ernie Green and 49 yards to Paul Warfield.

WEEK 6—The Browns register their first shutout in seven years with a 24-0 win over the Bears. A crowd of 83,183 flocks to Cleveland Stadium to see Gale Sayers' first game against the Browns, but the star running back is held out because of a leg injury. Fans do get to see Leroy Kelly rush for 111 yards, including a 22-yard touchdown run. Two other TDs come on Ryan-to-Gary Collins passes.

WEEK 9—The Browns lose, 55-7, to Green Bay at Milwaukee—the worst loss in franchise history. The Packers start quickly as Travis Williams returns the opening kickoff 87 yards for a touchdown and three Cleveland turnovers lead to three more Green Bay scores. The Browns get a 59-yard TD run from Green, but Williams returns the ensuing kickoff 85 yards for another TD.

WEEK 10—Kelly scores on a 1-yard run with 28 seconds remaining as the Browns defeat the Vikings, 14-10. Minnesota leads 10-7 and is trying to run out the clock when Jim Kanicki strips running back Dave Osborn and Walter Johnson recovers at the Vikings' 47, setting up the winning touchdown. Kelly finishes with 123 yards and scores both Cleveland TDs.

WEEK 11—In a game of big plays, the Browns beat the Redskins, 42-37. The Browns' first four TDs come on a 42-yard run by Kelly, a 70-yard interception return by linebacker Johnny Brewer, a club-record 104-yard kickoff return by Carl Ward and a 48-yard Ryan-to-Warfield pass.

WEEK 13—The Browns clinch their first Century Division title with a 20-16 victory at St. Louis. One touchdown comes on an 18-yard interception return by linebacker Jim Houston and the game ends when St. Louis tight end Jackie Smith catches a 41-yard pass and is dragged down at the Cleveland 18.

EASTERN CONFERENCE PLAYOFF—The battle of 9-5 teams goes to the Cowboys, who roar to a 52-14 victory at Dallas. The Browns fall behind 21-0 in the first quarter and never catch up. Dallas quarterback Don Meredith completes 11-of-13 passes for 212 yards, including an 86-yard touchdown bomb to Bob Hayes.

THE SEASON AT A GLANCE

HEAD COACH
Blanton Collier

REGULAR-SEASON RECORD
9-5 / 1st
Century Division

TOP DRAFT CHOICE (Rd.)
Bob Matheson, LB, Duke (1)

SCHEDULE/RESULTS

Dallas	L	14-21
at Detroit	L	14-31
at New Orleans	W	42-7
Pittsburgh	W	21-10
St. Louis	W	20-16
Chicago	W	24-0
at N.Y. Giants	L	34-38
at Pittsburgh	W	34-14
at Green Bay	L	7-55
Minnesota	W	14-10
Washington	W	42-37
N.Y. Giants	W	24-14
at St. Louis	W	20-16
at Philadelphia	L	24-28
Playoff Game		
at Dallas	L	14-52

1968

WEEK 3—The Rams, who left Cleveland for Los Angeles in 1946, record their first victory at Cleveland Stadium in more than 20 years, 24-6. The Rams hold the Browns to 129 total yards. Frank Ryan and Bill Nelsen share quarterback duty for the Browns, whose only points come on a 57-yard Ryan bomb to Paul Warfield.

WEEK 6—The 2-3 Browns record a 30-20 victory over a Baltimore team that would not lose again until Super Bowl III. While the offense piles up more than 300 yards, the defense forces five turnovers, including interceptions by Ben Davis, Bill Glass, Mike Howell and Bob Matheson. Colts quarterback Johnny Unitas, suffering from elbow tendinitis, makes his 1968 debut but completes just 1-of-11 passes and throws three interceptions.

WEEK 8—Leroy Kelly rushes for a career-high 174 yards and the Browns defeat the San Francisco 49ers, 33-21—the first meeting in six years between the former AAFC rivals. Rookie Don Cockroft, replacing the retired Lou Groza, kicks four field goals in five attempts.

WEEK 11—The Browns defeat the Eagles, 47-13, at Cleveland Stadium for their sixth straight win. Kelly rushes for 108 yards, but his first career completion, a 34-yard touchdown pass to Paul Warfield, breaks open a tight game and extends a 10-6 Browns lead. Kelly rushes for two more TDs in the third quarter.

WEEK 13—The Browns clinch their second straight Century Division title with their eighth straight win, a 24-21 decision at Washington. The Redskins lead at halftime, 14-7, before the Browns take the lead for good on touchdowns by Kelly and Warfield. The Browns' first points come on a 40-yard interception return by defensive back Erich Barnes.

EASTERN CONFERENCE PLAYOFF—The Browns avenge their 38-point playoff loss at Dallas the year before by defeating the Capitol Division-champion Cowboys, 31-20, at Cleveland. Kelly catches a 45-yard touchdown pass from Bill Nelsen and runs 35 yards for a TD. Linebacker Dale Lindsey steps in front of a Don Meredith pass intended for Bob Hayes and returns it 27 yards for another score.

NFL CHAMPIONSHIP GAME—The Colts whip the Browns, 34-0, in a 1968 rematch. Kelly is held to 28 rushing yards and the Browns never get inside the Baltimore 30. Colts runners roll up 184 yards and four touchdowns, three by Tom Matte.

THE SEASON AT A GLANCE

HEAD COACH

Blanton Collier

REGULAR-SEASON RECORD

10-4 / 1st
Century Division

TOP DRAFT CHOICE (Rd.)

Marvin Upshaw, DE,
Trinity (Texas) (1)

SCHEDULE/RESULTS

at New Orleans	W	24-10
at Dallas	L	7-28
Los Angeles	L	6-24
Pittsburgh	W	31-24
St. Louis	L	21-27
at Baltimore	W	30-20
Atlanta	W	30-7
at San Francisco	W	33-21
New Orleans	W	35-17
at Pittsburgh	W	45-24
Philadelphia	W	47-13
N.Y. Giants	W	45-10
at Washington	W	24-21
at St. Louis	L	16-27
Playoff Game		
Dallas	W	31-20
Championship Game		
Baltimore	L	0-34

Guard Gene Hickerson (66), forearm at the ready, clears a path for Kelly against Larry Wilson (8) and St. Louis.

Quarterback Bill Nelson was no match for Minnesota as the Vikings cruised past the Browns in the NFL title game.

1969

HIGHLIGHTS

WEEK 1—The Browns open with a 27-20 victory at Philadelphia, thanks to the efforts of rookie Ron Johnson, a first-round draft choice who replaces injured Leroy Kelly and rushes 17 times for 118 yards and two touchdowns. The Browns' other points come on a 35-yard Bill Nelsen pass to Gary Collins and two Don Cockroft field goals.

WEEK 2—The Browns defeat the Redskins, 27-23, as Johnson scores two touchdowns and Reece Morrison runs for 131 yards on 24 carries. It is the Browns' first regular-season win over Vince Lombardi, who defeated them five times as coach of the Packers before becoming the Redskins' coach.

WEEK 7—The Browns pound the Cowboys, 42-10, before a Cleveland Stadium crowd of 84,850. Nelsen is spectacular, completing 18-of-25 passes for 225 yards and four touchdowns. Cleveland's defensive front sacks Dallas quarterbacks six times.

WEEK 8—In a stunning one-week turnaround, the Browns fall to the Vikings at Minnesota, 51-3— just seven days after a 32-point win over Dallas.

The 48-point loss matches the worst defeat in Browns history. The Vikings outgain the Browns, 454 yards to 151 yards, and score nine times in 10 possessions.

WEEK 11—The Browns clinch their third straight Century Division title with a 28-24 victory over the Bears. Chicago leads, 14-0, before the Browns tie it at 21-21 on a one-handed, 24-yard catch by tight end Chip Glass. Collins, who catches six passes for 126 yards, makes two clutch receptions on an eight-play, 90-yard drive that ends with a 7-yard touchdown run by Johnson.

EASTERN CONFERENCE PLAYOFF—The Browns defeat the Cowboys in a first-round playoff game for the second straight year. The 38-14 victory is keyed by mistakes by Dallas, including a botched punt that turns into a Bo Scott score and an interception that Walt Sumner returns 88 yards for a touchdown. The Browns also score three rushing TDs against a Dallas defense that had allowed three all season.

NFL CHAMPIONSHIP GAME—The Vikings show their midseason 51-3 rout of the Browns was no fluke by beating them again, 27-7, at Minneapolis. Tough weather conditions affect play with a Sumner slip helping the Vikings to one touchdown and an Erich Barnes slip freeing Gene Washington for a 75-yard TD reception. The Browns finally score on Nelsen's 3-yard pass to Collins with 1:24 left.

THE SEASON AT A GLANCE

HEAD COACH
Blanton Collier

REGULAR-SEASON RECORD
10-3-1 / 1st Century Division

TOP DRAFT CHOICE (Rd.)
Ron Johnson, FB, Michigan (1)

SCHEDULE/RESULTS

at Philadelphia	W	27-20
Washington	W	27-23
Detroit	L	21-28
at New Orleans	W	27-17
Pittsburgh	W	42-31
St. Louis	T	21-21
Dallas	W	42-10
at Minnesota	L	3-51
at Pittsburgh	W	24-3
N.Y. Giants	W	28-17
at Chicago	W	28-24
Green Bay	W	20-7
at St. Louis	W	27-21
at N.Y. Giants	L	14-27
Playoff Game		
at Dallas	W	38-14
Championship Game		
at Minnesota	L	7-27

Tackle Walter Johnson closes in on quarterback Joe Kapp, who weathered the storm and guided the Vikings to a 27-7 championship game victory.

1970
HIGHLIGHTS

Phipps (15, left photo) arrived with the first-round pick acquired in the Warfield trade. Bob McKay (left) looked like a statue of mud while Bengals coach Brown (above) looked serious about his return to Cleveland.

WEEK 3—The Browns post their seventh straight win over the Steelers, 15-7, at Cleveland Stadium. Don Gault, a taxi squad player in 1968 and '69, opens at quarterback, but it doesn't take long for coach Blanton Collier to summon first-round draft pick Mike Phipps, who directs a 90-yard touchdown drive on his first possession and completes 3-of-5 passes for 86 yards. The Browns' defense intercepts Steelers rookie Terry Bradshaw three times and sacks him for a safety.

WEEK 4—In the first regular-season meeting between Paul Brown's old team and his new one, the Browns defeat the Bengals, 30-27, before 83,520 fans at Cleveland Stadium. It's an important win for the Browns, who were chastised for losing a preseason game to Cincinnati. Running backs Leroy Kelly and Bo Scott combine for 236 yards, and a fired-up defense sets the early tone when defensive tackle Walter Johnson sacks Bengals quarterback Virgil Carter for a safety.

WEEK 6—The Browns hand Miami Dolphins coach Don Shula his first home loss, 28-0. The Browns catch as many of Miami quarterback Bob Griese's passes as former teammate Paul Warfield, who was traded to the Dolphins in a controversial offseason deal. Erich Barnes, Walt Sumner and

Dale Lindsey make interceptions, with Lindsey returning his 56 yards for a touchdown.

WEEK 8—The first-ever meeting between the Browns and Raiders ends dramatically with Oakland prevailing, 23-20, on a 52-yard field goal by George Blanda that barely clears the crossbar with seven seconds left. The 43-year-old Blanda, replacing injured quarterback Daryle Lamonica, also throws a game-tying 14-yard TD pass to Warren Wells and directs the game-winning drive.

WEEK 12—Just days after Collier announces his retirement, the Browns travel to Houston and beat the Oilers, 21-10, in their first game at the Astrodome. Kelly rushes for 108 yards, but the highlight of the victory is a 99-yard touchdown drive that follows a goal-line stand and concludes with a 1-yard Nelsen-to-Gary Collins pass.

WEEK 14—The Browns, closing out the franchise's first non-winning season since 1956, send Collier into retirement on a high note, winning 27-13 at Denver. Nelsen completes 11-of-22 passes for 215 yards and two touchdowns and Scott scores twice, on a 23-yard pass and a 2-yard run.

THE SEASON AT A GLANCE

HEAD COACH
Blanton Collier

REGULAR-SEASON RECORD
**7-7 / 2nd
AFC Central**

TOP DRAFT CHOICES (Rd.)
Mike Phipps, QB, Purdue (1)

Bob McKay, T, Texas (1)

SCHEDULE/RESULTS

N.Y. Jets	W	31-21
at San Francisco	L	31-34
Pittsburgh	W	15-7
Cincinnati	W	30-27
Detroit	L	24-41
at Miami	W	28-0
San Diego	L	10-27
at Oakland	L	20-23
at Cincinnati	L	10-14
Houston	W	28-14
at Pittsburgh	L	9-28
at Houston	W	21-10
Dallas	L	2-6
at Denver	W	27-13

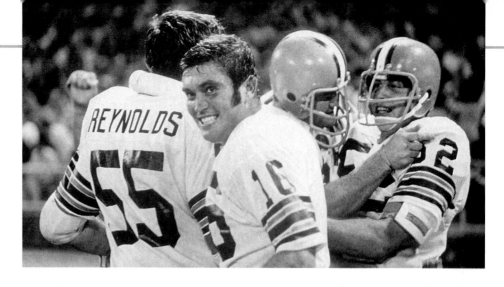

Andrews gets an escort from Erich Barnes (40) on his game-sealing 25-yard interception return (below) and celebrates (right, right photo) with teammates Chuck Reynolds (55), Nelsen (16) and John Demarie after the play. Jets running back Matt Snell (41, below right) runs for some of his 108 yards with an escort from Boozer (32), who finished the first Monday Night Football Game with two touchdowns.

The Monday Mania

An American tradition was born on September 21, 1970, when Howard Cosell, Don Meredith and Keith Jackson manned the microphones for the broadcast of ABC's first Monday Night Football Game—Joe Namath and the New York Jets vs. the Browns in a celebrated season opener.

A national television audience and record Cleveland Stadium crowd of 85,703 watched the Browns take a 14-0 lead on a Bill Nelsen-to-Gary Collins touchdown pass and a 2-yard TD run by Bo Scott. After New York's Emerson Boozer had cut the lead in half with a 2-yard first-quarter run, Homer Jones stretched it to 21-7 with a 94-yard return of the ensuing kickoff.

But the real back-breaking blow was delivered in the fourth quarter, after the Jets had cut the Browns' lead to 24-21 on Namath's 33-yard touchdown strike to George Sauer. With the Jets driving for a potential lead or tie, linebacker Billy Andrews stepped in front of a Namath pass, picked it off and ran 25 yards for the clinching touchdown in a 31-21 victory.

The interception was one of three thrown by Namath, who completed 19-of-32 passes for 299 yards. Nelsen countered with a 12-of-27 effort for 145 yards and one TD.

1971

WEEK 1—The Browns open the regular season by blasting the Oilers, 31-0, in Nick Skorich's first game as coach. Leroy Kelly scores the Browns' first two touchdowns on 1-yard runs, and Bill Nelsen and Mike Phipps both throw a touchdown pass. The Browns intercept five Houston passes (two by rookie cornerback Clarence Scott) and yield just 11 first downs.

WEEK 2—The Browns survive a late mistake and upset the defending Super Bowl-champion Colts, 14-13, at Baltimore. After Walt Sumner intercepts a Johnny Unitas pass with five seconds left (Cleveland's fifth interception), he attempts to lateral to Scott, who never even touches the ball as Baltimore's Ray Perkins recovers at the Cleveland 27. But the Colts, out of timeouts, watch the clock expire before they can get off a field-goal attempt.

WEEK 5—The Browns edge the Bengals, 27-24, at Cincinnati on Bo Scott's third touchdown—a 4-yard run with 39 seconds remaining. The win improves Cleveland's record to 4-1 and drops Paul Brown's defending AFC Central-champion Bengals to 1-4. The Browns get a break when defensive end Jack Gregory recovers a fumble at the Cincinnati 10, setting up a Nelsen-to-Scott TD pass.

WEEK 10—The Browns snap a four-game losing streak with a 27-7 win over the Patriots at Cleveland Stadium. Kelly rushes for 113 yards and scores two touchdowns, one on a 7-yard pass from Nelsen for the game's first score. The Browns intercept four passes by New England rookie Jim Plunkett, who has trouble adjusting on a windy day.

WEEK 12—The Browns clinch their first AFC Central Division title with a 31-27 win over Cincinnati at Cleveland. Kelly, who surpasses the 100-yard mark for the 26th time, scores the first and last touchdowns to complement a 224-yard passing performance by Nelsen.

DIVISIONAL PLAYOFF GAME—The Colts make amends for an early-season loss by whipping the Browns, 20-3, at foggy Cleveland Stadium. The game begins on a promising note when Bo Scott returns the opening kickoff 30 yards, but the drive ends when Colts rookie cornerback Rex Kern—a former star quarterback at Ohio State—strips the ball from wide receiver Fair Hooker at the Baltimore 12. The Browns' second possession ends when Bubba Smith blocks a Don Cockroft field-goal attempt, the first of two he would block in the game.

The old and new: First-year coach Skorich (wearing hat, top photo) delivers sideline instructions to Phipps while 13-year offensive tackle Dick Schafrath (above) ponders life during his final NFL season.

THE SEASON AT A GLANCE

HEAD COACH
Nick Skorich

REGULAR-SEASON RECORD
9-5 / 1st
AFC Central

TOP DRAFT CHOICE (Rd.)
Clarence Scott, CB, Kansas State (1)

SCHEDULE/RESULTS

Houston	W	31-0
at Baltimore	W	14-13
Oakland	L	20-34
Pittsburgh	W	27-17
at Cincinnati	W	27-24
Denver	L	0-27
Atlanta	L	14-31
at Pittsburgh	L	9-26
at Kansas City	L	7-13
New England	W	27-7
at Houston	W	37-24
Cincinnati	W	31-27
at New Orleans	W	21-17
at Washington	W	20-13
AFC Divisional Game		
Baltimore	L	3-20

1972

HIGHLIGHTS

When Doug Dieken (73 above) opened his first full season as the Browns' starting left tackle in 1972, he was the fourth player in the team's 27-year existence to man that position. Other contributors to that 10-4 season were offensive guard John Demarie (65) and running back Bo Scott (right).

WEEK 2—After an 0-6 exhibition season and a season-opening home loss to Green Bay, the Browns get on track with a 27-17 victory at Philadelphia. The Browns convert an interception and fumble into touchdowns in a 57-second span of the second quarter to take a 20-3 halftime lead, with Bo Scott plunging over from 1 yard out and Mike Phipps throwing 23 yards to Frank Pitts. Phipps runs 4 yards for the final Cleveland touchdown.

WEEK 6—After being outscored 48-7 in consecutive home losses, the Browns hand Houston a 23-17 defeat at the Astrodome. Phipps hooks up with Pitts for a 27-yard touchdown and Don Cockroft kicks three field goals, but the key is defense. The Browns sack Oilers quarterback Dan Pastorini three times and recover two fumbles.

WEEK 7—First-round pick Thom Darden picks off a Charley Johnson pass at the Cleveland 5—his first NFL interception—with 72 seconds left to preserve a 27-20 victory over the Broncos at snowy Denver. Johnson and Phipps each throw two touchdowns and Cockroft kicks two field goals, including a 57-yarder to break a team record set 21 years earlier by Lou Groza.

WEEK 9—Phipps, consistently completing third-down passes in key situations, leads the Browns to a 21-17 victory at San Diego. After the Chargers take a 17-14 lead on Mike Garrett's 3-yard run with 1:21 remaining, Phipps moves the Browns 64 yards on three plays—one a 38-yard touchdown pass to Pitts with 41 seconds remaining.

WEEK 10—The Browns win their fifth straight game, edging the Steelers, 26-24, on a 26-yard Cockroft field goal with 13 seconds left. Cockroft's winning kick comes less than two minutes after a 27-yard miss and moves the 7-3 Browns into a first-place AFC Central tie with Pittsburgh. Steelers rookie Franco Harris rushes for 126 yards, 75 coming on a fourth-quarter touchdown run. Both teams rush for more than 200 yards.

DIVISIONAL PLAYOFF GAME— The Browns lose, 20-14, to a Miami team that will complete its Super Bowl run without a loss or tie. The Browns take a 14-13 lead with eight minutes left when Phipps hits Fair Hooker for a 27-yard touchdown, but the Dolphins march 78 yards on seven plays with Jim Kiick scoring the winning TD on an 8-yard run. Phipps completes 9-of-23 passes and throws five interceptions.

THE SEASON AT A GLANCE

HEAD COACH

Nick Skorich

REGULAR-SEASON RECORD

**10-4 / 2nd
AFC Central**

TOP DRAFT CHOICE (Rd.)

**Thom Darden, DB,
Michigan (1)**

SCHEDULE/RESULTS

Green Bay	L	10-26
at Philadelphia	W	27-17
Cincinnati	W	27-6
Kansas City	L	7-31
Chicago	L	0-17
at Houston	W	23-17
at Denver	W	27-20
Houston	W	20-0
at San Diego	W	21-17
Pittsburgh	W	26-24
Buffalo	W	27-10
at Pittsburgh	L	0-30
at Cincinnati	W	27-24
at N.Y. Jets	W	26-10
AFC Divisional Game		
at Miami	L	14-20

WEEK 1—The Browns give rookie quarterback Bert Jones, son of former Cleveland great Dub Jones, a rough NFL initiation in a 24-14 season-opening win over Baltimore. The Browns sack Jones five times and limit him to six completions on 22 attempts. The Baltimore offense is held to 10 first downs and averages just two yards per play. Browns quarterback Mike Phipps completes 12-of-26 passes for 150 yards and two TDs, both to Frank Pitts.

WEEK 4—Defensive back Ben Davis triggers both scoring drives with fumble recoveries in the Browns' 17-10 win over Cincinnati. Davis pounces on a second-quarter Essex Johnson fumble at the Cleveland 37 and Leroy Kelly scores from 3 yards out nine plays later. Davis recovers a third-quarter fumble by Bengals rookie Boobie Clark, leading to a 7-yard touchdown run by Kelly. The Browns hold the Bengals to 11 first downs.

WEEK 6—The Browns crush hapless Houston, 42-13, before 61,146 fans at Cleveland Stadium. The Browns score six touchdowns and have two others nullified by penalties while keeping the Oilers winless for their 17th consecutive game. Houston finishes the afternoon with four first downs, 23 rushing yards and 83

passing yards. Phipps throws for two TDs and runs for two more.

WEEK 9—After coach Nick Skorich had threatened major roster changes after a dreadful 26-3 loss at Minnesota, the Browns respond with a 23-13 win at Houston. Don Cockroft kicks three field goals, but the big play is a 53-yard TD run by rookie Greg Pruitt, a second-round pick from Oklahoma.

WEEK 11—The Browns hold off Pittsburgh, 21-16, for their third straight win and leap into contention with the Steelers and Bengals in the AFC Central. Pruitt catches a 15-yard second-quarter touchdown pass from Phipps and runs 19 yards for the game-winner with less than two minutes remaining. Pruitt's winning score comes two plays after he catches a 42-yard pass from Phipps. The day ends with Pittsburgh in first place at 8-3, Cleveland at 7-3-1 and Cincinnati at 7-4.

WEEK 14—The Browns complete their season-ending 0-2-1 swoon by committing five turnovers in a 30-17 loss at Los Angeles. The Browns fail to make the playoffs for only the third time in 10 years.

THE SEASON AT A GLANCE

HEAD COACH
Nick Skorich

REGULAR-SEASON RECORD
7-5-2 / 3rd
AFC Central

TOP DRAFT CHOICE (Rd.)
Steve Holden, WR, Arizona State (1)

Pete Adams, G, USC (1)

SCHEDULE/RESULTS

Baltimore	W	24-14
at Pittsburgh	L	6-33
N.Y. Giants	W	12-10
Cincinnati	W	17-10
Miami	L	9-17
Houston	W	42-13
San Diego	T	16-16
at Minnesota	L	3-26
at Houston	W	23-13
at Oakland	W	7-3
Pittsburgh	W	21-16
at Kansas City	T	20-20
at Cincinnati	L	17-34
at Los Angeles	L	17-30

Milt Morin (top photo), a bulldozing tight end who ran over anybody who got in his way, and defensive tackle Walter Johnson (71, right photo) were veteran contributors for the early-1970s Browns. So was Cockroft, although this punt (above) never made it past the leaping Colts defender.

THE SEASON AT A GLANCE

HEAD COACH
Nick Skorich

REGULAR-SEASON RECORD
**4-10 / 4th
AFC Central**

TOP DRAFT CHOICE (Rd.)
**Billy Corbett, T,
Johnson C. Smith (2)**

SCHEDULE/RESULTS

at Cincinnati	L	7-33
Houston	W	20-7
at St. Louis	L	7-29
Oakland	L	24-40
Cincinnati	L	24-34
at Pittsburgh	L	16-20
Denver	W	23-21
at San Diego	L	35-36
at New England	W	21-14
Pittsburgh	L	16-26
Buffalo	L	10-15
San Francisco	W	7-0
at Dallas	L	17-41
at Houston	L	24-28

Defense, supplied in painful doses by tackle Jerry Sherk (72) and linebacker Charlie Hall (59, top photo), was the key to a Week 2 victory over Houston. Cornerback Clarence Scott (above) was a solid contributor through the difficult season.

WEEK 1—The Browns begin the second losing season in franchise history with a 33-7 clunker at Cincinnati. The game is tied 7-7 at halftime, but the Bengals run off 26 consecutive points in the second half. The Browns rush for 200 yards, but post 3 net passing yards.

WEEK 7—The Browns snap a franchise-worst four-game losing streak by scoring 14 fourth-quarter points in a 23-21 win over Denver at Cleveland Stadium. Backup quarterback Brian Sipe, who takes over from starter Mike Phipps in the fourth quarter with Denver leading 21-9, caps a 79-yard scoring drive by running 8 yards for one touchdown and scores the game-winner from 1 yard out in the final minute after Greg Pruitt returns a punt 72 yards to the Denver 3.

WEEK 8—Sipe, a collegiate star at San Diego State, returns home for his first NFL start and falls one point short in a 36-35 loss to the Chargers. The four-touchdown passing of second-year San Diego quarterback Dan Fouts rallies the Chargers from a 21-7 halftime deficit and a late Browns comeback dies when Sipe, trying to move the ball to the center of the field for a field-goal try, fumbles at the Chargers' 10-yard line with 18 seconds remaining.

WEEK 9—The Browns intercept four Jim Plunkett passes, two by Thom Darden, to key a 21-14 victory over New England at Schaefer Stadium. Darden also returns a fumble 29 yards for a touchdown, only minutes after Pruitt had returned the opening kickoff 88 yards for a score. Ken Brown's 4-yard fourth-quarter touchdown run provides the winning margin.

WEEK 12—The Browns post their first shutout in two seasons, beating the 49ers, 7-0, at windy, snowy Cleveland Stadium. The bad weather produces a no-show figure (29,000) higher than the actual attendance (24,559)—and the Browns' smallest home crowd in 18 years. The NFL's first scoreless tie since 1943 is averted when rookie safety Eddie Brown intercepts his third pass of the game with just over five minutes remaining and sets up a 1-yard touchdown run by Ken Brown. Darden picks off an end zone pass on the final play after the 49ers had driven to the Cleveland 28.

1975

WEEK 1—Despite scoring two touchdowns in 48 seconds, the Browns fall to the Bengals, 24-17, in an exciting opener at Cincinnati. Trailing 24-3 late in the third quarter, the Browns score on an 8-yard run by Greg Pruitt and moments later when linebacker Charlie Hall recovers a Ken Anderson fumble in the end zone. The Browns get the ball inside the Cincinnati 10 in the final minutes, only to be stopped on downs. For the game, the Bengals stop the Browns six times from the 1-yard line.

WEEK 3—The Browns are no match for the defending Super Bowl-champion Steelers, who post a 42-6 win at Cleveland. Pittsburgh wins despite losing two key players in the first half—quarterback Terry Bradshaw to a cut on his throwing hand and defensive tackle Joe Greene for fighting with Browns linemen Bob McKay and Tom DeLeone. Cleveland's only points come on a 7-yard TD run by Hugh McKinnis.

THE SEASON AT A GLANCE

HEAD COACH

Forrest Gregg

REGULAR-SEASON RECORD

**3-11 / 4th
AFC Central**

TOP DRAFT CHOICE (Rd.)

**Mack Mitchell, DE,
Houston (1)**

SCHEDULE/RESULTS

at Cincinnati	L	17-24
Minnesota	L	10-42
Pittsburgh	L	6-42
Houston	L	10-40
at Denver	L	15-16
Washington	L	7-23
at Baltimore	L	7-21
at Detroit	L	10-21
at Oakland	L	17-38
Cincinnati	W	35-23
New Orleans	W	17-16
at Pittsburgh	L	17-31
Kansas City	W	40-14
at Houston	L	10-21

WEEK 5—Don Cockroft kicks a team-record five field goals, but a 53-yarder by Denver's Jim Turner as time expires gives the Broncos a 16-15 victory at Mile High Stadium. The loss drops Cleveland to 0-5 and is its seventh straight loss since the end of 1974.

WEEK 7—The Browns lose to the Colts, 21-7, for their seventh straight loss. One week after losing to Washington for the first time since 1962, the Browns lose in Baltimore for the first time ever. The Browns mount just two scoring threats: a drive that ends at the Colts' 11 and their only touchdown—a 1-yard plunge by McKinnis.

WEEK 10—After beginning the season 0-9, the Browns upset the 8-1 Bengals, 35-23, at Cleveland. Billy Lefear returns the opening kickoff 92 yards to the Bengals' 2, only to suffer a season-ending broken leg. Pruitt scores the first of his two touchdowns on the next play. Pruitt rushes for 121 yards, catches seven passes for 106 and returns two punts for 41.

WEEK 13—Pruitt rushes for a career-high 214 yards and scores three touchdowns in leading the Browns to a 40-14 victory over Kansas City. Pruitt joins Jim Brown and Leroy Kelly as the only Browns to rush for 1,000 yards in a season and joins Brown and Bobby Mitchell as the only Browns to surpass 200 in a game. Almost overlooked is a six-catch, 130-yard performance by wide receiver Reggie Rucker.

Pruitt (top photo) provided most of the fireworks for new Browns coach Forrest Gregg (above right), who turned over his offense to 26-year-old quarterback Brian Sipe.

1976

HIGHLIGHTS

THE SEASON AT A GLANCE

HEAD COACH
Forrest Gregg

REGULAR-SEASON RECORD
**9-5 / 3rd
AFC Central**

TOP DRAFT CHOICE (Rd.)
Mike Pruitt, RB, Purdue (1)

SCHEDULE/RESULTS

N.Y. Jets	W	38-17
at Pittsburgh	L	14-31
at Denver	L	13-44
Cincinnati	L	24-45
Pittsburgh	W	18-16
at Atlanta	W	20-17
San Diego	W	21-17
at Cincinnati	L	6-21
at Houston	W	21-7
Philadelphia	W	24-3
at Tampa Bay	W	24-7
Miami	W	17-13
Houston	W	13-10
at Kansas City	L	14-39

Second-year coach Forrest Gregg waits his turn during pregame introductions (left) while the always-exuberant Browns fans offer encouragement (below) to big-play running back Greg Pruitt.

WEEK 1—Trailing 10-0 after the first quarter, the Browns roar back for a 38-17 season-opening win over the Jets. Greg Pruitt rushes for 124 yards and Reggie Rucker catches three touchdown passes, but a third-quarter goal-line stand provides the winning spark. On fourth down from the Browns' 1-yard line, New York rookie quarterback Richard Todd is stopped by linebacker Bob Babich.

WEEK 5—Losers of five straight games to Pittsburgh by a combined 150-69 score, the Browns shock the two-time defending Super Bowl-champion Steelers, 18-16, at Cleveland. What makes the upset even more surprising is that Cleveland wins behind third-string quarterback Dave Mays, a dentist and former World Football League player. Mays hits on 5-of-9 second-half passes after Brian Sipe suffers a concussion.

WEEK 6—Greg Pruitt rushes for 191 yards and two touchdowns as the Browns even their record with a 20-17 win at Atlanta. Pruitt sets up his 1- and 2-yard TDs with runs of 64 and 45. The Falcons, playing without injured quarterback Steve Bartkowski, fail to score despite moving inside the Browns' 40 three times in the fourth quarter.

WEEK 10—The Browns hold the Eagles to 21 net passing yards, sack quarterback Mike Boryla six times and intercept four passes in a 24-3 win at Cleveland. Ron Bolton returns one interception 37 yards for a touchdown, and a pick by Thom Darden sets up a 32-yard Don Cockroft field goal.

WEEK 12—Thanks to a mental lapse by Dolphins quarterback Bob Griese, the Browns escape with a 17-13 win at Cleveland. After Dolphins fullback Norm Bulaich plunges to the 3-yard line for a first down with 32 seconds left, Griese calls for another run, not realizing the clock has resumed after a measurement. Bulaich is stopped, the clock runs out and the Browns have their seventh win in eight weeks. Paul Warfield burns his former teammates with four receptions for 60 yards and a TD.

WEEK 14—Needing a final-day victory at Kansas City and a Steelers loss at Houston to squeak into the playoffs, the Browns get neither. The Browns turn the ball over six times in a 39-14 loss and Kansas City running back Ed Podolak torches their defense for 137 yards and three touchdowns.

The snarling Lambert (above), Bradshaw (12, top photo) and Greene (75, right photo) were thorns in the side of Cleveland fans, who were frustrated by the four Super Bowl titles the Steelers won during the 1970s.

doing my job. With the crowd and all, I didn't hear the whistle."

Steelers offensive lineman Gerry Mullins offered this take: "Maybe you could say throwing Terry down like that was a cheap shot. But they needed the win, and so did we." Pittsburgh wound up winning the '76 AFC Central title with a 10-4 record. Cleveland finished 9-5.

The scenario to which Mullins alluded is precisely the kind of high-stakes environment that has stoked the Cleveland-Pittsburgh series. From 1970, when the Browns and Steelers became AFC members, through the uprooting of the original Browns franchise after the 1995 season, Pittsburgh won 12 AFC Central championships and Cleveland accounted for six. When the two teams weren't going head-to-head for the Central Division crown, they were trying mightily to spoil the other club's title aspirations.

The Browns could only hope to assume such a spoiler role in another nasty meeting with the Steelers at Cleveland Stadium, this one coming the year before the Jones/Bradshaw incident. On the way to a 3-11 record, Cleveland thoroughly frustrated and angered the Steelers with its clutching blocking tactics. All-Pro defender Joe Greene, enraged over what he thought was flagrant holding by Browns linemen, couldn't contain himself and lashed out in a wild kicking melee involving Browns center Tom DeLeone.

"I asked everybody to stay cool," said Greene, who was ejected from the game. "I couldn't take my own advice. I thought I'd outgrown all that stuff."

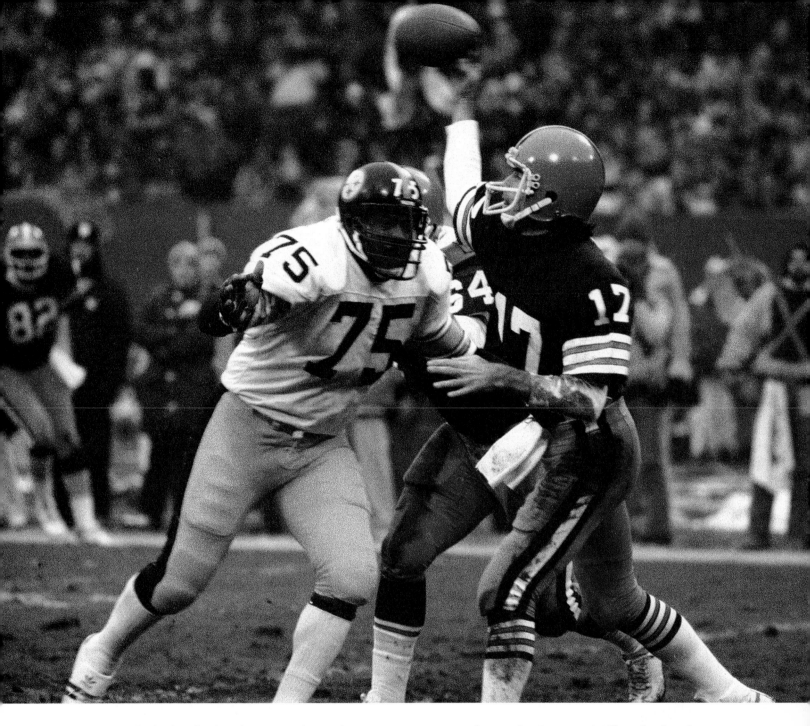

Steelers coach Chuck Noll, a key player on Paul Brown's Cleveland teams in the 1950s, managed to increase tensions between the two clubs. "Apparently some teams teach it (holding)," Noll said. "It was too consistent not to be intentional."

No matter. Pittsburgh won, 42-6.

The Steelers' domination of Cleveland during the era in which they won four Super Bowls and their tight grip on the Browns during the original Cleveland club's waning years heighten the perception that the Steel City has had the upper hand in this series. Not so.

Pittsburgh defeated Cleveland 18 times in a 22-game stretch from 1972 to 1983—the Steelers' 1974, 1975, 1978 and 1979 teams were Super Bowl champions—and the Steelers, under former

Browns player and assistant coach Bill Cowher, have been victorious in the teams' last six meetings, including a 1994 playoff game. Yet Cleveland leads the regular-season series, 52-40—thanks largely to the stranglehold of the early Paul Brown teams (they won their first eight meetings with the Steelers and 12 of the first 13) and two seven-game winning streaks in later years.

Beating the Steelers has long been a Browns priority—and passion. Other major rivals—the Bengals, Los Angeles Rams, Giants, Lions and Broncos—have stirred strong feelings, but the level of intensity just hasn't been the same.

Playing each other 93 times overall almost assures a spirited and special rivalry, of course. Browns-Steelers games evolved into such a happening that the two teams decided to make the matchup a

featured attraction from 1963 through 1970, playing the Cleveland portion of the series on Saturday nights in a highly charged atmosphere. It was festive. It was raucous. And it was just the prelude to what followed when the long-downtrodden Steelers emerged as an NFL power.

"They were such an extraordinary team," former Browns quarterback Brian Sipe said of the Steelers of the mid-'70s to early '80s. "How could you hate them? I was in awe of them, what they represented. I was always challenged by playing them. I wanted to beat them desperately."

The Bengals tend to bring out other sentiments. Founded in 1968 and first coached by Paul Brown (the creator and longtime coach/general manager of the Browns), Cincinnati is still viewed in some quarters as a relative Johnny-come-lately to the pro football wars. The in-state rivalry counts for something, to be sure, but Brown's controversial dismissal by Browns owner Art Modell in January 1963 and the coach's subsequent ties to the Bengals count for more.

"We had a different feeling about that team," Sipe said. "Those were always hard, tough games that were kind of like alley fights. It's hard to explain the emotion because it was more of an organization thing. It was a bigger deal for Modell, because of Paul Brown. It wasn't like there was great pressure, at least not for the

players. Maybe more for the coach."

Cleveland linebacker Clay Matthews, who played collegiately at Southern California, wasn't familiar with most regional rivalries when he joined the Browns in 1978.

"I thought the rivalry would really be between Cleveland and Cincinnati," he said. "(But) as a young player, that immediately became the benchmark, beating Pittsburgh. ... A lot of times there would be a rivalry among organizations, but the players turn over so quickly they don't feel it. But there was a tremendous rivalry with our players, especially the older players, with Pittsburgh. You learned how Joe Jones had slammed Bradshaw, how there had been fights with our linemen and their linemen.

"There was always a little extra spark when Pittsburgh came to town."

It was a spark that often turned into electricity, marked by such high-voltage performances as Sipe's four touchdown passes against the Steelers in his final Browns game in 1983 and Eric Metcalf's 91- and 75-yard punt-return touchdowns against Pittsburgh in 1993.

Bengals-Browns games haven't inspired that kind of drama, but Bob Golic says the Bengals' rise to prominence in the 1980s—they reached two Super Bowls in that decade—helped vault the Cincinnati-Cleveland rivalry to a notch just below the

 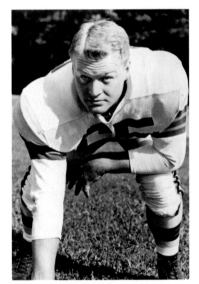

Greg Pruitt literally had to run for his life during games against the Steelers (left top), but Kosar didn't feel as much pressure against the Bengals (right top). Former Browns Cowher (53) and Noll (65) defected to the enemy and led Pittsburgh to championship heights as coaches.

Steelers-Browns clashes.

"But for me," said Golic, a Browns defensive standout in the 1980s, "it's always been the Browns-Steelers. That was the epitome of football. Especially when we played in Cleveland because everyone was covered with mud and dirt, blood and sweat, and it was the total opposite of any of these cushy little dome games."

Golic, offensive tackle Doug Dieken and tight end Ozzie

Newsome emphasize that the Pittsburgh rivalry has meant as much to the fans as it has to the players.

"One year I broke my arm and I actually played another quarter before the bone pulled apart," Golic said. "We're walking off before the end of the half and a bunch of Steeler fans are looking down over the railing and yelling, 'Golic, Golic. Go back out there and we'll break your other bleeping arm.'"

Dieken recalls that Cleveland fans would remind players of the Steelers' Super Bowl success and "they'd want to know if we were going to kick their butts this year."

Newsome, whose Browns career spanned three decades, remembers his introduction to Cleveland and its citizenry: "People would recognize me, and the first thing they would say is, 'You gotta win the game in Pittsburgh.'"

Winning any game in Pittsburgh took some doing for the Browns after Three Rivers Stadium opened in 1970. In fact, the Browns lost in their first 16 appearances there. The importance of breaking through at Three Rivers wasn't lost on Bernie Kosar.

"(The rivalry) was extra special for me, growing up in Youngstown, halfway between Pittsburgh and Cleveland," Kosar said. "Half the town was Browns fans. I had been a part of it since I

"You just couldn't lose to the Steelers. The fans had cousins, uncles and so on in Pittsburgh. It was bragging rights for the whole city."

— *Running back Earnest Byner*

Browns defenders Eric Turner (29), Michael Dean Perry (92) and Rick Lyle (95) put the crunch on Steelers quarterback Neil O'Donnell in a 1994 playoff loss at Pittsburgh.

was a kid. One of the highlights of my career was to be able to play so many games at Three Rivers and break that streak they had against us."

The Browns finally won at Three Rivers on October 5, 1986, when they rode Kosar's controlled passing, Earnest Byner's steady rushing and Gerald McNeil's 100-yard kickoff return to a 27-24 victory.

Offensive lineman Cody Risien, who played in that milestone game, said that over the years he "hated Pittsburgh but respected them. If you were going to pick a team that was dirty, it would probably have been the Steelers. But ... they were a tremendously talented, tough team."

Kosar, Risien and McNeil also were on hand in 1989 when the Browns and Steelers kicked off the season at Three Rivers. With former Pittsburgh defensive coordinator Bud Carson making his debut as Cleveland coach, the Browns got three touchdowns from their defense and, in a stunning display of domination, punished the Steelers, 51-0. It was the worst defeat in Pittsburgh history.

Remarkably, that victory was the Browns' fourth in a row at Three Rivers, but any thoughts that they had truly gotten the hang

of it there were dismissed a year later when the Steelers exacted revenge to the tune of 35-0.

Whether playing at Three Rivers Stadium or Cleveland Stadium, Byner maintains that "you just couldn't lose to the Steelers. The fans had cousins, uncles and so on in Pittsburgh. It was bragging rights for the whole city. The week in practice (before a Steelers game) was high energy, the most intense and hard hitting."

A week before a Bengals game might not have been a breather, either.

"Modell tried to make like it wasn't a big deal between him and Brown," Dieken said, "but you got the sense, especially the coach got the sense, of the importance of it."

Risien, though, detected a lack of respect for the Bengals among some Browns players. "If we didn't beat them," he said, "it was like we gave a game away."

Cleveland went 7-5 against Cincinnati while Brown was the Bengals' coach but eventually fell behind in the series, 24 victories to 20. But the Browns have defeated the Bengals seven consecutive times since then.

If the Bengals aren't quite the Steelers in this rivalry business, the same could be said of the Lions, Rams, Giants and Broncos.

Still, the Browns had outstanding '50s rivalries with the Lions and Rams, playing Detroit in four NFL title games and Los Angeles in three, and with the Giants, a fierce Eastern Conference rival whom they met twice in tiebreaker games to decide the Eastern (or American, as the conference was called early in that decade) representative in the league championship game.

Geographically, Detroit seems like a natural rival, but the Lions and Browns have never competed in the same conference or division and have met only 15 times in the regular season.

"They should realign (the NFL) and put Cleveland and Detroit in the same division," longtime Browns guard Gene Hickerson said.

Then there's Denver, which three times (1986, 1987, 1989) in a four-season stretch denied Cleveland a Super Bowl berth. "It's tough to (form) a rivalry when you don't play a team on a yearly basis," Dieken said of the Broncos. "They became more of a thorn in the side."

Somehow, being a thorn in the side doesn't quite measure up to the pain and suffering that the Browns and Steelers have been inflicting on each other for 50 years.

1979

HIGHLIGHTS

WEEK 1—The Browns nip the Jets, 25-22, in a wild season opener at Shea Stadium. After kicking a 35-yard field goal with four seconds left in regulation to force overtime, Don Cockroft kicks a 27-yarder with 15 seconds left in the extra session to win it. Brian Sipe moves the Browns 66 yards in 26 seconds with no timeouts for the first field goal, and a 33-yard interception return by Oliver Davis sets up the second.

WEEK 3—The Browns claim their third straight three-point win with a 13-10 triumph over Baltimore at Cleveland Stadium. The Browns tie the game on a 35-yard Sipe-to-Dave Logan touchdown pass in the third quarter and take the lead on a 28-yard Cockroft field goal with 1:55 remaining. Baltimore's Toni Linhart misses a 28-yard field goal with six seconds left—his third miss of the game.

WEEK 4—The Browns are impressive in a 26-7 victory over defending NFC-champion Dallas in a Monday night game at Cleveland. Sipe completes 7-of-10 passes in a 20-point first quarter, including touchdown throws of 24 yards to Logan and 52 yards to Ozzie Newsome. The Browns also score on Thom Darden's 39-yard return of a Roger Staubach interception and force five turnovers.

WEEK 7—The Browns let one get away and lose to Washington, 13-9, at Cleveland. With the Browns leading 9-6 and two minutes remaining, Joe Theismann leads the Redskins on an eight-play, 80-yard drive that ends with 27 seconds left on a 15-yard TD pass to Clarence Harmon.

WEEK 12—The Browns beat Miami, 30-24, as Sipe and Reggie Rucker hook up for a 39-yard touchdown 1:59 into overtime. Sipe, who completes 23-of-42 passes for 358 yards, sends the game into overtime with a 34-yard TD pass to Newsome with 1:21 left. He then dominates the overtime, running twice from scrimmage for 20 yards and completing two passes for 50 yards. The winner is Rucker's ninth reception for 177 yards—most by a Browns receiver in 19 years.

WEEK 16—A regular season-ending 16-12 loss at Cincinnati eliminates the Browns from playoff contention. After a 43-yard field goal by Chris Bahr gives the Bengals the lead with 1:51 left, the Browns drive 64 yards, only to lose when a fourth-down Sipe pass from the 5-yard line intended for Ricky Feacher is slapped down in the end zone.

THE SEASON AT A GLANCE

HEAD COACH
Sam Rutigliano

REGULAR-SEASON RECORD
**9-7 / 3rd
AFC Central**

TOP DRAFT CHOICE (Rd.)
Willis Adams, WR, Houston (1)

SCHEDULE/RESULTS

at N.Y. Jets	W	(OT)	25-22
at Kansas City	W		27-24
Baltimore	W		13-10
Dallas	W		26-7
at Houston	L		10-31
Pittsburgh	L		35-51
Washington	L		9-13
Cincinnati	W		28-27
at St. Louis	W		38-20
at Philadelphia	W		24-19
Seattle	L		24-29
Miami	W	(OT)	30-24
at Pittsburgh	L	(OT)	30-33
Houston	W		14-7
at Oakland	L		14-19
at Cincinnati	L		12-16

Running back Cleo Miller looks for daylight as tackle Doug Dieken (73) looks for a block in a victory over Miami.

WEEK 3—After totaling 18 yards rushing in his first two NFL games, first-round pick Charles White rushes for 59 yards and catches seven passes for 100 more yards in leading the Browns to a 20-13 win over Kansas City. The highlight comes in the third quarter when he breaks two tackles while converting a short pass from Brian Sipe into a 31-yard, game-winning touchdown.

WEEK 7—Sipe completes 24-of-39 passes for a career-high 391 yards and two touchdowns while leading the Browns to a dramatic 26-21 win over Green Bay at Cleveland Stadium. The game-winning TD comes with 16 seconds remaining when Sipe, facing a third-and-20 at the Packers' 46, connects with Dave Logan.

WEEK 8—Sipe completes a team-record 28 passes for 349 yards and four touchdowns as the Browns post a 27-26 victory over Pittsburgh. The Browns overcome deficits of 10-0, 20-7 and 26-14 to beat a crippled Steelers team playing without Terry Bradshaw, Lynn Swann, John Stallworth, Franco Harris and Jack Lambert. Two of Sipe's TD passes are caught by Greg Pruitt, but the 18-yard winner goes to Ozzie Newsome with 5:35 remaining.

WEEK 9—Sipe throws for 298 yards in a 27-21 victory over Chicago and becomes the Browns' all-time passing leader, surpassing the career totals of both Otto Graham and Frank Ryan. Sipe finishes with 13,534 career yards, but the winning touchdown comes on a 56-yard fourth-quarter run by Mike Pruitt.

WEEK 15—The "Kardiac Kids," winners of seven games by seven or fewer points, lose a heart-breaking 28-23 decision at Minnesota. Trailing 23-9 with 7:15 left, the Vikings score three touchdowns, two in the final 1:35, with the winner coming on a "Hail Mary" throw by Tommy Kramer as time expires. Kramer's pass, tipped by Browns safety Thom Darden, goes right to receiver Ahmad Rashad, who backs into the end zone. Kramer passes for 456 yards, the most ever by a Browns' opponent.

WEEK 16—Needing a win to clinch their first playoff berth since 1972, the Browns defeat the Bengals at Riverfront Stadium, 27-24. The winning points come on a 22-yard field goal by Don Cockroft with 1:25 left, but the victory isn't secured until Ron Bolton hauls down Bengals receiver Steve Kreider at the Cleveland 13 as time expires. Sipe finishes the season with the second-best yardage total in NFL history (4,132), the most touchdown passes in Cleveland history (30) and the league's best QB rating (91.4).

THE SEASON AT A GLANCE

HEAD COACH
Sam Rutigliano

REGULAR-SEASON RECORD
11-5 / T 1st AFC Central

TOP DRAFT CHOICE (Rd.)
Charles White, RB, USC (1)

SCHEDULE/RESULTS

at New England	L	17-34
Houston	L	7-16
Kansas City	W	20-13
at Tampa Bay	W	34-27
Denver	L	16-19
at Seattle	W	27-3
Green Bay	W	26-21
Pittsburgh	W	27-26
Chicago	W	27-21
at Baltimore	W	28-27
at Pittsburgh	L	13-16
Cincinnati	W	31-7
at Houston	W	17-14
N.Y. Jets	W	17-14
at Minnesota	L	23-28
at Cincinnati	W	27-24
AFC Divisional Game		
Oakland	L	12-14

Two weapons Sipe (top photo) utilized in leading the Browns to the playoffs were wide receiver Reggie Rucker (above) and Mike Pruitt (right photo), the club's leading rusher (1,034 yards).

Red Right 88

The words drifted through the steam-like haze emanating from a faceless helmet on a bitterly cold afternoon at Cleveland Stadium. "Red Right 88," said Browns quarterback Brian Sipe with a calm that never again would be associated with that simple pass play. Few people heard the call, and nobody who did could have imagined how the words would echo through the city for generations to come—with emotion ranging from sadness and disappointment to fascination and painful resignation.

Red Right 88.

Everybody was expecting a photo finish in the Browns' AFC divisional playoff game against the Oakland Raiders on January 4, 1981, when Cleveland woke up to sub-zero temperatures and a minus-37 wind chill, courtesy of 28-mph gusts blowing off frozen Lake Erie. These were, after all, the Kardiac Kids—winners of six last-minute games en route to an 11-5 record, competitors in 24 games decided in the final two minutes over a 32-game stretch. The 1980 Browns were not your average, everyday division champions. They exposed their heart every Sunday and dared opponents to cut it out.

"The Kardiac Kids years were something real special," recalled offensive tackle Cody Risien. "Brian Sipe, Dave Logan and Calvin Hill, Greg Pruitt and Lyle Alzado and all the gang. We had a heck of a lot of fun, we had a good team and people who made plays and were really tight. There was a camaraderie there. It was a special feeling."

Special, in large part, because of Sipe, who orchestrated the franchise's first playoff run in nine years with a 4,132-yard passing performance that earned him a league MVP award and status as the third NFL player to reach the lofty 4,000-yard plateau. Several of his 30 touchdown throws were responsible for heart-stopping victories;

Sipe and Rutigliano (above) decided to go for the touchdown and Raiders cornerback Davis (36, right photo) made them pay with an end zone interception in front of Newsome.

several more came in gut-wrenching defeats.

But when Sipe surveyed the icy, snow-rimmed field on that memorable playoff Sunday, he knew the Browns would need more than flashy numbers to get past the Raiders and make a serious run at their first Super Bowl.

SPOTLIGHT: BRIAN SIPE

Almost 20 years later, the name still elicits painful smiles and sends shivers down the spines of devoted Cleveland football fans. Brian Sipe. No. 17. The original Kardiac Kid. The most popular player who ever broke his city's heart.

That happened in January 1981 when Sipe threw a pass to Oakland defensive back Mike Davis instead of Lake Erie. Sipe's errant pass secured the Raiders' playoff victory and ended the Browns' season. It marked the end of Camelot, that one brief, shining moment when Sipe was not only the best quarterback in Cleveland, but the best in all of football. Forget Red Right 88. The personable, articulate Sipe always will be revered as the third quarterback to pass for 4,000 yards in a season—the player who helped restore football dignity to the City by the Lake.

"I wasn't amazed. I sort of expected it," Sipe recalled when asked about the 4,132-yard 1980 performance that helped the Browns post an 11-5 record and their first AFC Central championship since 1971. "I just wanted there to be more. It was a rare time for me as a quarterback. I just didn't want it to end."

Sipe was, in fact, a thirtysomething quarterback when he opened the 1979 season and took the Browns on an incredible two-season roller-coaster ride during which 24-of-32 games were decided in the final two minutes. After years of insecurity on the Cleveland sideline under coaches who doubted his ability, Sipe blossomed under Sam Rutigliano, who encouraged him to take chances, improvise and go for broke in a free-wheeling system that maximized his resourcefulness under pressure.

"He wasn't your physically-perfect, John Elway-type quarterback, but he found a way to get it done," recalled former Browns linebacker Clay Matthews. "I think Brian was small and not that fast and his arm wasn't that strong. But he could make plays when he had to."

Sipe, a former national passing champion under Don Coryell at San Diego State, did not command a lot of excitement in the 1972 draft. The 6-1, 195-pounder with a questionable arm was buried in the 13th round, the 330th player chosen, and he spent his first two professional seasons on the Browns' taxi squad.

It wasn't until Rutigliano arrived in 1978 that Sipe got his big chance. His stock rose swiftly during the final four games of that season.

"It was like a light going on upstairs," Sipe said in a 1979 interview. "All of a sudden everything started falling into place and I was sorry we didn't have more time left in the season."

In 1979, throwing to such receivers as Dave Logan, Ozzie Newsome and Reggie Rucker, Sipe passed for 3,793 yards and 28 touchdowns as the Browns finished 9-7. He added a team-record 30 touchdown passes in his incredible 1980 campaign. Sipe topped the 3,500-yard mark two more times before ending his NFL career in 1983 with 23,713 passing yards, but the Kardiac Kid magic was gone.

His special place in Cleveland history, however, remains to this day.

"Looking back, I really have come to appreciate the Cleveland fans more than when I played there," Sipe said. "They're special. They still like me, even though I broke their heart."

"It was miserable, just a miserable day," he recalled years later. "It was the worst weather I had ever played in. There was no way to keep your hands and feet warm. If they were ever going to call off a game because of the weather, I thought that would be it."

The players had to settle for heated benches that had been trucked in from Philadelphia and the knowledge that everybody was playing on the same icy field. Running the ball was difficult because of bad footing. Throwing and catching was difficult because of frozen hands and fingers. Sometimes, just standing was an adventure.

"On my two touchdowns, I was scared to death I was going to slip," said running back Mark van Eeghen, who accounted for both Oakland scores on a pair of 1-yard runs. "In my stance, I was on a sheet of ice. But their linebackers and linemen were on skates, too."

The Raiders could muster only 208 total yards, but two sustained drives produced touchdowns. The Browns totaled 254 yards, but the offense failed to

generate a touchdown and Sipe completed only 13-of-40 passes for 182 yards—with three interceptions. Still, the Browns carried a 12-7 lead into the fourth quarter, thanks to Ron Bolton's 42-yard second-period runback of a Jim Plunkett interception and two Don Cockroft field goals.

Van Eeghen's second TD capped an 80-yard drive and gave the Raiders a 14-12 lead with a little more than four minutes remaining. When the Raiders recovered a Sipe fumble at the Cleveland 25-yard line moments later, it appeared time was running out on another miracle. But that changed when the Raiders, facing fourth-and-inches near the 15, disdained a field-goal attempt and ran van Eeghen to try to get a first down. The Browns held and got the ball back with 2:22 remaining.

"The Raiders had a chance to ice the game with about two minutes left," recalled tight end Ozzie Newsome. "They had the ball, and we stopped them. It became, 'Oh, here we go again!' The whole stadium

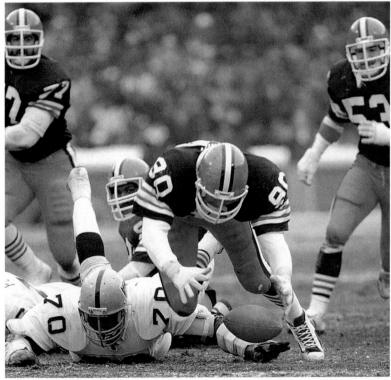

Bolton's second-quarter interception return (top photo) gave the Browns an early lead and warmed up freezing Cleveland fans, as did a fumble recovery (above) by end Marshall Harris (90). Bill Cowher (53) watches Harris dive for the loose ball.

The disappointment of Sipe (above) and Newsome (left, sitting) contrasts the Raiders' jubilation after Davis' game-saving interception.

just came to a roar. We take it down and get ourselves in position to score."

The 72-yard drive featured a 29-yard pass to Newsome, a pass interference penalty and a 14-yard run by Mike Pruitt. Suddenly the Browns, needing only a field goal to win, faced a second down with less than a minute remaining at the Oakland 13. Decision time: two runs and a kick or go for broke?

Red Right 88.

"Yes and no," Risien recalled when asked if he was surprised by the call. "We had not had success kicking field goals that day, especially at that end of the stadium. And we had been winning in that fashion all year long."

Cockroft, in fact, had missed two field-goal attempts and had an extra point blocked. And the winds were swirling off the lake, making coach Sam Rutigliano's decision all the more difficult.

"Our plan was to run on first and third downs, and throw on second," Rutigliano explained after the game. "Then, if we didn't get the first down, we'd run the clock down, call a time out and try the field goal."

Sipe was instructed to "throw the ball into Lake Erie" if nobody was open on a pattern that targeted Logan, with Newsome and Reggie Rucker clearing out coverage on crossing patterns. But Newsome appeared to break free.

"I beat (cornerback) Mike Davis clean off the line and Brian saw it and he threw the ball," Newsome said. "It got caught in the wind. It would have been easy (without the wind), an easy touchdown."

Instead, Davis recovered, cut in front of Newsome and made the end zone interception with 41 seconds remaining. The Raiders ran out the clock on the Kardiac Kids.

"I was shocked, but only because, having won so many games at the end, it just never occurred to us that we wouldn't win the game, or that we wouldn't have another opportunity to win it," recalled linebacker Clay Matthews. "We had never really had to deal with that."

The interception turned Cleveland Stadium into a frigid mausoleum—so quiet you could hear 77,655 dreams drop.

"It was like dead silence, very eerie," Newsome recalled.

"It was eerie, complete silence," agreed Risien. "But then there was a round of applause for the great season we had had."

After the game, in a stunned Cleveland locker room, Sipe expressed the defiant sentiment befitting a Kardiac Kid.

"We did things in dramatic fashion all year," he said. "It's only fitting that we lose in dramatic fashion."

WEEK 3—After opening the season with two losses, the Browns bounce back to beat the Bengals, 20-17. Mike Pruitt scores the game-winning touchdown in the fourth quarter on a 12-yard draw play.

WEEK 7—In a game reminiscent of 1980, the Browns nip the Saints, 20-17, by driving 78 yards in the final minutes for a 1-yard Mike Pruitt touchdown run. Brian Sipe completes four passes on the drive to Greg Pruitt, who finishes with seven catches for 113 yards. The Saints, who get a club-record 79-yard TD run from rookie George Rogers, miss a chance to tie when Benny Ricardo hooks a 37-yard field-goal attempt with 1:11 left.

WEEK 8—Sipe breaks Otto Graham's 29-year-old team record for single-game passing yardage (401) by throwing for 444 yards and four touchdowns in a 42-28 win over Baltimore. Sipe, who enters the game with seven TD passes, tosses scoring strikes to Ozzie Newsome, Greg Pruitt and Dave Logan in the first half and Ricky Feacher in the second, nullifying a three-TD performance by Colts quarterback Bert Jones. The Browns roll up 562 total yards.

WEEK 10—The Browns fall to 4-6 and drop into the AFC Central cellar with an 23-20 overtime loss at Denver. The Browns tie the game on Matt Bahr's 32-yard field goal with 29 seconds left and get the first possession in overtime, but Calvin Hill fumbles near midfield after hauling in a 23-yard pass. Broncos quarterback Craig Morton's 33-yard pass to Rick Upchurch sets up a 30-yard, game-winning field goal by Fred Steinfort.

WEEK 11—The Browns beat eventual Super Bowl champ San Francisco, 15-12, when Bahr connects on a 24-yard field goal with 43 seconds left at Candlestick Park. The Browns, who snap a seven-game 49ers winning streak, tie the game on a 21-yard touchdown pass from Sipe to Reggie Rucker and set up the winner on a 38-yard Sipe-to-Rucker completion in the final minute.

WEEK 16—In a fitting conclusion to a disappointing season, the Browns commit 10 turnovers (two shy of the NFL record) and are pounded by the Seahawks, 42-21. The Browns fumble a team-record nine times, losing seven. Seattle converts six turnovers into touchdowns, including an 82-yard interception return by rookie safety Kenny Easley and a 31-yard fumble return by Greggory Johnson.

THE SEASON AT A GLANCE

HEAD COACH
Sam Rutigliano

REGULAR-SEASON RECORD
**5-11 / 4th
AFC Central**

TOP DRAFT CHOICE (Rd.)
**Hanford Dixon, CB,
Southern Mississippi (1)**

SCHEDULE/RESULTS

San Diego	L	14-44
Houston	L	3-9
at Cincinnati	W	20-17
Atlanta	W	28-17
at Los Angeles	L	16-27
at Pittsburgh	L	7-13
New Orleans	W	20-17
Baltimore	W	42-28
at Buffalo	L	13-22
at Denver	L	(OT) 20-23
at San Francisco	W	15-12
Pittsburgh	L	10-32
Cincinnati	L	21-41
at Houston	L	13-17
N.Y. Jets	L	13-14
at Seattle	L	21-42

In '81, Charles White (top) gains 342 rushing yards and Logan (above) catches 31 passes as one of Sipe's primary targets.

1982
HIGHLIGHTS

Sipe (left) tossed four touchdown passes in his six games and spent much of the season eluding rushers. Bahr (9) led the club in scoring with 38 points.

WEEK 1—Less than nine months after closing the 1981 season with a dismal loss at Seattle, the Browns return to the Kingdome and defeat the Seahawks, 21-7. Mike Pruitt accounts for 136 of Cleveland's 200 rushing yards and scores two touchdowns. The Browns sack Dave Krieg eight times, three by rookie linebacker Chip Banks.

WEEK 3—In their first game after a players' strike that wipes out almost half the regular season, the Browns fight their way through a heavy Cleveland fog and beat New England, 10-7, on Matt Bahr's 24-yard field goal as time expires. Bahr's winner comes three plays after Browns safety Clinton Burrell recovers a fumble by Mark van Eeghen at the Patriots' 20.

WEEK 5—James Brooks scores two touchdowns and Dan Fouts completes 18-of-23 passes as San Diego pounds the Browns, 30-13, at Cleveland. Despite the loss, Brian Sipe completes 14 straight passes and stretches his overall streak to a club-record 33. He also surpasses the 20,000-yard career mark. Tight end Ozzie Newsome catches a career-high 10 passes and extends his streak of consecutive games with at least one reception to a club-record 45.

WEEK 7—Hanford Dixon intercepts three passes and the Browns keep their playoff hopes alive with a 10-9 win over Pittsburgh at rainy, muddy Cleveland Stadium. The poor conditions affect Steelers quarterback Terry Bradshaw more than Paul McDonald, who starts his first game in place of the slumping Sipe. Nose tackle Bob Golic enjoys a big game with eight tackles and one sack.

WEEK 8—The Browns escape Houston with a 20-14 win, thanks to two critical fumbles by running back Earl Campbell. The first comes at the Cleveland 4 and the second sets up the Browns' winning touchdown in the fourth quarter. Dave Logan scores one TD on a 56-yard pass from McDonald and Charles White scores the winner on a 1-yard run.

AFC FIRST-ROUND GAME—The Los Angeles Raiders knock the Browns out of the playoffs for the second time in three years, 27-10. Raiders quarterback Jim Plunkett completes a 64-yard bomb to Cliff Branch on the game's first play, setting up a Chris Bahr field goal. The game is secured in the second half when Plunkett moves the Raiders 89 yards on 12 plays, with rookie Marcus Allen's 3-yard run increasing the lead to 20-10.

THE SEASON AT A GLANCE

HEAD COACH

Sam Rutigliano

REGULAR-SEASON RECORD

4-5 / T 8th AFC

TOP DRAFT CHOICE (Rd.)

Chip Banks, LB, USC (1)

SCHEDULE/RESULTS

at Seattle	W	21-7
Philadelphia	L	21-24
New England	W	10-7
at Dallas	L	14-31
San Diego	L	13-30
at Cincinnati	L	10-23
Pittsburgh	W	10-9
at Houston	W	20-14
at Pittsburgh	L	21-37
AFC First-Round Game		
at L.A. Raiders	L	10-27

WEEK 2—Brian Sipe throws four touchdown passes to lead the Browns to a 31-26 win at Detroit. Sipe becomes Cleveland's career leader, raising his TD total to 135 (surpassing Frank Ryan) with throws to Ricky Feacher, Mike Pruitt, Ozzie Newsome and Dave Logan. Pruitt also rushes for 137 yards.

WEEK 4—Harry Holt, a 25-year-old NFL rookie, catches a 48-yard touchdown pass from Sipe on Cleveland's fourth play of overtime as the Browns beat the Chargers, 30-24, at San Diego. Holt catches his first NFL touchdown after Matt Bahr forces overtime with a 32-yard field goal with 18 seconds left in regulation.

WEEK 6—Linebacker Tom Cousineau records 15 tackles, one interception and one fumble recovery while leading Cleveland to a 10-7 win over the New York Jets. His interception stops a Jets drive at the Browns' 5-yard line and his fumble recovery stops New York at the Cleveland 9. The Browns' only touchdown is scored by wide receiver Bobby Jones on a 32-yard pass from Sipe.

WEEK 8—The Browns lose a tough one at Cincinnati, 28-21, when Bengals cornerback Ken Riley intercepts a Sipe pass and returns it

1983
HIGHLIGHTS

42 yards for a touchdown midway through the fourth quarter. Riley's 60th career interception spoils a three-TD pass performance by Sipe.

WEEK 12—After going eight seasons without a shutout, the Browns make it two straight with a 30-0 rout of the Patriots at Foxboro. One week after posting a 20-0 win over Tampa Bay, Pruitt runs for 136 yards and Bahr kicks three field goals. The defensive star is linebacker Chip Banks, who returns an interception 65 yards for a touchdown and records two sacks. Cousineau and Hanford Dixon each intercept two passes.

WEEK 13—Newsome catches eight passes for 108 yards to spark a 41-23 victory over Baltimore at Cleveland. Newsome, who surpasses Gary Collins as the Browns' all-time receptions leader, catches a 66-yard TD pass from Sipe—one of three he would throw in the game.

WEEK 16—Sipe throws four touchdown passes and leads Cleveland to a 30-17 win over Pittsburgh in his last game as quarterback of the Browns. Sipe's finest career performance against the Steelers is not enough to secure a playoff berth, thanks to Seattle's later-day victory over New England.

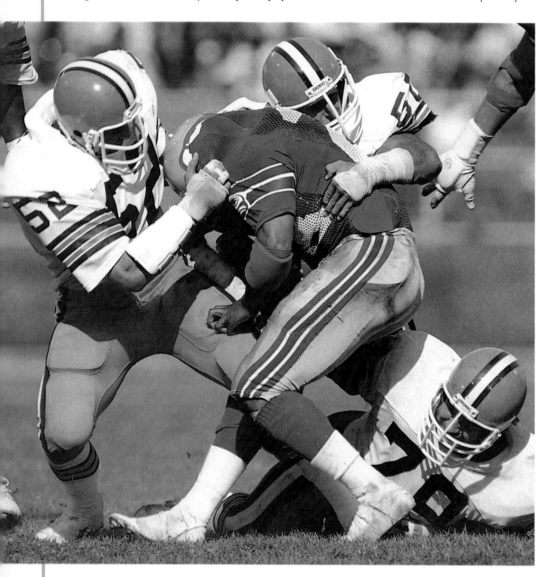

THE SEASON AT A GLANCE

HEAD COACH
Sam Rutigliano

REGULAR-SEASON RECORD
**9-7 / 2nd
AFC Central**

TOP DRAFT CHOICE (Rd.)
**Ron Brown, WR,
Arizona State (2)**

SCHEDULE/RESULTS

Minnesota	L	21-27
at Detroit	W	31-26
Cincinnati	W	17-7
at San Diego	W	(OT) 30-24
Seattle	L	9-24
N.Y. Jets	W	10-7
at Pittsburgh	L	17-44
at Cincinnati	L	21-28
Houston	W	(OT) 25-19
at Green Bay	L	21-35
Tampa Bay	W	20-0
at New England	W	30-0
Baltimore	W	41-23
at Denver	L	6-27
at Houston	L	27-34
Pittsburgh	W	30-17

Cleveland defenders Bob Golic (79), Dick Ambrose (52) and Cousineau won this battle, but Seattle won the war with a 24-9 Week 5 victory over the Browns.

WEEK 1—The Browns open with a 33-0 loss at Seattle—the first opening-game shutout loss in club history. The game is never in doubt as the Seahawks roll up 307 yards and hold the Browns to 120 yards. The Browns commit five turnovers, allow seven sacks and go 0-for-11 on third-down plays.

WEEK 4—The Browns roll up 413 yards in a 20-10 win over Pittsburgh—their first victory of the season after three losses. After the Steelers' Sam Washington intercepts a pass and returns it 69 yards for the game's first touchdown, Paul McDonald settles down and throws for 222 yards and two second-half touchdowns in a 20-3 blitz.

WEEK 6—The Browns can't hold a 16-3 lead and drop a tough 17-16 decision to New England. The Patriots take their first lead on a 2-yard touchdown run by Tony Collins with 50 seconds left, but the Browns storm back, only to see McDonald's pass, intended for Duriel Harris near the goal line, intercepted by Raymond Clayborn.

WEEK 9—Sam Rutigliano is fired and replaced by defensive coordinator Marty

Schottenheimer, but the Browns lose again, 16-14, to New Orleans in a dramatic conclusion. The game, Cleveland's fifth straight loss by five or fewer points, is decided on the final play when Morten Andersen bombs a 53-yard field goal—the longest ever at Cleveland Stadium. The Saints start their game-winning drive at their own 23 with 59 seconds left and no timeouts.

WEEK 10—The 1-8 Browns snap a five-game losing streak by beating winless Buffalo, 13-10. Turnovers produce both touchdowns in a game played in pouring rain. The Bills' Chris Keating returns a fumble 34 yards for Buffalo's score and Earnest Byner picks up a teammate's fumble and runs 55 yards for his first NFL TD. Boyce Green rushes for 156 yards, the most by a Cleveland player in six years.

WEEK 14—The Bengals beat the Browns, 20-17, on a 35-yard Jim Breech field goal on their first possession of overtime after tying the game on the final play a regulation. The tying touchdown comes on a 1-yard Boomer Esiason TD pass to Anthony Munoz on a tackle-eligible play—Munoz's first reception since high school.

McDonald (16) and Green (30) were regulars in the backfield and first-round pick Don Rogers (top photo) stepped in at free safety and played two seasons before his death following the 1985 season.

THE SEASON AT A GLANCE

HEAD COACHES
Sam Rutigliano (1-7) /
Marty Schottenheimer (4-4)

REGULAR-SEASON RECORD
5-11 / 3rd
AFC Central

TOP DRAFT CHOICE (Rd.)
Don Rogers, S, UCLA (1)

SCHEDULE/RESULTS

at Seattle	L		0-33
at L.A. Rams	L		17-20
Denver	L		14-24
Pittsburgh	W		20-10
at Kansas City	L		6-10
New England	L		16-17
N.Y. Jets	L		20-24
at Cincinnati	L		9-12
New Orleans	L		14-16
at Buffalo	W		13-10
San Francisco	L		7-41
at Atlanta	W		23-7
Houston	W		27-10
Cincinnati	L	(OT)	17-20
at Pittsburgh	L		20-23
at Houston	W		27-20

WEEK 1—The Browns open the season with a 27-24 loss to St. Louis—a game decided by a 35-yard Neil O'Donoghue field goal in overtime. The Browns, who trail by two touchdowns with 11:43 left, score three times in 7:15 to take a 24-17 lead. But the Cardinals drive 63 yards in 34 seconds to force overtime on a 5-yard Neil Lomax TD pass to Pat Tilley.

WEEK 5—Rookie Kevin Mack rushes for 115 yards and catches five passes for 85 yards to key a 24-20 victory over the Patriots. Wide receiver Brian Brennan adds to the fun with seven catches for 104 yards and throws a 33-yard touchdown pass to Ozzie Newsome. The game marks the NFL debut of Browns quarterback Bernie Kosar, a Boardman, Ohio, native who comes in after starter Gary Danielson strains his shoulder.

WEEK 6—Kosar leads the Browns to a 21-6 win at Houston in his first NFL start. The Oilers lead 6-0 at the half before Kosar throws a 68-yard third-quarter touchdown pass to Clarence Weathers. Chip Banks and Carl Hairston combine for four of the Browns' seven sacks of quarterbacks Warren Moon and Mike Moroski.

WEEK 9—The Browns lose at Pittsburgh, 10-9, on a 25-yard field goal

1985

HIGHLIGHTS

Linebacker Eddie Johnson records 148 tackles, including a season-high 15 against the Bills.

by Gary Anderson with nine seconds left. The game's memorable play comes in the third quarter with the Browns leading 6-0 and Kosar in shotgun formation. Kosar looks to the officials for help in quieting a loud Pittsburgh crowd just as center Mike Baab snaps the ball past the startled quarterback, who recovers for a 12-yard loss. After a short Cleveland punt, the Steelers score their only touchdown.

WEEK 15—Kosar throws for three touchdowns and runs for another as the Browns move into sole possession of first place in the AFC Central with a 28-21 win over Houston. Kosar's first TD pass is caught by Newsome, the 500th reception of the tight end's career.

DIVISIONAL PLAYOFF GAME—The 8-8 Browns, the first team in NFL history to win a division title with a non-winning record, lose at Miami, 24-21, in their first playoff game in five years. The Browns grab a 21-3 lead when Earnest Byner runs 66 yards for a touchdown on their first second-half possession. But Miami rallies behind quarterback Dan Marino, who connects 10 times with running back Tony Nathan. Miami's 18-point comeback, the biggest in AFC playoff history, ruins a Cleveland playoff-record 161-yard performance by Byner.

THE SEASON AT A GLANCE

HEAD COACH
Marty Schottenheimer

REGULAR-SEASON RECORD
8-8 / 1st AFC Central

TOP DRAFT CHOICE (Rd.)
Greg Allen, RB, Florida State (2)

SCHEDULE/RESULTS

St. Louis	L	(OT) 24-27
Pittsburgh	W	17-7
at Dallas	L	7-20
at San Diego	W	21-7
New England	W	24-20
at Houston	W	21-6
L.A. Raiders	L	20-21
Washington	L	7-14
at Pittsburgh	L	9-10
at Cincinnati	L	10-27
Buffalo	W	17-7
Cincinnati	W	24-6
at N.Y. Giants	W	35-33
at Seattle	L	13-31
Houston	W	28-21
at N.Y. Jets	L	10-37
AFC Divisional Game		
at Miami	L	21-24

In '85, Mack (34) tops 1,000 yards and rookie Kosar (right photo), shown in the playoffs, excels at times.

1986
HIGHLIGHTS

WEEK 1—The Browns open with a 41-31 loss to defending Super Bowl-champion Chicago at Soldier Field. Kevin Mack and Earnest Byner, who in 1985 became only the third NFL teammates to rush for 1,000 yards in the same season, are held to a combined 68 yards while Walter Payton rushes for 113 and scores two touchdowns for the Bears.

WEEK 3—On a Thursday night, the Browns lose, 30-13, to rival Cincinnati before 78,779 at Cleveland Stadium. The Browns have no answer for Larry Kinnebrew (three rushing touchdowns) or James Brooks (118 yards) while yielding their highest rushing total (257 yards) in four years. The game is memorable for Bengals Vice President and G.M. Paul Brown, who had coached both teams for a combined 25 years.

WEEK 5—After 16 straight losses, the Browns finally win at Pittsburgh's Three Rivers Stadium, 27-24. After the Steelers score to take a 14-10 lead, Gerald "Ice Cube" McNeil returns the ensuing kickoff 100 yards—the third kickoff return of at least 100 yards in Browns history and the first since 1967.

WEEK 12—The Browns register their first sweep of the Steelers since 1969 as Bernie Kosar completes 28-of-46 passes for a career-high 414 yards in a 37-31 overtime win at Cleveland. Pittsburgh forces overtime on Gary Anderson's 40-yard field goal with seven seconds left, but the Browns prevail on Kosar's second TD pass—a 36-yarder to rookie Webster Slaughter. The win ties the Browns and Bengals for first in the AFC Central.

WEEK 13—Five days after being signed to replace injured Matt Bahr, veteran Mark Moseley kicks a 29-yard field goal with 16 seconds left in overtime to give Cleveland a 13-10 win over Houston. Moseley hits his game-winner after Frank Minnifield intercepts his second Oliver Luck pass in overtime, returning it 20 yards to the Houston 38—one of six Cleveland interceptions in the game.

Kosar (above) was the right arm for offensive coordinator Lindy Infante (left) and coach Marty Schottenheimer during a big 1986 season. McNeil (right photo) was a big-play man who helped beat Pittsburgh with a 100-yard kickoff return.

WEEK 15—The Browns win their second straight AFC Central title by crushing the Bengals, 34-3, at Riverfront Stadium—the largest margin of victory in a Browns-Bengals game. Kosar and Reggie Langhorne hook up for a 66-yard completion to the Cincinnati 2-yard line on the game's first play, setting up a 1-yard touchdown run by Mack. The Browns do not commit a turnover and hold the Bengals' top-ranked offense to one possession inside their 20.

The Drive

The Drive. Those two words are suspended in time, an arrow piercing the heart of a city that should have recovered from its pain many years ago. They were coined and choreographed by John Elway, a name that cuts through the very fabric of Cleveland football like the passes he used to cut through the swirling winds of Lake Erie on a fateful January day in 1987.

"We were a game away from the Super Bowl, minutes away," remembers former Browns offensive tackle Cody Risien, who played against Elway and the Broncos in that 1986 AFC championship game and two others in the decade. "It's still very difficult, year in and year out when the Super Bowl comes on after the championship games—it's invariably frustrating to think that three times I was in position where I was a game away from the Super Bowl. I'm not over it yet."

Memories die hard in Cleveland, especially those associated with a 1986 team that dangled championship hopes in the eyes of success-starved fans and then saw Elway snatch them away. To capture the high and the low of an amazing season, you

Carl "Big Daddy" Hairston (78) couldn't catch Denver running back Winder (above) and the Cleveland defense couldn't catch Elway (right photo) when he led the Broncos to their game-winning touchdown.

need look no further than the two playoff games following a 12-4 regular season that gave the Browns distinction as the best team in the AFC.

"I think the 1980 and the 1986 teams were the best two teams I played on," recalled linebacker Clay Matthews, who played 16 seasons for the Browns. "Talent-wise, they might not have been as good as some other teams, but generally

"When John got the ball on the 2 and started driving, I remember that if he needed 4 yards, he got 5; if he needed 13, he got 14. It just seemed like anything he needed he got a couple yards more. And he just moved the ball down the field."

— *Defensive tackle Bob Golic*

SPOTLIGHT: BERNIE KOSAR

The first thing you noticed about Bernie Kosar was his gangly awkwardness and the unorthodox, sidearm motion that delivered passes from every position imaginable. He wasn't pretty, but that was not part of the quarterback job description in blue-collar Cleveland. Kosar was productive. He was dramatic. And he was a home-grown Ohio boy—a perfect fit for an imperfect city.

"Growing up in Youngstown, Ohio, I was a Browns fan from when I was a kid," recalled Kosar, who gave up two years of eligibility at the University of Miami so Cleveland could select him in a 1985 supplemental draft. "I just wanted to go back (to northern Ohio) because my family's there, that was my team, I love that part of the country."

The feeling was mutual. From the moment he made his Cleveland Stadium debut in the fifth game of the 1985 season, Kosar was a fixture in the hearts of Browns fans and the offensive scheme of coach Marty Schottenheimer, who guided the Browns to three straight AFC Central Division titles with Kosar. The 1986, '87 and '89 Browns, with Bud Carson replacing Schottenheimer, lost to Denver in AFC title games.

"We had won our division in 1985, but '86 is when we went to a more

evolved offensive system," Kosar said—a philosophy change forced by early 1986 injuries to running backs Kevin Mack and Earnest Byner. "More of the onus was put on myself throwing the ball. The '86 and '87 seasons were fun for all of us in Cleveland, with the exception of losing at the end to Denver.

"But the team, the city—we hadn't been at that level, one of the elite teams in the league, for quite a while and the enthusiasm that was there was just incredible."

Kosar triggered that enthusiasm with a 3,854-yard, 17-touchdown passing performance in 1986 before exploding for 489 passing yards in a dramatic, come-from-behind playoff victory over the Jets. He threw for 3,033 yards and 22 TDs despite playing only 12 games in a 1987 season shortened by a players' strike. He would top 3,000 yards two more times in eight-plus Cleveland seasons. The honeymoon came to an unexpected end midway through the 1993 season when Kosar, who was having philosophical differences with coach Bill Belichick, was released.

"In 1993, I get released after the Denver game and we're still in first place," Kosar said. "I had never envisioned playing for another team and it seemed like the end of the world. But all of a sudden, four days later, I'm playing for the Cowboys, defending Super Bowl champs, and we go on to win another Super Bowl."

That championship was followed by three backup seasons with the Miami Dolphins before an April 1997 retirement and a consultant role with the reborn Browns.

---

you really had a good feeling about the team. You really enjoyed playing with them. And it showed up in the win/loss column."

The 1986 spotlight focused on second-year quarterback Bernie Kosar, who became the high-powered trigger man for coach Marty Schottenheimer's offense after running backs Kevin Mack and Earnest Byner went down with early injuries. After a 4-3 start, Kosar began piling up impressive passing numbers and the inspired Browns began piling up victories.

"He (Kosar) came in and had a lot of success and there was a lot of excitement," said former nose tackle Bob Golic. "The fans loved Bernie. I think just having a young, exciting quarterback—we just felt we had taken a step in the right direction."

Kosar, who was born and raised in northeast Ohio, did not have a classic throwing motion or evasive speed, but his direction was definitely up. After a 3,854-yard passing season that helped the Browns gain home-field advantage throughout the AFC playoffs, he cemented a permanent spot in team lore with a Houdini-caliber performance in a divisional playoff

matchup against the wild-card Jets.

The need for some well-timed magic was the result of two Kosar interceptions, one in the end zone early in the fourth quarter when the Browns were on the verge of wiping out a 13-10 Jets advantage and the other on Cleveland's next series, setting up Freeman McNeil's 25-yard touchdown run. The consecutive interceptions, Kosar's first in 133 passes, and the 20-10 deficit cast an understandable pall over the 78,106 fans at Cleveland Stadium. But Kosar's next venture into the huddle, with 4:08 left on the clock, would be different.

"Bernie comes into the huddle and says, 'We're going to take this game,'" left tackle Paul Farren said after the game. "It's incredible the way he brought us together as a unit, one play at a time."

The Browns, facing a second-and-24, got a big break when New York defensive end Mark Gastineau was flagged for a late hit on Kosar. Five pass completions later, Mack bulled into the end zone from the 1-yard line and a Mark Moseley conversion cut the deficit to 20-17 with 1:57 remaining.

Slaughter's 37-yard reception (above) stunned the Jets and put the Browns in position for a game-tying field goal, which was delivered by Moseley (3, right photo) with seven seconds remaining in regulation.

Cleveland's onside kick failed, but the Browns' inspired defense held and Kosar got the ball back on his own 33 with 51 seconds on the clock. A pass interference penalty and a 37-yard strike to Webster Slaughter took the ball to the Jets' 5-yard line, setting up Moseley's 22-yard game-tying field goal with seven seconds left in regulation. Miracle No. 1 was complete.

"We knew what kind of character the team had and I think that when we got ourselves in trouble against the Jets, nobody really panicked," Golic recalled. "I think the character of that team was to keep punching away, keep punching away and hope for the best. When we tied it up, I think at that point there was no way we were going to lose that game."

They didn't. Moseley, kicking on first

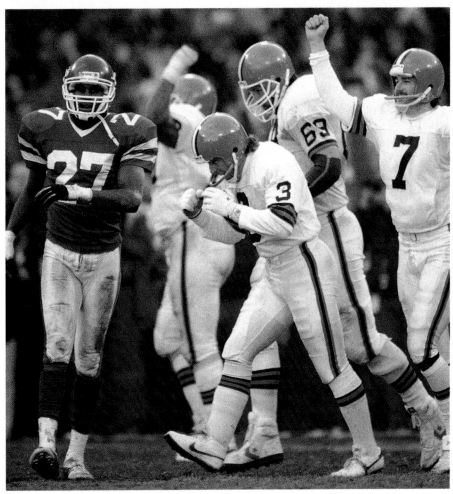

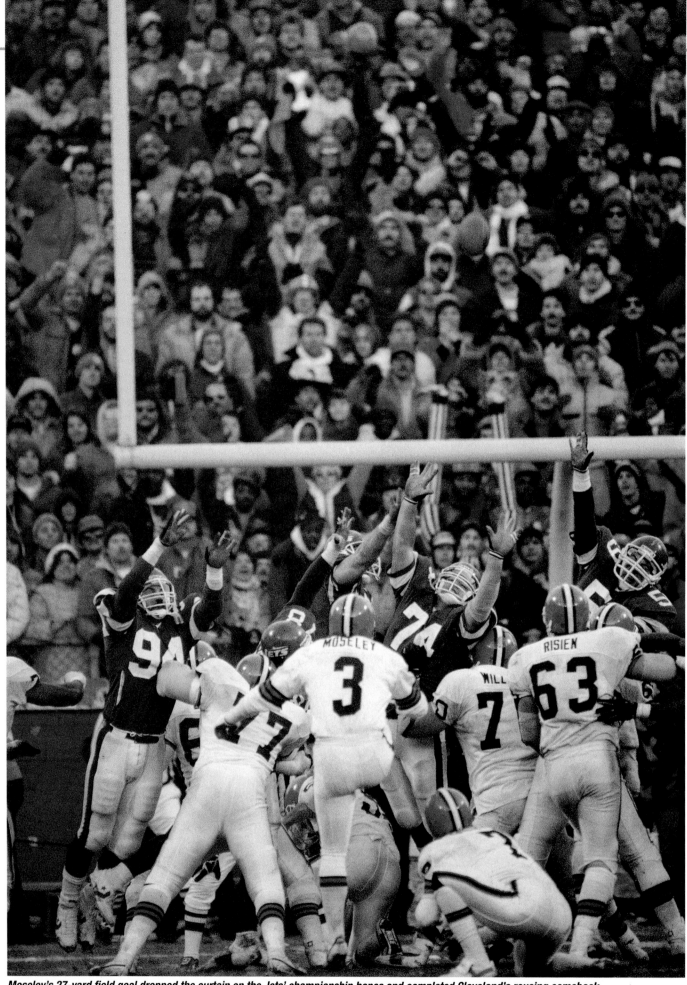

Moseley's 27-yard field goal dropped the curtain on the Jets' championship hopes and completed Cleveland's rousing comeback.

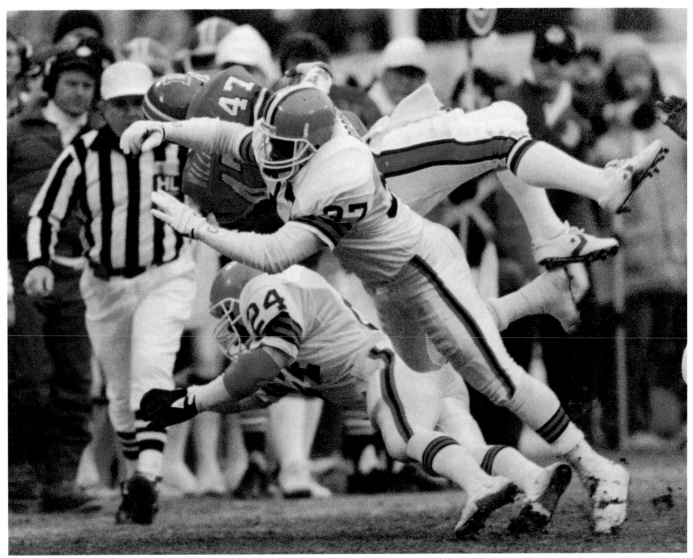

down, could have made it easy on the Browns with a 23-yard field goal at the closed end of Cleveland Stadium in the first overtime. But he missed and the game stretched into a second extra period before Kosar drove the Browns into position for another field-goal attempt by the 38-year-old Moseley. This time, he connected on a 27-yard game-winner into the swirling wind, ending the third-longest game in NFL history, 23-20, after 17:02 of overtime.

"I felt like I had 80,000 people on my shoulder and they all had knives in my back," Moseley said in the winning locker room. "But I've been in these situations before."

Kosar's dramatics included 33 completions, tying a playoff record, and postseason marks of 64 attempts and 489 passing yards. And, of course, what Risien called the "incredible finish."

That description also would apply the following week—only this time the spotlight would fall on Elway, the Broncos'

fourth-year quarterback who would have to overcome cold, gusty winds, the clock and 79,915 screaming Browns fans in a do-or-die march for the tying touchdown. In a role reversal from the Jets game, the Browns carried a 20-13 lead into the final 5:32 of regulation, thanks to a 48-yard, fourth-quarter touchdown strike from Kosar to Brian Brennan. When Denver's Ken Bell mishandled the ensuing kickoff, the Broncos got the ball at their own 2-yard line.

"When John got the ball on the 2 and started driving, I remember that if he needed 4 yards, he got 5; if he needed 13, he got 14," Golic said. "It just seemed like anything he needed he got a couple yards more. And he just moved the ball down the field."

With the Browns playing a prevent defense, Elway moved his team out of trouble with a 5-yard pass to Sammy Winder and two Winder runs that gave him a key first down at the 12. Now Elway had room to operate.

Brennan (86) dropped a 48-yard fourth-quarter bomb on the Broncos, but it wasn't enough to overcome Elway's last-minute magic.

> "To watch (The Drive) unfold was horrible.
> We were so deflated we just couldn't bounce back."
>
> — *Tight end Ozzie Newsome*

Jackson's sliding end zone catch (above) completed The Drive and tied the championship game at 20-20. Karlis' 33-yard field goal (right) ended the game and touched off a high-flying Broncos celebration.

Winder ran for 3 more yards and Elway scrambled for 11 before throwing a 22-yard swing pass to Steve Sewell and a 12-yarder over the middle to wide receiver Steve Watson. The first down at Cleveland's 40-yard line set the stage for the key play of the drive.

After Browns defensive tackle Dave Puzzuoli finally got to the scrambling Elway on second down and forced Denver into a third-and-18 situation at the 48, the sideline decision was to go for half the distance on third down and the rest on fourth. But Elway saw something he liked.

"Their safety (Ray Ellis) was real deep, so I just took a shot at it," said Elway, whose 34-yard scramble had set up the Broncos' first touchdown. His "shot" was a 20-yard sideline strike to

rookie Mark Jackson and a first down at the 28 with 1:19 remaining. A 14-yard pass to Sewell and a 9-yard scramble to the 5 set up the coup de grace—a low bullet pass to a sliding Jackson for the touchdown. Kicker Rich Karlis tied the game, 20-20, with 37 seconds left.

"When he brought that team back, I don't want to say we were broken, but we were so emotionally beat up the week before against the Jets," Golic recalled. "We saw what John had done, it was tough to keep it up."

"To watch (The Drive) unfold was horrible," recalled tight end Ozzie Newsome. "We were so deflated we just couldn't bounce back."

The Broncos, like the Browns a week earlier, used the

momentum to prevail in overtime—after Cleveland had gone three-and-out on its first possession. The winning drive was a paltry 60 yards, but it reeked of Elway magic. There was a 22-yard pass to tight end Orson Mobley and a 28-yarder to Watson, a play on which defensive back Felix Wright fell down. When Karlis drilled his game-ending, 33-yard field goal 5:48 into overtime, the Broncos were in the Super Bowl. Ironically, the final score, like the week before, was 23-20.

After the game, several players questioned the prevent defense that opened the field for Elway, who had been contained most of the afternoon by the relentless Browns. The nagging questions have not gone away.

"Hindsight is 20-20," Risien said, "but it seemed like the whole game we had the wraps on John, we were just going after him. Teams year in and year out, game in and game out, they go into that prevent defense and rush three and give the quarterback time, a guy like Elway, to do anything they want to do."

Consider: Elway, after completing 14-of-26 pass attempts for 124 yards in the game's first 55 minutes, connected on 8-of-12 for 120 yards on Denver's last two possessions.

"I understand if you go with the normal attack defense and get burned deep, you look like an idiot," Golic said. "But how many times do you put the prevent in and have somebody move right down the field on you?"

This time, on a drive forever etched among the most memorable moments in football history.

1987

HIGHLIGHTS

Kosar fires a pass over the hard-charging Colts during the Browns' AFC divisional playoff victory over Indianapolis.

WEEK 2—The Browns get their first win of 1987 by scoring 17 points in a 2:25 span of the fourth quarter and beating Pittsburgh, 34-10. The Browns' sixth straight win over the Steelers at Cleveland Stadium is their most lopsided win over Pittsburgh in 21 years. Linebacker Clay Matthews keys the victory by intercepting two Mark Malone passes, returning the first 26 yards for a touchdown.

WEEK 7—After a home game against Denver is cancelled because of labor problems and a team of "replacement players" compiles a 2-1 record, the regular Browns return and defeat the Rams, 30-17. A Cleveland Stadium crowd of 76,933 watches the Browns jump out to a 20-0 lead, with Felix Wright's 40-yard interception return highlighting the explosion. Bernie Kosar and Brian Brennan hook up on a 53-yard touchdown pass for the Browns' final points.

THE SEASON AT A GLANCE

HEAD COACH
Marty Schottenheimer

REGULAR-SEASON RECORD
10-5 / 1st AFC Central

TOP DRAFT CHOICE (Rd.)
Mike Junkin, LB, Duke (1)

SCHEDULE/RESULTS

at New Orleans	L	21-28
Pittsburgh	W	34-10
Denver *(cancelled because of strike)*		
at New England*	W	20-10
Houston*	L	10-15
at Cincinnati*	W	34-0
L.A. Rams	W	30-17
at San Diego	L	(OT) 24-27
Atlanta	W	38-3
Buffalo	W	27-21
at Houston	W	40-7
at San Francisco	L	24-38
Indianapolis	L	7-9
Cincinnati	W	38-24
at L.A. Raiders	W	24-17
at Pittsburgh	W	19-13
AFC Divisional Game		
Indianapolis	W	38-21
AFC Championship Game		
at Denver	L	33-38

* games played with replacement players

WEEK 11—The Browns take sole possession of first place in the AFC Central with a 40-7 win at Houston. Kevin Mack rushes for 114 yards, Earnest Byner scores two touchdowns and Kosar throws for two more. The Browns force six Houston turnovers, sack quarterback Warren Moon three times and yield 43 rushing yards. Frank Minnifield intercepts three passes.

WEEK 14—The Browns snap a two-game losing streak by defeating the Bengals, 38-24, at Cleveland. After scoring one offensive touchdown in their previous seven quarters, the Browns explode for 28 second-quarter points, tying a club record. Kosar throws a career-high four TD passes and Mack rushes for 133 yards.

WEEK 16—The Browns win their third straight AFC Central title and second straight game at Pittsburgh, defeating the Steelers, 19-13. The Browns hold the Steelers to 10 first downs, do not allow an offensive touchdown and keep possession of the ball for all but 21 seconds of the fourth quarter. The Steelers' only offensive play of the quarter results in an interception by Hanford Dixon.

AFC DIVISIONAL PLAYOFF GAME—Byner makes amends for a regular-season fumble that costs his team a win over the Colts by rushing for 122 yards and scoring two touchdowns in a 38-21 win over Indianapolis. Byner's second TD, a 2-yard run late in the third quarter, caps a 13-play, 86-yard drive that gives the Browns a 21-14 lead—one they never relinquish. The Browns convert 11-of-14 third-down plays and punt once.

The Fumble

The play loops in slow motion through the memory of every Browns fan, always playing and replaying to the same inevitable conclusion. Earnest Byner takes the handoff from Bernie Kosar and cuts left to daylight. Denver cornerback Jeremiah Castille reaches for the ball and pokes it free as Byner's momentum carries him into the end zone. Big bodies converge near the 3-yard line. A foot-stomping roar from 75,993 fans engulfs Mile High Stadium and pronounces another death knell on Cleveland's Super Bowl hopes.

Like the Red Right 88 bomb that blew up a potentially fruitful 1980 postseason and The Drive, executed to perfection by John Elway a year earlier in the 1986 AFC championship game, The Fumble would take on a life of its own, remembered and disdained as the reason Cleveland lost again. More than a decade after the 1987 AFC title game, former Browns cringe at such shortsighted analysis.

"The fumble was the one thing people pointed at as the reason we didn't go to the Super Bowl," Byner recalled. "But the whole game was filled with penalties, fumbles, dropped

Kosar, protected (above) by Risien (63), fired 41 passes at the Broncos' defense on a frantic come-from-behind afternoon at Denver's Mile High Stadium. But the lingering memory is of fallen hero Byner kneeling solemnly in the end zone (right photo) as referees tried to separate bodies at the 3-yard line in search of his game-turning fumble.

passes. We did some things that could have caused us to not even be in that game."

Kosar put it more succinctly. "Earnest gets a lot of attention for the play at the end of the game where we almost scored," he said. "But Earnest Byner had just a heck of a game that day. He had 120 yards receiving (on seven receptions), 67 yards rushing and two touchdowns. When he was going for second effort at the end, the ball comes out. Without his effort, I don't think we would have been in that position."

The Browns might not have even reached the championship game if not for Byner,

169

Tight end Ozzie Newsome hauls in a 25-yard first-quarter pass from Kosar as Broncos safety Tony Lilly closes in for the tackle.

who was a consistent contributor throughout the strike-shortened 1987 regular season and rushed for 122 yards in a 38-21 divisional playoff victory over the Colts. And against the Broncos, Byner's second-half effort was a big reason why the late fumble even mattered.

Before the game was four minutes old, the AFC West-champion Broncos had a 7-0 lead, thanks to a deflected interception by Freddie Gilbert and Elway's 8-yard scoring pass to Ricky Nattiel. At 11:06 of the first quarter, Denver's Steve Sewell scored on a 1-yard run after the Broncos recovered a Kevin Mack fumble. By halftime, the Browns trailed, 21-3, and were reeling.

"The first half was—well, terrible would be an understatement," recalled Kosar, who had passed for 3,033 yards and 22 touchdowns during the regular season. "We fall behind 21-3. We went into the second half and basically scrapped the

game plan and went into this throwing, two-minute mode to try to get ourselves back into it."

The building Mile High crescendo was muffled briefly when Felix Wright intercepted Elway on Denver's first second-half possession and Kosar connected on an 18-yard touchdown strike to Reggie Langhorne. Elway answered with an 80-yard touchdown bomb to Mark Jackson, but the Browns regained momentum with an 80-yard drive of their own, capped by Byner's first touchdown on a 32-yard pass from Kosar.

"It's not fun being down," Kosar said, "but it's fun when you start clicking and you know that you've got your offense rolling. We got into a really good groove and a good sync and started putting points on the board. Our goal was to get one score and get it to 21-10; then get a defensive stop and another score. Just try to close the gap."

And close it did. The Browns, showing the offensive form that had driven them to a 10-5 regular-season record and a third straight AFC Central title, pulled to within 28-24 on Byner's 4-yard run. Rich Karlis lifted the Broncos' lead to 31-24 with a 38-yard field goal on the final play of the third quarter before the Browns finally pulled even. Cleveland's game-tying drive, their fourth touchdown in as many second-half possessions, covered 86 yards—53 on a Kosar pass to Byner—and ended with a 4-yard pass to Webster Slaughter. Now the Broncos were reeling.

"I knew we had to get some points on the board at that point," Elway said after the game, "because Bernie was throwing the ball all over the place." In a situation reminiscent of his game-saving 1986 drive, Elway called his offense into the huddle, 75 yards from the Browns' end zone, with 5:14 remaining. Again he was up to the task, but this time he left too much time on the clock.

The drive took five plays—two of them 26-yard passes to Nattiel—and ended with 4:01 remaining on a 20-yard dump-off screen to Sammy Winder. Like Elway, Kosar would get the chance to take his team 75 yards and Byner's 17-yard run got the drive off to a rousing start.

Mile High Stadium quieted to a nervous rumble as the Browns moved quickly downfield—14 and 19-yard passes to Brian Brennan, a 6-yard run by Byner. With 1:12 remaining, the Browns faced second-and-5 at the Denver 8. Kosar called a simple Trap 13 play, Byner up the middle, and his cut left appeared to give him daylight to the end zone. Only Castille blocked the path to a game-tying touchdown.

"You thought he was there and then, boom, you saw these bodies converge and you knew it wasn't good," recalled former Browns offensive tackle Doug Dieken, who

Earnest Byner will never forget. Nobody will let him. The Fumble, an unfortunate misplay that sent shock waves through a Super Bowl-hungry city more than a decade ago, is entwined with his personal and football psyche, attached to his name like a shadow.

"It took me three or four years to get over that game emotionally," Byner recalled. "I continued to play and be successful and all that, but I never really dealt with it. I probably should have gone through some type of debriefing. It really was a traumatic situation. A lot of people joked about it, pointed the finger at me."

Browns fans remember the play all too well. Byner, the popular running back who had spearheaded Cleveland's emotional second-half comeback from a big deficit in the 1987 AFC championship game, took a handoff and was stripped of the ball at the Broncos' 3-yard line, just as he was about to explode into the end zone with the tying touchdown. Only 1:01 remained on the clock, but the moment would endure forever.

"The media was more harsh on me than the fans," Byner said. "There's always gotta be somebody to point the finger at and I was the one. It made me who I am now. I wouldn't wish it on anybody—nobody should have to go through what I went through. Personally, it was really hard and really very personal as far as what was being said about me, how people perceived me."

Before the fumble, Cleveland fans perceived Byner (5-10, 225) as a hard-working runner/receiver who wouldn't back down from anyone. He was always dangerous, whether running the ball or catching a swing pass out of the backfield. In 1985, the second-year East Carolina product rushed for 1,002 yards, combining with Kevin Mack (1,104) as the third NFL teammate combination to top 1,000 yards rushing in the same season.

But the perception changed after 1987. "I was one of the most loved and hated guys in Browns history," said Byner, who lasted through 1988 (576 rushing yards, 576 receiving yards) before being traded to Washington.

"Earnest Byner was traded because they (the Browns) thought he was jinxed," former Browns offensive tackle Doug

Dieken said. In Washington, Byner recorded two more 1,000-yard rushing seasons and was a member of a Super Bowl championship team (1991 season). But then a strange thing happened: Byner was invited back to the scene of the crime.

"I never dreamed of going back to Cleveland, never thought about it," he said. "When Ozzie (Newsome) called me in that offseason and asked me what I thought about coming back, it was a little bit shocking."

In retrospect, Byner's return for the 1994 and 1995 seasons—coinciding with the franchise's emotional farewell—sealed a special bond with Cleveland fans that had been shrouded briefly, but never lost. Byner played two more seasons with the Ravens and ended his 14-year career with 8,261 rushing yards and 4,605 receiving yards. But what if. ...

"If I had scored that touchdown, God would not have gotten his message to me," Byner said. "I don't know who I would have become or what I would have been."

Byner, chased by Denver's Karl Mecklenburg (77), heads into the end zone with one of his two third-quarter touchdowns.

watched the play from Cleveland's broadcast booth. "The defensive back made a great play. It was just one of those things."

Castille recovered with 1:01 remaining and Denver ran down the clock before taking an intentional safety with eight seconds left. Final score: Broncos 38, Browns 33. Denver would return to the Super Bowl for a second straight year—at the expense of the Browns.

"That was most frustrating for me, and I think the rest of the team, to be that close two years in a row," offensive tackle Cody Risien recalled. "The first year we were thinking, 'Hey, we'll be

back next year.' The second year you begin to realize how much work, how much good fortune it takes to get into that situation. And you can't count on those opportunities year in and year out."

Equally frustrating is the memory of watching Denver lose both Super Bowls—to the Giants and Redskins. "I definitely think that if we had gotten by John Elway, we could have shown up and had a much better chance to beat an NFC team," Risien said. "I think we matched up better against both New York and the Redskins in those years."

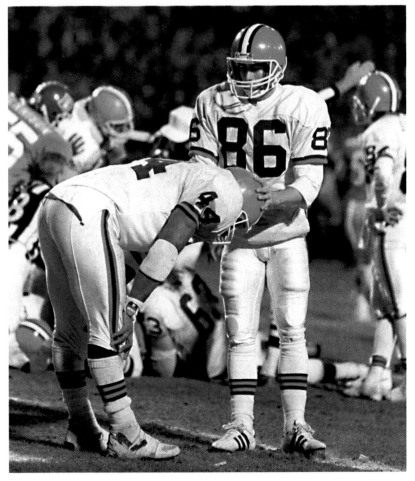

The thrill of victory, the agony of defeat.
Denver's Winder (23) gets a victory hug (above)
from teammate Gene Lang; a grief-stricken
Byner (left) is consoled by Brennan (86) after
his fumble. Winder's game-deciding touchdown
(top photo) came when he caught a 20-yard
Elway screen pass and sprinted past linebacker
David Grayson (56).

1988
HIGHLIGHTS

WEEK 1—The Browns' first season-opening win in six years—6-3 at Kansas City—is marred by injuries to quarterback Bernie Kosar, cornerback Frank Minnifield, fullback Kevin Mack, nose tackle Bob Golic, receiver Webster Slaughter and kick returner Gerald McNeil. The Browns prevail on a 38-yard field goal by Matt Bahr with 25 seconds left.

WEEK 2—Injuries pile up as the Browns lose quarterback Gary Danielson to a broken ankle and cornerback Hanford Dixon to a sprained ankle in a 23-3 loss to the Jets. The Browns do little offensively, mustering 12 first downs and 27 yards rushing. It marks the first time since 1973 the Browns fail to score a touchdown in back-to-back games.

THE SEASON AT A GLANCE

HEAD COACH
Marty Schottenheimer

REGULAR-SEASON RECORD
10-6 / T 2nd AFC Central

TOP DRAFT CHOICE (Rd.)
Clifford Charlton, LB, Florida (1)

SCHEDULE/RESULTS

at Kansas City	W	6-3
New York Jets	L	3-23
Indianapolis	W	23-17
at Cincinnati	L	17-24
at Pittsburgh	W	23-9
Seattle	L	10-16
Philadelphia	W	19-3
at Phoenix	W	29-21
Cincinnati	W	23-16
at Houston	L	17-24
at Denver	L	7-30
Pittsburgh	W	27-7
at Washington	W	17-13
Dallas	W	24-21
at Miami	L	31-38
Houston	W	28-23
AFC Wild-Card Game		
Houston	L	23-24

WEEK 6—The Browns lose their third quarterback and third game, 16-10 to Seattle. Mike Pagel, playing only because Kosar and Danielson can't, suffers a separated shoulder while making a tackle after a blocked field-goal attempt. Longtime Dolphins backup Don Strock replaces Pagel but cannot rally the Browns, who dominate statistically but can't overcome four turnovers that lead to all 16 Seattle points.

WEEK 11—Denver records its 10th straight victory over the Browns, 30-7. The Broncos score on all six first-half possessions to take a 30-0 halftime lead. Twenty points come after Cleveland turnovers, including three in a span of 3:43 of the second quarter. Kosar is sacked six times and the Browns never begin a drive beyond their own 30.

WEEK 13—Two weeks after getting beat by the loser of Super Bowl XXII (Denver), the Browns beat the winner (Washington), 17-13. The Browns hand the Redskins their third straight defeat and drop them below .500 (6-7) as Earnest Byner runs 27 yards for the game-winning touchdown with 1:49 left.

WEEK 16—Needing a victory to clinch an AFC wild-card berth, the Browns rally from a 23-7 deficit with 21 unanswered points and record a 28-23 win over the Oilers at Cleveland Stadium. Strock completes 25-of-42 passes for 326 yards and two touchdowns, the last coming on a 22-yard pass to Slaughter with 6:23 left.

AFC WILD-CARD GAME—In a rematch of the season finale, the Oilers defeat the Browns, 24-23, in the first round of the playoffs. The Browns lead, 16-14, after three quarters before the Oilers rally on Lorenzo White's 1-yard touchdown run and a 49-yard Tony Zendejas field goal. Marty Schottenheimer resigns under pressure as Browns coach three days later.

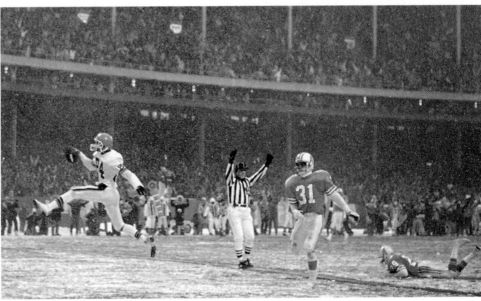

Mack and Reggie Langhorne (34 and 88, top photo) found time to stay loose during a time out at Cleveland Stadium, but there was no rest for Slaughter (above), who made five catches and scored two touchdowns against the Oilers in a 24-23 playoff loss. Strock (12, left) was the chief engineer of a regular season-ending 28-23 win over Houston.

The referee signals touchdown after a 9-yard run by Keith Jones (26) in the third quarter of a 38-24 home-opening victory over the New York Jets in 1989.

1989

HIGHLIGHTS

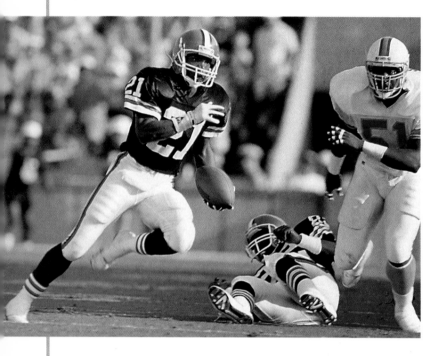

THE SEASON AT A GLANCE

HEAD COACH
Bud Carson

REGULAR-SEASON RECORD
9-6-1 / 1st AFC Central

TOP DRAFT CHOICE (Rd.)
Eric Metcalf, RB, Texas (1)

SCHEDULE/RESULTS

at Pittsburgh	W	51-0
N.Y. Jets	W	38-24
at Cincinnati	L	14-21
Denver	W	16-13
at Miami	L	(OT) 10-13
Pittsburgh	L	7-17
Chicago	W	27-7
Houston	W	28-17
at Tampa Bay	W	42-31
at Seattle	W	27-7
Kansas City	T	10-10
at Detroit	L	10-13
Cincinnati	L	0-21
at Indianapolis	L	(OT) 17-23
Minnesota	W	(OT) 23-17
at Houston	W	24-20
AFC Divisional Game		
Buffalo	W	34-30
AFC Championship Game		
at Denver	L	21-37

Matthews (right photo) lies on the ground as Felix Wright (22) and Robert Lyons (49) congratulate him after a game-saving interception against Buffalo. Other top players were Metcalf (top), who broke Paul Warfield's club rookie record for receptions with 54 catches and hard-charging defensive tackle Michael Dean Perry (92).

WEEK 1—Bud Carson begins his Browns head coaching career with a memorable 51-0 victory over the Steelers at Pittsburgh. It is the most lopsided victory in the 79-game series between the teams and the Browns' biggest shutout ever. Carson, Pittsburgh's former defensive coordinator, watches his team force eight turnovers, record seven sacks and score three touchdowns (two by linebacker David Grayson).

WEEK 4—The Browns snap a 10-game losing streak to Denver with a controversial 16-13 win at Cleveland. The game is decided by a Matt Bahr 48-yard field goal as time expires—a kick that barely clears the crossbar. Bahr's field goal comes after referee Tom Dooley orders the teams to switch ends of the field, thanks to rowdy Dawg Pound fans who pelt the Broncos with dog biscuits, eggs and other debris. The switch gives the Browns a timely wind advantage.

WEEK 7—Wide receiver Webster Slaughter catches eight passes for 186 yards in leading the Browns to a 27-7 win over the Bears in a Monday night game at Cleveland Stadium. One of the catches is a 97-yard touchdown from Kosar—the longest play from scrimmage in Browns history.

WEEK 8—For the first time in more than a decade Ozzie Newsome fails to catch a pass, but the Browns still beat Houston, 28-17. The Browns explode for 326 second-half yards as Kosar throws touchdown passes of 80 and 77 yards to Slaughter. Newsome's club-record streak of 150 consecutive games with a reception ends.

WEEK 11—Former coach Marty Schottenheimer, returning to Cleveland with his Chiefs, has to settle for a 10-10 tie as Kansas City kicker Nick Lowery misses three makeable field-goal attempts: 45- and 39-yarders in the final 10 seconds of regulation and a 47-yarder with

seven seconds left in overtime. The Browns fumble four times, throw one interception and punt a club record-tying 12 times.

WEEK 16—With the AFC Central title and a wild-card berth at stake, the Browns blow a 17-point lead before bouncing back to defeat the Oilers, 24-20, at the Astrodome. The Browns march 58 yards with no timeouts and Kevin Mack scores on a 4-yard touchdown run with 39 seconds left to save the day.

AFC DIVISIONAL PLAYOFF GAME—The Browns hold off visiting Buffalo, 34-30, when linebacker Clay Matthews intercepts a Jim Kelly pass intended for Thurman Thomas at the goal line with nine seconds left. Matthews' interception comes one play after a wide-open Ronnie Harmon drops a pass from Kelly in the end zone. The Browns get a 90-yard kickoff return by rookie Eric Metcalf in the third quarter and three touchdown passes from Kosar.

Play It Again, John

The John Elway show played to familiar reviews as the Broncos knocked the Browns out of the Super Bowl picture for the third time in four years. But this time Elway did not need a miracle finish, directing Denver to a 37-21 victory at Mile High Stadium.

Elway completed 20-of-36 passes for 385 yards and three touchdowns—including a 70-yard bomb to Michael Young and a 39-yarder to Sammy Winder.

Browns quarterback Bernie Kosar, who played with injuries to his shoulder, elbow and finger, threw three interceptions and had six passes batted down at the line. But he did rally the Browns to a 24-21 deficit in the third quarter on 27- and 10-yard TD passes to Brian Brennan before the Broncos posted the final 13 points.

The Browns had Elway on the run briefly when safety Felix Wright returned a third-quarter fumble to the Denver 1, setting up a touchdown. But the Broncos were in control most of the day, sacking the banged-up Kosar (left) four times.

The Dawg Pound

I t was sound logic, a motivational appeal using one of the most basic conflicts known to man.

"We were thinking of a dog and a cat, the quarterback being the cat and the defensive line being the dog," explained former Browns cornerback Hanford Dixon, referring to an idea that he and fellow corner Frank Minnifield developed during the Browns' 1985 summer training camp at Lakeland Community College in Mentor, Ohio. It was simply a ploy to get the linemen motivated to chase the quarterback all out during passing situations.

"If we did our thing—what they now call a coverage sack—or if the defensive line got to the quarterback, that's when we started barking," Minnifield recalled. "The fans were very, very close to the practice field. We would do it in practice when something good happened, then all of a sudden the fans were doing it on the sideline. That carried right over to the games."

From the first inspirational bark that Dixon and Minnifield delivered on that practice field sprang the Dawg Pound—one of the most celebrated, feared and reviled fan groups ever created. The barking continued on the field, but the concept exploded beyond anyone's wildest imagination away from it.

Suddenly the vast section of

Dixon (29) and Minnifield (31) were barking up the right tree when they played cat and mouse in the Browns' 1985 training camp. John 'Big Dawg' Thompson (right photo) grabbed the Dawg Pound bone and ran with it.

bleachers at the open end of Cleveland Stadium was filled on Sundays with barking, snarling, cheering fans wearing dog masks, dog bones, painted faces and other animalistic regalia. They were rowdy, fanatic and dedicated, armed with dog biscuits they could throw at opposing players and an emotional frenzy that could influence games.

"When we would go to play at other places, they all had their advantage we had to overcome," Minnifield said. "In Seattle, it was the deafening roar of the crowd. In Denver, it was the altitude. But if you came to Cleveland in good weather, there was nothing you had to overcome. There really wasn't an advantage.

"But when the Dawg Pound was created, it was really an obstacle. They (opponents) had to deal with the Dawg Pound at all times. When the Dawg Pound was created, we were all glad because the other people would get treated like the enemy when they left home. They (Dawg Pounders) got really good at it. It became a national issue."

Not only did the Pound provide an emotional advantage, it became a symbol for bonding between fans and players—a special bond that Cleveland fans lifted to unprecedented heights. The following fan testimonials provide a glimpse of the fervor, dedication and enjoyment the Dawg Pound has brought to Browns football.

Creativity and passion are prerequisites for Dawg Pound members, who embrace conquering heroes like Eric Metcalf (right photo) with the same fervor they use to harass Browns opponents.

Dawg Pound Memories

"Some of the happiest times of my life, and some of the fondest memories, are about times spent in the Dawg Pound. One thing that often goes unnoticed among the masks and bones, biscuits and barking, is the closeness of the fans in the Pound. If you miss a

game or two, everybody wants to know where you have been and if everything is all right with your family and home. It's more than just fans sitting together, it's like family. There is a bond between everybody. I think one of the things that has been missed the most is that closeness, that extended family that was torn apart. Although I have moved to another part of the country and will not

Linebacker Eddie Johnson (51) and safety Felix Wright (22) were integral parts of the original Dawg Pound mania that became part of Cleveland Stadium's football mystique.

be in the Dawg Pound any more, those are memories I will carry to my grave."

—Raymond Lemon
Orlando, Fla.

"I am a Steelers fan living in Toledo and I went to the game with three other Cleveland Browns fans. We had seats in the Dawg Pound. Of course, I was wearing my Steelers garb, and I was hounded the entire game by Dawg Pounders. This happened to be one of the best games ever played between the teams. It was the game Eric Metcalf ran back two punts for touchdowns. Even though the Steelers lost, it was one of the best times I ever had."

—Rich Cartwright
Toledo, Ohio

"After the Phoenix game in 1994, Vinny ran down to the Dawg Pound and tossed the game ball into the stands. He threw it right to me! Section 51, row 24, seat 1. I made a great catch. The ball still looks great. Go Browns in '99."

—J. Matt
Tipp City, Ohio
From the Wall of Memories on Cleveland Browns.com

"My most lasting memory would be sitting in the Dawg Pound for the last Cleveland home game and standing bawling in the stands with my heart broken into a million pieces. Then the next thing I know some of the players come running back onto the field and the forever-faithful Steve Everitt jumps into the stands no more than 3 feet from me. He looked up with the same tears I had and I knew he would be back if the team ever came back. God willing, he will be. I know he will."

—Christine
Columbus, Ohio
From the Wall of Memories on Cleveland Browns.com

"I have been to one Browns game—the final home game at Municipal Stadium. It was a Christmas present from my fiance (the best present I ever got) and we sat in the Dawg Pound. I remember sitting there, in awe for the whole game. I cried on the way there and on the way home. I remember breaking off pieces of the Dawg Pound, wearing the dawg mask and ears my dad had lent me, that he had worn in the same Dawg Pound many times before. I still have that piece of the Pound. It sits on the TV in my dorm room."

—Josh
Perrysburg, Ohio
From the Wall of Memories on Cleveland Browns.com

"I have been a season-ticket holder in the Dawg Pound since 1989. ... I have many memories of the Pound. They are all great, but the memories that stand out have to do with the other Dawg Pounders. We tailgate together, cheer together, travel together, share stories and, most important as fans, we win and lose together. The Dawg Pound will never go quiet."

—Bob Harley
North Royalton, Ohio

1990

HIGHLIGHTS

THE SEASON AT A GLANCE

HEAD COACHES
Bud Carson (2-7) /
Jim Shofner (1-6)

REGULAR-SEASON RECORD
3-13 / 4th AFC Central

TOP DRAFT CHOICE (Rd.)
Leroy Hoard, RB,
Michigan (2)

SCHEDULE/RESULTS

Pittsburgh	W	13-3
at N.Y. Jets	L	21-24
San Diego	L	14-24
at Kansas City	L	0-34
at Denver	W	30-29
at New Orleans	L	20-25
Cincinnati	L	13-34
at San Francisco	L	17-20
Buffalo	L	0-42
Houston	L	23-35
Miami	L	13-30
L.A. Rams	L	23-38
at Houston	L	14-58
Atlanta	W	13-10
at Pittsburgh	L	0-35
at Cincinnati	L	14-21

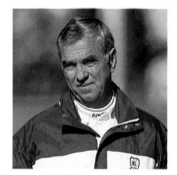

It was mostly a down season for Kosar (19) and Carson (above right), who was replaced by interim coach Shofner (right).

WEEK 1—The Browns open with a 13-3 win over the Steelers at Cleveland Stadium. Quarterback Bernie Kosar is sacked seven times and completes 13-of-30 passes as the Browns are held to 11 first downs and 200 total yards. But Cleveland's defense holds the Steelers to 49 rushing yards and scores the game's only touchdown on a 30-yard fumble return by cornerback Anthony Blaylock.

WEEK 5—The Browns get a 30-yard last-second field goal from Jerry Kauric and snap a seven-game losing streak at Denver with a 30-29 Monday Night Football victory over the AFC-champion Broncos. Kosar throws three touchdown passes, including a 24-yarder to Brian Brennan with 3:21 remaining. Trailing 29-27, the Browns begin their 61-yard final drive with 2:04 left.

WEEK 8—The 2-5 Browns come close, but the undefeated 49ers pull out a 20-17 victory on a 45-yard Mike Cofer field goal with five seconds remaining at San Francisco. The Browns rally from a 17-3 deficit and force a tie on a 4-yard touchdown pass from backup quarterback Mike Pagel to tight end Ozzie Newsome with 1:10 left. But quarterback Joe Montana drives the defending Super Bowl champions 44 yards for the game-winning points.

WEEK 9—Bud Carson's final game as coach ends with the worst shutout defeat in Browns' history: a 42-0 hammering by Buffalo at Cleveland. The Bills score one touchdown in each of the first three quarters and three in the fourth. The clincher is a 60-yard interception return by Cleveland native Darryl Talley with 2:31 left.

WEEK 10—Houston quarterback Warren Moon throws five touchdown passes to five different receivers and the Oilers hand the Browns and new coach Jim Shofner a 35-23 beating at Cleveland. The only bright spots are Webster Slaughter, who catches six passes for 104 yards, and Newsome, who catches his 47th and final touchdown pass.

WEEK 13—The Oilers get four touchdowns from Lorenzo White and the Browns surrender 30 or more points for the fifth straight game in a 58-14 loss at Houston. It is the most points allowed by the Browns in a regular-season game and most points scored by the Oilers. Cleveland's eighth straight loss is brightened by two Metcalf touchdowns—a 101-yard kickoff return and a 31-yard reception.

WEEK 16—The Browns close out the worst season in franchise history with a 21-14 loss at Cincinnati. The game is Shofner's last as interim coach.

1991

WEEK 2—After losing their opener to Dallas, the Browns shut out the Patriots, 20-0, and give Bill Belichick his first NFL coaching win. Playing before a small crowd (35,377) at Foxboro Stadium, the Cleveland defense roughs up quarterback Tommy Hodson with four sacks and two interceptions. The Browns hold the Patriots to eight first downs and 143 total yards and don't allow a penetration inside the 26-yard line.

WEEK 3—The Browns defeat the Bengals, 14-13, at sold-out Cleveland Stadium on Matt Stover's fourth field goal—a 45-yarder with four seconds left. Most of Cleveland's points are generated by the defense—Van Waiters and Michael Dean Perry force fumbles that lead to field goals and rookie tackle James Jones tackles Bengals running back James Brooks in the end zone for a safety.

THE SEASON AT A GLANCE

HEAD COACH
Bill Belichick

REGULAR-SEASON RECORD
6-10 / 3rd AFC Central

TOP DRAFT CHOICE (Rd.)
Eric Turner, S, UCLA (1)

SCHEDULE/RESULTS

Dallas	L	14-26
at New England	W	20-0
Cincinnati	W	14-13
at N.Y. Giants	L	10-13
N.Y. Jets	L	14-17
at Washington	L	17-42
at San Diego	W	(OT) 30-24
Pittsburgh	W	17-14
at Cincinnati	L	21-23
Philadelphia	L	30-32
at Houston	L	24-28
Kansas City	W	20-15
at Indianapolis	W	31-0
Denver	L	7-17
Houston	L	14-17
at Pittsburgh	L	10-17

WEEK 7—In their only overtime game of the season, the Browns defeat the Chargers, 30-24, on linebacker David Brandon's 30-yard interception return of a John Friesz pass midway through the extra period. Bernie Kosar completes 26-of-42 passes for 303 yards and two touchdowns, including a 15-yarder to Leroy Hoard with 4:09 left to force overtime. The Browns overcome deficits of 17-3 and 24-17.

WEEK 10—The Browns blow a 23-0 lead and lose to Philadelphia, 32-30, at Cleveland Stadium. The Browns take their early lead on a 50-yard field goal by Stover, a 42-yard interception return by rookie Eric Turner, a 65-yard Kosar pass to Hoard and an 18-yard Kosar-to-Webster Slaughter TD pass. But the Eagles storm back with 17 points on their next three possessions. Kosar breaks Bart Starr's NFL record of 294 consecutive throws without an interception before Philadelphia's Ben Smith ends the streak late in the second quarter.

WEEK 13—The Browns turn four consecutive turnovers into 24 points just before halftime and go on to whip the Colts, 31-0, at Indianapolis. Cleveland's only score not aided by a turnover is a 51-yard touchdown run by Kevin Mack.

WEEK 15—The Browns lose a heartbreaker to the Oilers, 17-14, when Stover misses a 19-yard field-goal attempt with four seconds left. After the Oilers take their first lead with 2:19 left, the Browns drive 81 yards to the Houston 1, Kosar coming up just short of the end zone on an 11-yard scramble to set up Stover's miss. The loss officially eliminates the Browns from playoff contention.

In '91, Clay Matthews (above) plays his 200th game for the Browns and Rob Burnett (90) tallies three sacks in Belichick's first season as the Browns' coach.

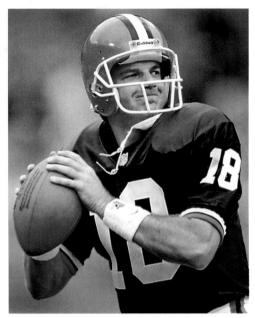

1992
HIGHLIGHTS

Tomczak (18) started eight games for the Browns, rookie Vardell (44) rushed for 369 yards and Eric Turner (right photo) kept his head on straight long enough to tally 119 tackles.

THE SEASON AT A GLANCE

HEAD COACH

Bill Belichick

REGULAR-SEASON RECORD

7-9 / 3rd AFC Central

TOP DRAFT CHOICE (Rd.)

Tommy Vardell, RB, Stanford (1)

SCHEDULE/RESULTS

at Indianapolis	L	3-14
Miami	L	23-27
at L.A. Raiders	W	28-16
Denver	L	0-12
Pittsburgh	W	17-9
Green Bay	W	17-6
at New England	W	19-17
at Cincinnati	L	10-30
at Houston	W	24-14
San Diego	L	13-14
at Minnesota	L	13-17
Chicago	W	27-14
Cincinnati	W	37-21
at Detroit	L	14-24
Houston	L	14-17
at Pittsburgh	L	13-23

WEEK 2—Trailing 20-3 with less than 12 minutes remaining, the Browns score 20 straight points before losing to Miami, 27-23, on a 1-yard run by Mark Higgs with seven seconds on the clock. Quarterback Bernie Kosar, playing on what would later be diagnosed as a broken ankle, leads the improbable comeback with a 6-yard, fourth-down touchdown pass to Michael Jackson and a 3-yard TD throw to Mark Bavaro sandwiched around linebacker David Brandon's 32-yard fumble return for a touchdown. The Dolphins start their winning drive at their own 16 with 1:15 remaining.

WEEK 3—Eric Metcalf catches five passes for 177 yards and scores four touchdowns while keying a 28-16 win over the Raiders at Los Angeles. Todd Philcox makes his first NFL start in place of the injured Kosar and throws three touchdown passes. But the story is Metcalf, who becomes the first Cleveland player to score four TDs in a game since Leroy Kelly in 1968.

WEEK 7—The Browns defeat the Patriots, 19-17, on Mike Tomczak's 6-yard pass to tight end Scott Galbraith with 31 seconds left. Matt Stover supplies Cleveland's first nine points with field goals on the first three possessions. The defense does the rest, forcing fumbles on three straight New England

possessions, leading to 10 Cleveland points.

WEEK 11—The Vikings score two touchdowns in the final 10 minutes for a 17-13 victory over the Browns at Minnesota. The Browns blow a 13-0 halftime lead with the winning points coming on a 25-yard interception touchdown by Vikings cornerback Audray McMillian, who makes a diving catch of a pass that bounces off Bavaro's hands. It is the third interception of the game for McMillian.

WEEK 13—Kosar completes a club-record 82.6 percent of his passes (19-of-23) as the Browns defeat the Bengals, 37-21, at Cleveland Stadium. Kosar throws second-half touchdown passes to Metcalf (35 yards) and Jackson (45) as the Browns score three times in 1:35 to take command.

WEEK 15—With a playoff berth still a possibility, the Browns give up 14 points in the final three minutes and lose, 17-14, to Houston. The playoff-bound Oilers erase a 14-3 deficit with scoring drives of 85 and 74 yards. The late collapse overshadows a fine performance by the Browns' defense, which sacks Houston quarterback Cody Carlson six times, intercepts two passes and recovers a fumble.

Pleasant (98) and Michael Dean Perry (92) brought down quarterback Steve Young, and the Browns brought down the 49ers in a Week 2 upset.

1993 HIGHLIGHTS

WEEK 1—Second-year running back "Touchdown Tommy" Vardell scores the first touchdown of his career in the Browns' 27-14 season-opening win over Cincinnati at Cleveland Stadium. Vardell, Cleveland's No. 1 draft pick in 1992, ties the game at 14-14 with a 1-yard run late in the first half as the Browns overcome an early 14-0 deficit. The game is the 217th of Clay Matthews' Browns career, surpassing Lou Groza's club record of 216.

WEEK 3—The Browns go to 3-0 for the first time since 1979 with a 19-16 win over the Raiders at Los Angeles. The Browns score all their points in the fourth quarter while overcoming deficits of 13-0 and 16-3. Vinny Testaverde makes his quarterback debut early in the fourth quarter, replacing an ineffective Bernie Kosar, and leads the team on an 11-play, 53-yard drive that produces a 32-yard field goal by Matt Stover. The winning touchdown comes on Eric Metcalf's 1-yard run with two seconds remaining.

WEEK 5—Miami, playing most of the game without injured quarterback Dan Marino, rallies behind backup Scott Mitchell for a 24-14 victory over the Browns at Cleveland Stadium. Cornerback Najee Mustafaa greets Mitchell with a team-record 97-yard touchdown interception on his first pass, but Mitchell rebounds to throw his first two NFL touchdown passes for the victory.

The shocking release of quarterback Kosar upset Browns fans and opened the door for Testaverde (above). Fans showed up at Cleveland Stadium wearing Cowboys jerseys sporting Kosar's new No. 18.

WEEK 7—Eric Metcalf ties an NFL record with two punt return touchdowns in a 28-23 Browns victory over Pittsburgh. Metcalf joins six other players in the elite two-TD club with an amazing 91-yard return in the second period and a 75-yard game-decider with 2:05 remaining. Metcalf finishes with 237 combined yards, countering a 355-yard passing performance by Pittsburgh quarterback Neil O'Donnell.

WEEK 9—Six days after coach Bill Belichick's controversial release of the popular Kosar, the Browns lose 22-5 at Seattle. Cleveland commits seven turnovers while Kosar is coming off the bench in his Cowboys debut to spark a 20-15 victory over Phoenix.

WEEK 12—The Browns snap a four-game losing streak with a 17-13 victory over New Orleans. The Cleveland defense sacks quarterback Wade Wilson nine times and holds the Saints to 127 total yards. Seven Browns are credited with sacks, with Anthony Pleasant and Rob Burnett getting two apiece.

WEEK 15—Having been eliminated from the AFC playoff picture, the Browns pound the Rams, 42-14, at Anaheim. After falling behind 7-0, the Browns explode for six straight touchdowns—two on Testaverde-to-Keenan McCardell passes. Testaverde completes 21-of-23 passes for an NFL-record .913 completion percentage.

THE SEASON AT A GLANCE

HEAD COACH
Bill Belichick

REGULAR-SEASON RECORD
7-9 / 3rd AFC Central

TOP DRAFT CHOICE (Rd.)
Steve Everitt, C, Michigan (1)

SCHEDULE/RESULTS

Cincinnati	W	27-14
San Francisco	W	23-13
at L.A. Raiders	W	19-16
at Indianapolis	L	10-23
Miami	L	14-24
at Cincinnati	W	28-17
Pittsburgh	W	28-23
Denver	L	14-29
at Seattle	L	5-22
Houston	L	20-27
at Atlanta	L	14-17
New Orleans	W	17-13
at Houston	L	17-19
New England	L	17-20
at L.A. Rams	W	42-14
at Pittsburgh	L	9-16

Three key contributors for the Browns were Turner (top photo), who tied for the NFL lead in interceptions with nine, left offensive tackle Tony Jones (above), who anchored a line that gave up an NFL-low 14 sacks, and linebacker Pepper Johnson (right), who led the team with a career-high 207 tackles.

WEEK 1—Randy Baldwin (85 yards with a kickoff) and Eric Metcalf (92 yards with a punt) return kicks for touchdowns in a 28-20 win at Cincinnati. The returns come less than three minutes apart as the Browns build a 25-7 lead. In the first quarter, Tom Tupa becomes the first NFL player to score a two-point conversion.

WEEK 3—The Browns register their first home shutout in 11 years with a 32-0 win over the Cardinals. The score is 3-0 at the half before the Browns score 29 straight points, the final two touchdowns coming on an 81-yard Testaverde pass to Derrick Alexander and a 93-yard interception return by Eric Turner.

WEEK 7—The Browns are 6-1 for the first time since 1963 following their fifth straight win, 37-13 over the Bengals at Cleveland Stadium. Special teams play a big role, as Travis Hill recovers a blocked punt in the end zone for a touchdown, Metcalf returns a punt 73 yards for a score and Bennie Thompson recovers a fumbled punt, leading to a Matt Stover field goal.

WEEK 14—The Browns win a thriller in Dallas, 19-14, as Turner makes contact with Cowboys tight end Jay Novacek just short of the goal line on the final play to preserve the victory. Turner's play caps a solid performance by the Browns' defense, which forces four turnovers. Stover kicks four field goals to extend his streak for consecutive field goals to 20 as the Browns clinch their first playoff berth in five years.

THE SEASON AT A GLANCE

HEAD COACH
Bill Belichick

REGULAR-SEASON RECORD
11-5 / 2nd AFC Central

TOP DRAFT CHOICES (Rd.)
Antonio Langham, CB, Alabama (1)

Derrick Alexander, WR, Michigan (1)

SCHEDULE/RESULTS

at Cincinnati	W	28-20
Pittsburgh	L	10-17
Arizona	W	32-0
at Indianapolis	W	21-14
N.Y. Jets	W	27-7
at Houston	W	11-8
Cincinnati	W	37-13
at Denver	L	14-26
New England	W	13-6
at Philadelphia	W	26-7
at Kansas City	L	13-20
Houston	W	34-10
N.Y. Giants	L	13-16
at Dallas	W	19-14
at Pittsburgh	L	7-17
Seattle	W	35-9
AFC Wild Card Game		
New England	W	20-13
AFC Divisional Game		
at Pittsburgh	L	9-29

AFC WILD-CARD GAME: The Browns defeat the Patriots, 20-13, at Cleveland Stadium. The difference is the quarterbacks, as Testaverde outplays Drew Bledsoe, completing just one fewer pass in 20 fewer attempts. At one point in the second half Testaverde, playing in his first NFL postseason game, completes 11 straight passes. The recipient of most of the passes is Michael Jackson, who catches seven for 122 yards, and Alexander, who catches five for 69.

AFC DIVISIONAL GAME: In Pittsburgh, the Steelers beat the Browns for the third time this season, 29-9, in the first postseason meeting between the rivals. Pittsburgh grabs a 17-0 lead and keeps the mistake-prone Browns at bay. Alexander and Earnest Byner each drop two passes on the Browns' first three possessions and Testaverde completes 13-of-31 passes with two interceptions in the Browns' eighth straight road playoff loss.

1995

HIGHLIGHTS

WEEK 2—After losing their season-opener at New England, the Browns bounce back by beating the Buccaneers, 22-6, at Cleveland Stadium. It is the Browns' 200th regular-season home victory since entering the NFL in 1950. Vinny Testaverde completes 17-of-27 passes for 256 yards and two touchdowns, both to Keenan McCardell. The defense tallies seven sacks and two interceptions of quarterback Trent Dilfer.

WEEK 5—The Browns and Bills engage in a seesaw game at Cleveland Stadium that isn't decided until Steve Christie kicks his third field goal, a 33-yarder with five seconds left, to give the Bills a 22-19 win. The game is tied four times and the lead changes hands three times before the game-winning points.

THE SEASON AT A GLANCE

HEAD COACH

Bill Belichick

REGULAR-SEASON RECORD

5-11 / 4th AFC Central

TOP DRAFT CHOICE (Rd.)

Craig Powell, LB, Ohio State (1)

SCHEDULE/RESULTS

at New England	L		14-7
Tampa Bay	W		22-6
at Houston	W		14-7
Kansas City	W		35-17
Buffalo	L		19-22
at Detroit	L		20-38
Jacksonville	L		15-23
at Cincinnati	W	(OT)	29-26
Houston	L		10-37
at Pittsburgh	L		3-20
Green Bay	L		20-31
Pittsburgh	L		17-20
at San Diego	L		13-31
at Minnesota	L		11-27
Cincinnati	W		26-10
at Jacksonville	L		21-24

WEEK 8—Looking to snap a three-game losing streak, the Browns find an agreeable foe in the Bengals, who succumb to Cleveland for the sixth straight time, 29-26, on Matt Stover's career-high fifth field goal—a 28-yarder at 6:30 of overtime. But the Browns don't make it easy on themselves, blowing a 10-point lead with 2:51 left in regulation time. Eric Zeier becomes the first rookie quarterback to throw for more than 300 yards in his first NFL start while winning the game. Zeier, starting for the ineffective Testaverde, helps the Browns roll up 480 yards of offense, the club's highest total in nearly 10 years.

WEEK 9—In Zeier's second start, the Browns commit five turnovers in a 37-10 loss to Houston. Three of the turnovers are Zeier interceptions, one of which is returned 62 yards by Blaine Bishop for the game's final touchdown. The turnovers are so pivotal that the Browns run 80 offensive plays to the Oilers' 50, enjoy a 367 to 277 advantage in total yards and never punt—yet lose by 27 points.

WEEK 10—One week after owner Art Modell announces his intention of moving the Browns to Baltimore by the start of the 1996 season, the Browns play awful in losing a Monday night game at Pittsburgh, 20-3. Clearly affected by the fallout from the Modell announcement, the Browns do little right, totalling 120 yards in offense, converting 1-of-10 third downs and seven first downs—all in the first half. They go three-and-out on five of their six second-half possessions, netting just 10 total yards. It is the Steelers' 23rd victory in 27 games against the Browns at Three Rivers Stadium.

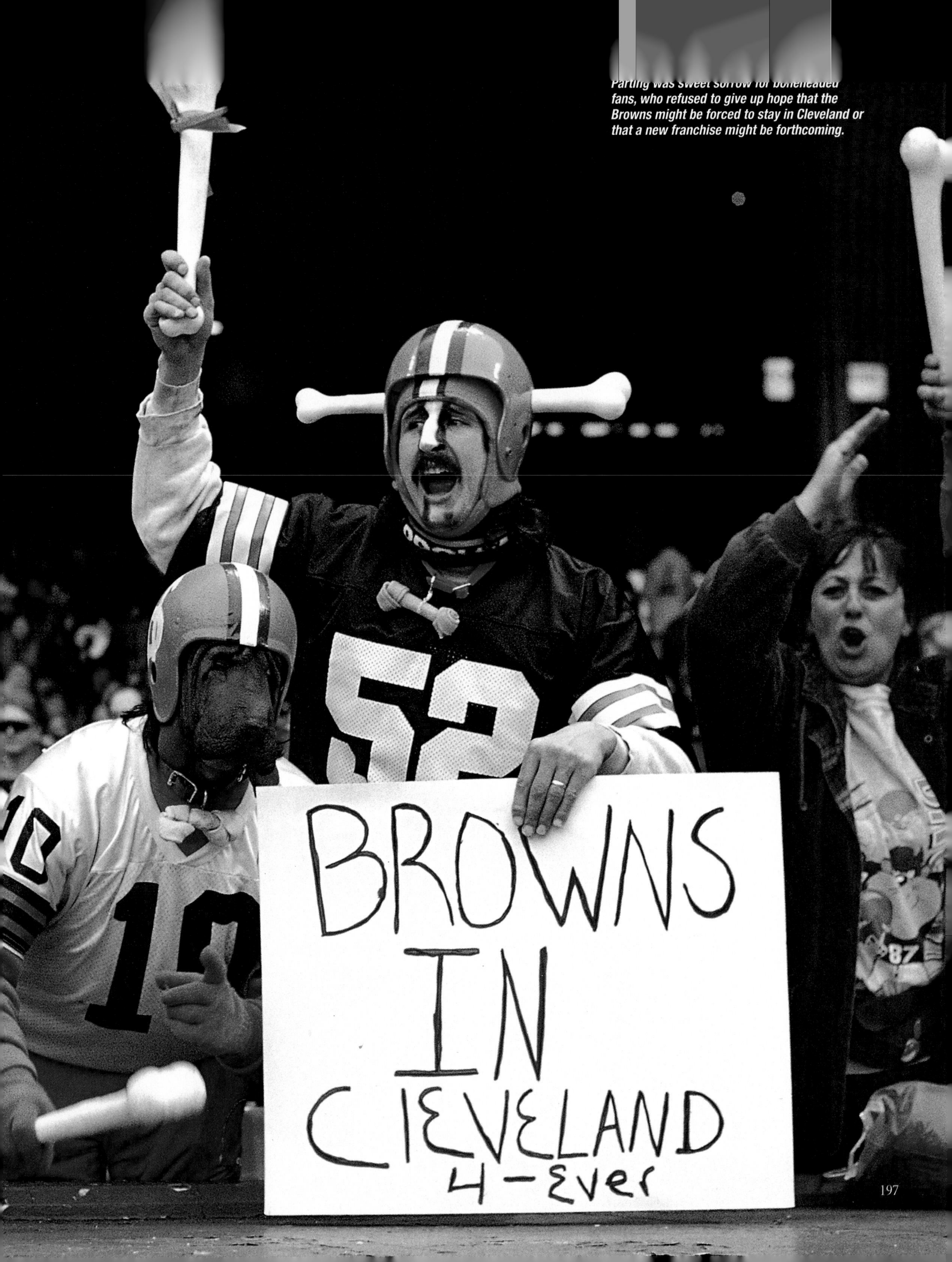

BROWNS IN CLEVELAND 4-Ever

197

"I remember I went down there six hours before the game. I just wanted to be down there as long as I could that day. I don't remember that much about the actual game. But you could just feel it. Once the second half started, the fans started ripping out the bleachers—it was really a strange feeling. You could tell it was over."

— *Center Steve Everitt*

A Surreal Goodbye

Instead of being introduced individually, the Browns were introduced as a group (left photo). Testaverde (above) scrambles in the 26-10 win.

The eerie sounds cascaded through cavernous Municipal Stadium—the rantings of pain and grief being experienced by 55,875 wailing, heart-broken lovers. For most of the afternoon of December 17, 1995, the Fans by the Lake poured out festering emotions as their Browns staged one last public display of reciprocated affection. When the anger had subsided, the barking had ceased, the sobs had died and the last tears had been wiped away, a city celebrated one final victory by mourning a loss.

The victory was over rival Cincinnati—a 26-10 romp that would have inspired ecstasy in years gone by. The loss was to Baltimore—the city that would inherit the 50-year-old Browns franchise and a piece of Cleveland's soul. The final game at the Stadium was about betrayal, goodbyes and disbelief.

"I remember when the press conference came on and they announced they were leaving," recalled former Browns linebacker Clay Matthews, who was a member of the Falcons on that November 6, 1995 day when Art Modell announced he was moving his team to Baltimore. "When that press conference came on, all I thought about was all those folks that, wherever I went, they told me how they would pray, or they would wish, or where they were, or what they were doing when certain games were on. And I was thinking how much more it would hurt them than it would hurt the players. And it

was tough. I really thought about the loss for the people."

The pain and anger from that announcement had snowballed over the confusing final weeks of the 1995 season and loomed like a thick fog when fans began their tailgating routines on a cold Sunday afternoon outside the Stadium. The last game that would ever be played at Cleveland Municipal Stadium opened amid an eerie sensation that it would be like no other experienced by players or fans.

"It was really weird," said center Steve Everitt, who can still recall the defiant atmosphere of that afternoon. "I remember I went down there six hours before the game. I just wanted to be down there as long as I could that day. I don't remember that much about the actual game. But you could just feel it. Once the second half started, the fans started ripping out the bleachers—it was really a strange feeling. You could tell it was over."

The players, who had lost five straight games since the stunning news was delivered by Modell, didn't want it to be over any more than their rabid fans. Motivated to give the fans one

last winning memory, the Browns vaulted to a 17-3 halftime lead behind Vinny Testaverde's two touchdown passes and the running of Earnest Byner, who finished with 121 yards. But the cheers celebrating the Browns' second-half dominance became muffled by the frightful, ugly sounds of scavenger fans pounding bleacher planks, ripping apart rows of chairs and angrily throwing debris and firecrackers into the open end zone.

"I left in the third quarter; I just didn't want to be there," said former offensive tackle Cody Risien, who was one of many former players who showed up for the historic finale. "In a way, people were in kind of a celebratory mood because, hey, it was the last game. That's why I left, because I didn't want to see it at the end. Emotions were running high and it was the end of the Browns as we knew it."

And when the crowd's roaring "5-4-3-2-1" countdown pronounced the official end, the emotional floodgates really opened.

"The game was pretty much over and myself and Tony Jones

were sitting on the sideline, just kind of looking around," Byner recalled. "We were looking at the Dawg Pound and all of a sudden, when the game was over, nobody said anything, we all just went over to the Dawg Pound to say thanks. And that ended up being everybody kind of going around the whole stadium."

The passionate exchange of affection between players and fans that followed might never be matched at the professional level. It became a hugfest, a final emotional bonding that would never be forgotten in Cleveland.

Fans prepare to throw seats they have ripped out (left photo) and embrace Everitt (top). Byner (above) fights for yards in the final home game.

"This city is just like me," offensive tackle Jones said after the game, fighting back tears. "I wasn't drafted. I had to fight for everything. This city is fighting now. I knew it was going to get emotional, and it did."

Emotional might have been an understatement.

"We saw people crying," Byner said. "People didn't want to let you go. They wanted to hold your hand. They'd shake your hand and then grab it with both of their hands, and you almost had to pull them out of the stands to get your hand back. It was a difficult situation."

Everitt says the reality of the moment "still eats me up."

"It was really kind of weird," he said. "Everyone was so pumped up before the game. After the game it blew me away. There were old men crying, all different ages of people—I shook as many hands as I could, we went over and sat and were hugging people. It seemed like five minutes, but I think we were actually out there close to an hour."

Which, in retrospect, seems hardly more than a speck in the half century of unrelenting support given to Browns football.

"It was all kind of a disbelief that such a great thing was coming to an end," recalled former offensive tackle Doug Dieken, who watched the final moments from the perspective of the broadcast booth. "There were a lot of pissed-off people, a lot of people who felt they had been betrayed. There was a lot of anger. It was a combination of everything. Disappointment is not strong enough because the loyalty they had put into the organization went beyond disappointment.

"The thing that got me as I walked out of the stadium was that people in tears would come up to you and thank you for all the good years. I thought, 'I didn't ever buy a ticket. You're the people. I should be thanking you.'"

After the final handshake, the final hug, the final exchange of affection, Everitt was left with one final memory.

"What was really bad was when we walked back across the field to the dugout, where we go into the locker room," he said. "You gotta walk all the way, 120 yards, across the field. That last walk, I think that's when it really sunk in that it was over."

A postgame proclamation bids a fitting farewell to the Browns (above). Defensive tackle Larry Webster (79) and offensive tackle Orlando Brown (77) say goodbye to the fans.

The New Browns

J im Pyne's agent couldn't wait to tell him the good news: The Cleveland Browns were going to make Pyne the first pick in the expansion draft.

"I was pumped," Pyne said. "Then Tony (Agnone), my agent, says, 'Jim, make sure you bring your best suit,' And I'm like, 'Why?' "

Pyne had heard some of the stories about Cleveland and its football fans before the old Browns moved to Baltimore after the 1995 season. But he had no idea the fervor had grown to the point where 4,000 fans would rearrange their Tuesday afternoon so they could jam themselves into Canton Memorial Civic Center to watch the draft on a sunny, unseasonably warm February 9, 1999.

"We gave the tickets away," said Joe Horrigan, vice president of public relations for the Pro Football Hall of Fame. "They were gone in 20 minutes. Before we were done giving them away, guys were in our parking lot scalping them."

Pyne hears the story and laughs.

"I didn't think it was going to be that big of a deal," he said. "But when we got to the (Civic Center), you knew these weren't your typical fans."

Standing backstage behind a curtain—and wearing his best gray suit—Pyne heard his name announced. "It was dark and I went to take a step," Pyne said. "Then I heard the loudest roar I think I ever heard. I almost tripped and went rolling onto the stage. That wouldn't have been too cool for a No. 1 draft pick."

When he got on stage, Pyne was met with a standing ovation.

"The roar surprised us all," said Dwight Clark, the team's vice president and director of football operations. "I'm standing there thinking to myself, 'Man, I barely know who Jim Pyne is.' "

It didn't matter. Jim Pyne could have been Joe Schmo. Not since December 17, 1995—the old Browns' final home game—had Browns fans been introduced to a real, live, active Browns player. It also had been three years to the date that NFL owners had approved a deal whereby Art Modell was allowed to move his team to Baltimore—while leaving the Browns' nickname and colors behind for another team that was promised by 1999. That promise was delivered on March 23, 1998.

First pick Pyne (right photo with Lerner and Policy) was the toast of the expansion draft. Coach Palmer (above) is pointing to the future.

"I didn't think it was going to be that big of a deal. But when we got to the (Civic Center), you knew these weren't your typical fans."

— *Offensive lineman Jim Pyne*

The owner

The winner of the Browns sweepstakes was Al Lerner, the Shaker Heights resident who was awarded the new Browns franchise on September 8, 1998, with a $530 million bid. Here's something you should know about the team's new owner:

"I remember a game in Cincinnati in the early '90s," said Doug Dieken, a former Browns' player who was working as the team's color analyst at the time. "Art, David (Modell) and Al Lerner go into the owner's loge and there's no television. Art and David go crazy and demand that someone bring them a TV. Al Lerner's just sitting there quietly. Finally, he reaches into his pocket and takes out $600, gives it to David and tells him to go buy a television."

There was plenty of reason for Policy (left) and Lerner (right) to smile during the expansion draft, where every selection was greeted with enthusiasm by a capacity audience (top photo).

Dieken laughs because he knows Lerner's pockets go much deeper than 600 bucks. When the Browns needed someone to head security, Lerner hired Lewis Merletti, director of the U.S. Secret Service. When the new Cleveland stadium scoreboard wasn't big enough, Lerner paid for a bigger one. When someone asked about the millions of dollars he could make off the naming rights of the stadium, Lerner said he preferred Cleveland Browns Stadium.

"We're going to see what first class really is," Dieken said. "The days of flying coach are over. Al Lerner will be a great owner."

Lerner, who is chairman and chief executive officer of MBNA Corp., the second-largest credit card issuer in the United States, also was credited by Cleveland Mayor Mike White and NFL commissioner Paul Tagliabue with organizing the corporate community support that was critical to getting a team placed back in Cleveland.

"Al Lerner has the wherewithal to support the team without it having any impact whatsoever on his personal or other business life," said Carmen Policy, the Browns' president and chief executive officer. "He is the ultimate owner, and not only because of his money. He also cares about the community, he's a very prideful, smart and wise man, he cares about the team.

"And he understands that autonomy is absolutely necessary relative to the people who are responsible for running this franchise on a day-to-day basis. He almost to a fault tries to give us the space we need. I can't imagine a better owner than that. Then, when you put it all together, you add one last ingredient to the mixture: He's a very good man. Yes, he can have a tough side, but he does not possess a dark side."

Lerner laughs when people express shock over his "hands-off" approach.

"I did not get qualified by osmosis when the NFL took my money," he said. "I did not acquire any intelligence or experience or knowledge that minute. I feel we are in the hands of people who really know what they're doing, and that doesn't include me.

"I'm hands-on where I know something. That's why I'm hands-off here. I'm hands-off when I go to the Cleveland Clinic (where he is president and trustee) also. You don't want me messing with you there, either. There is just a whole lot I don't know."

Lerner resisted several opportunities to join the ownership race until a chance meeting with Policy through Dennis Swanson, the head of the NBC affiliate in New York and a mutual friend. Lerner was impressed, an admiration that was not one-sided.

"This is how impressed I was by Al Lerner," Policy said. "The first time I ever laid eyes on the man was on Monday, July 20. I had breakfast, lunch and dinner with him. By Tuesday night, July 21, he and I agreed to be partners."

Policy decided to leave San Francisco because of the uncertainty surrounding the 49ers' front office and a strained relationship with owner Eddie DeBartolo Jr. He announced his resignation July 22 and was on Lerner's jet that night. The next day, he and Lerner were sitting together in front of an overflowing crowd of reporters inside the Wyndham Cleveland Hotel.

The architect

"When Carmen called me, that changed everything," Lerner said. "The offer was irresistible. The thought of creating for Cleveland something the caliber of what they have in San Francisco was too much to ignore. And I was the only way it was going to happen for Carmen."

Policy also was the only way it was going to happen for Lerner.

"If Carmen were to walk out of this room right now, you couldn't give me this team for free," Lerner said that July afternoon. In explaining his support, White called Policy "the Yoda of football."

Clark, the man who would follow Policy from San Francisco to Cleveland on November 30, 1998, put it another way.

"Carmen is the Joe Montana of the business world," Clark said. "Joe could take players around him and make them better than they ever thought they could be. As a manager, Carmen is the same way."

Dieken put it yet another way in late September 1998.

"This team doesn't have a coach or one player yet," he said, "but I think it's closer to the Super Bowl than before the other team left."

Policy was practicing law in his native Youngstown when he joined the 49ers as vice president and general counsel in 1983. He became executive vice president in 1989 and was promoted to president and chief executive officer in 1991. In 1994, he was named NFL Executive of the Year by THE SPORTING NEWS after finding a way to keep the 49ers intact despite the league's new salary cap. The ability to manipulate the cap paid off when the team won its fifth Super Bowl title.

"We had the highest payroll in the league when the salary cap was instituted," Policy said. "The only way to survive was to do some very, very creative things. You definitely pay a price later. As you can see now, it's become almost impossible to keep the 49ers together. But I think we were smart in doing what we did because we won a Super Bowl by doing it."

Policy thinks the Browns won't have a problem with the salary cap because they started from scratch knowing the rules. But just to be sure, Policy hired the league's salary cap expert, Lal Heneghan. Before joining the Browns as assistant director of football operations and general counsel, Heneghan was director of labor relations for the NFL. One of his duties was supervising and interpreting the salary cap.

Policy also helped the Browns get off to a fast start by convincing the league to let Clark leave the 49ers early rather than wait until after the season.

"If we do this thing right, we have some advantages available to us that the 49ers didn't have," Policy said. "If we are able to transport all of the good things that we were part of with the 49ers and bring it all to Cleveland with the fan base and the new stadium being sold out and ownership as committed and having the wherewithal that it has, we might be able to do something very significant here."

Policy said it's unreasonable to think the Browns can win more than five to seven games in 1999. But he expects a challenge for the

The new Browns are being constructed in the image of Policy (above), who will watch them play in new Cleveland Browns Stadium (top photo).

playoffs in 2000. "I don't know when we could see ourselves in the Super Bowl," he said. "But if we're not there in five years, I will personally feel I haven't accomplished a goal that I set for myself before I even knew who the players and coaches and the personnel people would be for this new team."

The receiver

Clark isn't afraid to mention the Super Bowl either. Asked if he could envision a time when the Browns will struggle with the salary cap like the 49ers did after the 1998 season, Clark said, "Not until after the third or fourth Super Bowl."

Clark spent 19 years with the 49ers, nine as a wide receiver and the last 10 in the front office. On the field, he went from being a 10th-round draft choice from Clemson in 1979 to the guy who made "The Catch" to beat the Cowboys in the 1981 NFC Championship Game and vault the 49ers to their first Super Bowl. When he retired, Clark was the team's all-time leading receiver.

"Then Dwight took that work ethic on the field and applied it to the front office," Policy said. "He works harder than anyone I know. He dealt with the pressure of leaving San Francisco, relocating and then was able to get everyone in his department working together as though they had been doing it for years.

"There were people in the football operations department who were hired by the league who were paranoid and didn't know what to do or how to do it. Dwight got them all to buy into our way of doing things without making any promises. He got them to buy into it on the basis of self pride, and then they started working as though they all had four-year contracts with us."

On January 21, 1999, Clark said he was "absolutely blown away" by Chris Palmer, the Jaguars' offensive coordinator. Nineteen days later, Palmer was the new Browns' head coach and he helped Clark pick 37 players in the expansion draft. The idea was to grab them young and cheap, saving more money for free agency.

"Our philosophy is to find players we think will still be here in three years," Clark said when asked why the team didn't select some of the older, well-known stars in the draft. "We are building for the future. We aren't trying to impress anybody in 1999."

In three hours, Clark picked 18 offensive players, 19 on defense. Nine were offensive linemen, including four of the top seven picks. The average age was 25.6, with one player over 30; and the average salary cap number was $500,000, with two players at more than $1 million. The final bill was $18 million, leaving the Browns $39 million to spend on free agency and the college draft.

Clark's three-year plan is developing much faster than anticipated, thanks in large part to the 49ers, his old team.

Clark was able to spin three more starters off of the expansion draft. The Bills traded middle linebacker Chris Spielman and the 49ers traded defensive end Roy Barker and tight end Irv Smith to the Browns as compensation for taking some unwanted salaries off of their cap. The last pick in the expansion draft was 49ers cornerback Antonio Langham, the first former Brown to be brought home. Langham had a huge cap figure ($3 million) and was coming off of a poor season. Clark got him to agree to restructure his contract, so Clark got Barker, Smith and Langham as potential starters at a much lower salary.

"When I was with the 49ers, it used to upset me when a guy left

and he'd come back and raid the team," Clark said. "When I left, I told myself I wasn't going to do that." But the 49ers found themselves $28 million over the salary cap. And there was Clark waiting to benefit from the problem he and Policy created so the 49ers could remain among the elite teams.

"It's ironic, isn't it?" said Bill Walsh, the 49ers' general manager. Maybe it's an indication that all of Cleveland's misfortunes—The Drive, The Fumble, Red Right 88—went to Baltimore with the old Browns.

"At first, all I wanted to do was sign Terry Kirby and Marquez Pope as free agents," Clark said. "Then the 49ers started making offers I couldn't refuse. Before you knew it, I had six or seven starters from there, and all it cost was a fourth- and a fifth-round draft pick."

At one point, the Browns had 13 former 49ers on the roster. Seven—Langham, Kirby, Pope, Smith, Barker, Marc Edwards and Ty Detmer—were projected starters entering training camp. By the beginning of May, Clark had solidified the starting lineup with 16 experienced veterans via free agency or trade.

The offensive line was the club's first priority and the Browns signed three of the top free-agent linemen (tackles Orlando Brown and Lomas Brown and center Dave Wohlabaugh). Three defensive starters were brought in from the Vikings—cornerback Corey Fuller, end Derrick Alexander and tackle Jerry Ball. Suddenly, the locker room didn't look like an expansion team.

"Nothing here reminds me of an expansion team," Lomas Brown said. "To me, it looks like a team that just had a down year and is reloading with some new players."

Clark still finds it hard to believe an expansion team can make the playoffs in its first year. But his acquisition of Ball, 34, in late April indicated he was starting to waver a little. "He goes a little

Langham (above), a first-round 1994 draft pick of the original Browns, was acquired from the 49ers, Spielman (far right) was picked up from Buffalo and free agent Lomas Brown was signed to anchor the offensive line. All were expected to be 1999 starters.

against our philosophy of wanting players we think will still be here in three years," Clark said. "But the guys in this locker room expect to win right away. Chris Spielman kept asking me for a big body to put in front of him. I won't do anything stupid to jeopardize our future, but I am trying to give these guys as much ammunition to fight with this year as I can.

"How far we go in 1999 depends on the desire of the players. We're a longshot to make the playoffs. And, yeah, I would be surprised if we did make it. But if you look at the type of character we have on the team, it wouldn't be out of the question."

As for the long term, Clark is much more optimistic.

"What we hope to do here," he said, "is take the very best of the 49ers and in conjunction with new ideas and Mr. Lerner and make this an even better organization."

The coach

It was a subtle sentence, spoken in front of a crowded room of reporters, bright lights and several former Browns players. Chris Palmer said his favorite book is *P.B.: The Paul Brown Story*.

"I thought that was interesting, and a real good sign," said Hall of Famer Dante Lavelli, an original Brown who attended the January 21 press conference.

"What Paul Brown said in the '50s and '60s holds true today," Palmer said months later. "He believed speed at every position is a

tremendous factor in the game. His thoughts on execution, blocking and tackling were obviously right on. And his preparation, his organization, everything are examples you want to follow."

Palmer doesn't look like a football coach. That's the first thing Policy said about him. "But the guy is so solid, so sincere, so up front," Policy said. "We were convinced the players would love him, not from a buddy standpoint, but from the way he shows them respect, honesty. Players detest insincerity or people who engage in mind games."

Palmer was always on the Browns' short list of coaching candidates, but the first meeting did not take place immediately. It was worth the wait.

"Chris was one of the first guys we wanted to talk to," Clark said. "But we had to put him on the back burner because Jacksonville didn't want us speaking to him until after the playoffs. "

Palmer finally got his interview and quickly displayed the passion Policy and Clark were hoping to find.

"We didn't want to decide that day," Clark said. "We wanted to wait a couple of days and maybe call him back. But he blew all of us away."

The interview took place in Lerner's Beachwood MBNA office. Palmer was grilled by Clark, Policy and even Lerner. "Al was zinging him with tough, tough questions about his professional life, his personal life and tough philosophical questions," Policy said. "And Chris just sat there and dealt with every one of them. He's unflappable. He'd make a great witness on the stand under even the most difficult cross-examination."

The group took a break and Policy and Lerner called Bill Parcells, Palmer's head coach when he was in New England, Patriots owner Robert Kraft and Jacksonville owner Wayne Weaver. All gave Palmer glowing recommendations. Unsolicited recommendations already

Couch opened the 1999 season as No. 2, but he was No. 1 in the hearts of delighted Browns fans. The team's hopes for a quick rise to prosperity are tied to his powerful right arm and the coaching of Palmer (left page).

Palmer may look like a gentle college professor, but players have found him tough and strict. On March 23, the start of the team's offseason conditioning program, 15-year veteran Lomas Brown leaned against a wall and called it the hardest first-day workout he had ever experienced. When right guard Ben Cavil met Palmer after the expansion draft, the coach looked at his 356-pound body and told him, "There's only going to be one fat guy in Cleveland—me." Cavil was down to 319 by May.

"If you work hard and stay in shape, coach Palmer is your best friend," Fuller said. "You can't ask for anything more than that."

Palmer said he hasn't had time to realize he's standing in the same shoes Paul Brown stood in when he assembled the original Browns in 1946.

"Some day it'll hit me," he said. "But right now, it's such a great challenge that takes a lot of time. It's funny. A week before I got the job, I thought I was a long shot. I wasn't expecting to get the job. But I knew deep down in my heart that I was the perfect man for this job."

The rookie

If Palmer becomes a success in Cleveland, chances are good quarterback Tim Couch will be by his side. Couch (6-5, 227) left Kentucky a year early because he wanted to play in Cleveland as the No. 1 pick in the college draft. He got his wish just hours before the draft when he agreed to a seven-year contract.

"We would have traded the pick if Tim hadn't agreed to a contract before the draft," Policy said. "The first pick had to be totally committed to the Browns. Obviously, he is going to maintain a significant position from a leadership standpoint. There could be no holdback coming into this excursion that we're all on."

With his contract signed, Couch was able to have 30 practices and several more hours of instruction from Palmer before training camp even started.

"If he hadn't been signed early," Policy said, "it could have set us back a number of years."

Couch came from a laid-back Kentucky offense that didn't even use a playbook to Palmer's complex offense that is a combination of nine different pro concepts and has a playbook that's more than 300 pages and three inches thick.

"I needed to be in here from Day 1," said Couch, who passed for 8,835 yards and 74 touchdowns at Kentucky. He completed 72 percent of his passes in 1998 and he finished with 26 school records, 14 SEC marks and four NCAA records. Yet his selection came down to a workout in Lexington six days before the draft. That's when Palmer became convinced Couch was the franchise

had been flooding in from about two dozen players who had worked with Palmer, including Drew Bledsoe, Doug Flutie and Mark Brunell.

"Palmer just seemed to have it all, plus he loved the idea of being head coach of the Cleveland Browns," Policy said. "We felt coming on board at this point, a coach had to be more than just ambitious. He had to believe this is something special. He had to know he was embarking on a journey that is historic in nature."

Palmer, who signed for five years, brought 27 years of coaching experience to his new job—the last two as Jacksonville's offensive coordinator. He was a head coach at Boston University and the University of New Haven, and also coached as an assistant in the USFL, the CFL and nine years in the NFL with the Oilers, Patriots and Jaguars. A noted quarterback guru, Palmer not only has helped develop Bledsoe, a No. 1 overall draft pick, but he also helped the Jaguars to back-to-back playoff appearances despite having to use five quarterbacks because of injuries.

Couch (right photo) understands the fan pressure that is part of the Cleveland equation, but he says he wouldn't have it any other way.

quarterback he wanted.

"His field vision is incredible, his arm is strong enough and anybody who completes 72 percent of his passes has a chance to be someone special," Palmer said. "I think we found the right guy."

The fans

April 17, the day Couch was drafted, there were 5,000 Browns fans inside the Great Lakes Science Center right outside the new stadium. There would have been four or five times as many had the Browns been able to find a place big enough to hold their fan draft party.

"There probably is more pressure playing here because of the fans and the history of the team," Couch said. "But as a player, you wouldn't want it any other way." For the first time in Browns' history, the stadium sold out before the season started. And many more fans are paying $20 a year to keep their names on a waiting list.

"We sold 53,000 PSLs and could have sold out the entire stadium just on PSLs," Policy said. "We have a waiting list for tickets. We have a waiting list for our luxury suites, even though we added 35 of them to make the total number of suites 148. It really is unbelievable."

When the new team's first preseason game (the Hall of Fame game vs. the Cowboys) was scheduled for August 9 in Canton, the Hall of Fame could make only 500 end zone tickets and 500 standing-room-only tickets available to the general public. When the Hall announced two drawings would be held for the tickets, it received more than 5,000 applications from all 50 states and Canada.

"The whole situation is very moving," Policy said. "Al Lerner and I were in Columbus as keynote speakers for a charity luncheon. While we were down there, we were invited to visit the Ohio Senate and the House. We're standing on the floor of the House and everybody gives us a standing ovation. And then we hear legislators barking at the top of their voices."

Though hard to believe, the mood of Browns' fans is as high today as it was low the morning of November 5, 1995, when word of the Baltimore move leaked out before a home game against the Oilers.

"I could never forgive (Art Modell) personally for the decision he made," said John "Big Dawg" Thompson, the team's now-infamous No. 1 fan, during an on-line chat session at the college draft. "But since our fight became so positive and our true colors are now showing, I wish he would have moved 10 years ago."

THEY WORE THE COLORS

ALL-TIME CLEVELAND BROWNS ROSTER, 1946-1995

Player, (position) college	Years
Abrams, Bobby (LB) Michigan	92
Adamle, Tony (FB) Ohio State	47-51, 54
Adams, Chet (T) Ohio	46-48
Adams, Pete (G) USC	74, 76
Adams, Stefon (DB) Auburn	90
Adams, Vashone (DB) Eastern Michigan	95
Adams, Willis (WR) Houston	79-85
Aeilts, Rick (TE) S.E. Mississippi St.	##89
Agase, Alex (G) Illinois	48-51
Akins, Al (RB) Washington State	46
Aldridge, Allen (DE) Prairie View	74
Alexander, Derrick (WR) Michigan	94-95
Allen, Ermal (QB) Kentucky	47
Allen, Greg (RB) Florida State	85
Alzado, Lyle (DE) Yankton	79-81
Ambrose, Dick (LB) Virginia	75-83
Amstutz, Joe (C) Indiana	57
Anderson, Herbie (DB) Texas A&I	##92
Anderson, Preston (DB) Rice	74
Anderson, Stuart (LB) Virginia	84
Andrews, Billy (LB) S.E. Louisiana	67-74
Arvie, Herman (T) Grambling	93-95
Askin, John (OG) Notre Dame	*87
Athis, Pete (DB) Tennessee	75
Atkins, Doug (DE) Tennessee	53-54
Baab, Mike (C) Texas	82-87, 90-91
Babich, Bob (LB) Miami (Ohio)	73-78
Bahr, Matt (K) Penn State	81-89
Baker, Al (DE) Colorado State	87, 89-90
Baker, Sam (P-K) Oregon State	60-61
Baker, Tony (RB) East Carolina	86,88
Baldwin, Keith (DE) Texas A&M	82-85
Baldwin, Randy (RB) Mississippi	##91-94
Ball, Jerry (DT) SMU	93
Bandison, Romeo (DL) Oregon	#94
Banker, Ted (G) S.E. Mississippi St.	89
Banks, Carl (LB) Michigan State	94-95
Banks, Chip (LB) USC	82-86
Banks, Fred (WR) Liberty	85
Banks, Robert (DE) Notre Dame	89-90
Barisich, Carl (DT) Princeton	73-75
Barnes, Erich (DB) Purdue	65-71
Barnett, Harlon (S) Michigan State	90-92
Barnett, Vincent (S) Arkansas State	*87
Barney, Eppie (WR) Iowa State	67-68

Bassett, Maurice (RB) Langston	54-56
Bates, Michael (WR-KR) Arizona	95
Battle, Jim (DE) Southern University	66
Baugh, Tom (C) Southern Illinois	89
Bavaro, Mark (TE) Notre Dame	92
Beach, Walter (DB) Central Michigan	63-66
Beamon, Autry (DB) E. Texas State	80-81
Beauford, Clayton (WR) Auburn	*87
Bedosky, Mike (OL) Missouri	##94
Belk, Rocky (WR) Miami (Fla.)	83
Bell, Terry (WR) Indiana State	*87
Benz, Larry (DB) Northwestern	63-65
Berry, Latin (DB) Oregon	91-92
Best, Greg (S) Kansas State	84
Bettridge, Ed (LB) Bowling Green	64
Beutler, Tom (LB) Toledo	70
Biedermann, Leo (T) California	78
Bishop, Harold (TE) LSU	95
Black, James (RB) Akron	84
Blandin, Ernie (T) Tulane	46-47
Blaylock, Anthony (DB) Winston-Salem	88-91
Bloch, Ray (T) Ohio	#81
Boedeker, Bill (DB) No College	47-49
Bolden, Leroy (RB) Michigan State	58-59
Bolden, Rickey (T) SMU	84-89
Bolton, Ron (DB) Norfolk State	76-82
Bolzan, Scott (T) No. Illinois	#85
Booth, Issac (DB) California	94-95
Borton, John (QB) Ohio State	57
Bosley, Keith (OT) Eastern Kentucky	*87
Bostic, Keith (DB) Michigan	90
Bradley, Harold (G) Iowa	54-56
Bradley, Henry (DT) Alcorn State	79-82
Brady, Donny (DB) Wisconsin	95
Braggs, Stephen (DB) Texas	87-91
Brandon, David (LB) Memphis State	91-93
Brannon, Robert (DE) Ark.-Fayetteville	*87
Braziel, Larry (CB) USC	82-85
Brennan, Brian (WR) Boston College	84-91
Brewer, Johnny (TE-LB) Mississippi	61-67
Brewster, Darrell (WR) Purdue	52-58
Briggs, Bob (DE) Heidelberg	71-73
Briggs, Greg (S) Texas Southern	##93
Brockman, Lonnie (LB) West Virginia	##91
Brooks, Clifford (DB) Tennessee State	72-74
Brooks, James (RB) Auburn	92
Brown, Dean (DB) Fort Valley State	69

Retired numbers

14	Otto Graham
32	Jim Brown
45	Ernie Davis
46	Don Fleming
76	Lou Groza

Brown, Eddie (DB) Tennessee	74-75
Brown, Jerome (DL) Mississippi State	##93
Brown, Jim (RB) Syracuse	57-65
Brown, John (T) Syracuse	62-66
Brown, John III (WR) Houston	##92
Brown, Ken (RB) No College	70-75
Brown, Orlando (T) South Carolina St.	94-95
Brown, Preston (KR) Vanderbilt	84
Brown, Richard (LB) San Diego State	91-92
Brown, Stan (WR) Purdue	71
Brown, Terry (DB) Oklahoma State	76
Brown, Thomas (DE) Baylor	81, 83
Buben, Mark (DT) Tufts	82
Buchanan, Charles (DE) Tennessee State	88
Buczkowski, Bob (DL) Pittsburgh	90
Buddenberg, John (OL) Akron	##89
Buehler, George (G) Stanford	78-79
Bumgardner, Rex (RB) West Virginia	50-52
Bundra, Mike (DT) USC	64
Burnett, Rob (DE) Syracuse	90-95
Burrell, Clinton (DB) LSU	79-84
Burton, Leonard (OL) South Carolina	91
Butler, Dave (LB) Notre Dame	*87
Butler, Ray (WR) USC	#89
Byner, Earnest (RB) East Carolina	84-88, 94-95
Caldwell, Mike (LB) Middle Tenn. St.	93-95
Caleb, Jamie (RB) Grambling	60, 65
Camp, Reggie (DE) California	83-87
Campbell, Milt (RB) Indiana	57
Capers, James (LB) Central Michigan	*87
Carollo, Joe (T) Notre Dame	72-73
Carpenter, Ken (RB) Oregon State	50-53
Carpenter, Lew (RB) Arkansas	57-58
Carpenter, Preston (RB) Arkansas	56-59
Carraway, Stanley (WR) West Texas State	87
Carreker, Vince (DB) Cincinnati	*87
Carrier, Mark (WR) Nicholls State	93-94
Carter, Alex (DE) Tennessee State	*87
Carver, Dale (LB) Georgia	83
Cassady, Howard (RB) Ohio State	62

Catlin, Tom (LB) Oklahoma	53-54, 57-58
Caylor, Lowell (DB) Miami (Ohio)	64
Charlton, Clifford (LB) Florida	88-89
Cheroke, George (G) Ohio State	46
Childress, Freddie (T) Arkansas	92
Christensen, Jeff (QB) Eastern Illinois	*87
Clancy, Sam (DE) Pittsburgh	85-88
Clark, Monte (T) USC	63-69
Clarke, Frank (WR) Colorado	57-59
Clarke, Leon (WR) USC	60-62
Clayborn, Raymond (CB) Texas	90-91
Cline, Ollie (RB) Ohio State	48
Cockroft, Don (K-P) Adams State	68-80
Cole, Emerson (RB) Toledo	50-52
Colella, Tom (P-DB) Canisius	46-48
Coleman, Greg (P) Florida A&M	77
Collins, Gary (WR-P) Maryland	62-71
Collins, Larry (RB) Texas A&I	78
Collins, Shawn (WR) Northern Arizona	92
Colo, Don (T) Brown	53-58
Conjar, Larry (RB) Notre Dame	67
Connolly, Ted (G) Tulsa	63
Conover, Frank (DL) Syracuse	91
Contz, Bill (T) Penn State	83-86
Cooks, Johnie (LB) Mississippi State	91
Cooper, Scott (DE) Kearney State	*87
Copeland, Jim (G) Virginia	67-74
Coppage, Alton (DE) Oklahoma	46
Cornell, Bo (RB) Washington	71-72
Costello, Vince (LB) Ohio	57-66
Cotton, Fest (DT) Dayton	72
Cotton, Marcus (LB) USC	90
Cousineau, Tom (LB) Ohio State	82-85
Cowan, Bob (RB) Indiana	47-48
Cowher, Bill (LB) North Carolina St.	80-82
Cox, Arthur (TE) Texas South	91
Cox, Steve (P-K) Arkansas	81-84
Craig, Neal (DB) Fisk	75-76
Craig, Reggie (WR) Arkansas	77
Craven, Bill (DB) Harvard	76
Crawford, Mike (RB) Arizona State	*87
Crawford, Tim (LB) Texas Tech	*87
Crespino, Bob (WR) Mississippi	61-63
Crews, Ron (DE) UNLV	80
Crosby, Cleveland (DE) Arizona	#80
Cureton, Will (QB) East Texas State	75
Cvercko, Andy (G) Northwestern	63
Dahl, Bob (OL) Notre Dame	92-95
Daniell, Jim (C) Ohio State	46
Danielson, Gary (QB) Purdue	85, 87-88
Darden, Thom (DB) Michigan	72-74, 76-81
Dark, Steve (TE) Middle Tennessee St.	##93
Darrow, Barry (T) Montana	74-78

Davis, Ben (DB) Defiance	67-68, 70-73
Davis, Bruce (WR) Baylor	84
Davis, Dick (RB) Nebraska	69
Davis, Gary (RB) Cal Poly-SLO	#81
Davis, Johnny (RB) Alabama	82-86, *87
Davis, Michael (CB) Cincinnati	95
Davis, Oliver (DB) Tennessee State	77-80
Davis, Willie (DE) Grambling	58-59
Dawson, Doug (G) Texas	94
Dawson, Len (QB) Purdue	60-61
DeLamielleure, Joe (G) Michigan St.	80-84
DeLeone, Tom (C) Ohio State	74-84
DeLeone, Tony (P) Kent State	*87
Dellerba, Spiro (RB) Ohio State	47
DeMarco, Bob (C) Dayton	72-74
DeMarie, John (G-T) LSU	67-75
Dennis, Al (G) Grambling	76-77
Dennison, Doug (RB) Kutztown State	79
Denton, Bob (DT) College of Pacific	60
Deschaine, Dick (DE) No College	58
Devries, Jed (OL) Utah State	##94
Devrow, Billy (DB) Southern Mississippi	67
Dewar, Jim (RB) Indiana	47
Dickey, Curtis (RB) Texas A&M	85-86
Dieken, Doug (T) Illinois	71-84
Dimler, Rich (DT) USC	79
Dixon, Gerald (LB) South Carolina	93-94
Dixon, Hanford (CB) Southern Miss.	81-89
Donaldson, Gene (G) Kentucky	53
Douglas, Derrick (RB) Louisiana Tech	91
Dressel, Chris (TE) Stanford	#88
Driver, Stacey (RB) Clemson	*87
Dudley, Brian (S) Bethune-Cookman	*87
Dumont, Jim (LB) Rutgers	84
Dunbar, Jubilee (WR) Southern Univ.	74
Duncan, Brian (RB) SMU	76-77
Duncan, Ron (TE) Wittenberg	67
East, Ron (DE) Montana State	75
Eaton, Chad (DL) Washington State	*95
Echols, Donnie (TE) Oklahoma State	*87
Edwards, Earl (DT) Wichita	76-78
Elkins, Mike (QB) Wake Forest	#91
Ellis, Ken (DB) Southern University	77
Ellis, Ray (S) Ohio State	86-87
Engel, Steve (RB) Colorado	70
Ethridge, Ray (WR) Pasadena City	#95
Evans, Fred (RB) Notre Dame	46
Evans, Johnny (QB-P) N.C. State	78-80
Everett, Major (RB) Miss. College	86, *87
Everitt, Steve (C) Michigan	93-95
Fairchild, Greg (G) Tulsa	78
Farren, Paul (T) Boston University	83-91
Feacher, Ricky (WR) Miss. Valley St.	76-84

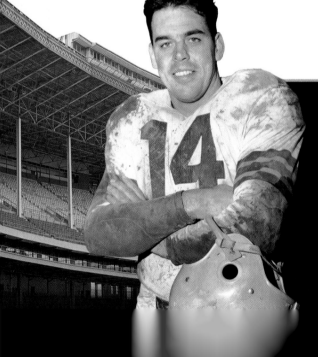

BROWNS ENSHRINED IN THE PRO FOOTBALL HALL OF FAME

OTTO GRAHAM

ENSHRINED, 1965

He was the first player signed by Paul Brown and the trigger man for seven of Cleveland's eight championship teams. It seems only appropriate Graham would be the first Browns player to be enshrined in Canton.

PAUL BROWN

ENSHRINED, 1967

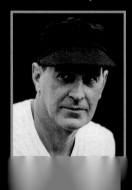

MARION MOTLEY

ENSHRINED, 1968

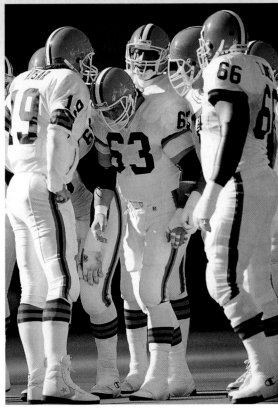

Fekete, Gene (RB) Ohio State — 46
Ferguson, Charley (DE) Tennessee A&I — 61
Ferguson, Vagas (RB) Notre Dame — 83
Ferrell, Kerry (WR) Syracuse — ##93
Fichtner, Ross (DB) Purdue — 60-67
Figaro, Cedric (LB) Notre Dame — 91-92
Fike, Dan (G) Florida — 85-92
Fiss, Galen (LB) Kansas — 56-66
Fleming, Don (DB) Florida — 60-62
Flick, Tom (QB) Washington — 84
Flint, Judson (DB) Memphis State — 80-82
Florence, Anthony (DB) Beth.-Cookman — 91
Foggie, Fred (DB) Minnesota — 92
Fontenot, Herman (RB) LSU — 85-88
Footman, Dan (DE) Florida State — 93-95
Ford, Henry (RB) Pittsburgh — 55
Ford, Len (DE) Michigan — 50-57
Forester, Herschel (G) SMU — 54-57
Fortune, Elliott (DL) Georgia Tech — #95
Francis, Jeff (QB) Tennessee — 90, #92
Franco, Brian (K) Penn State — *87
Franklin, Bobby (DB) Mississippi — 60-66
Franks, Elvis (DE) Morgan State — 80-84
Frederick, Andy (T) New Mexico — 82
Frederick, Mike (DE) Virginia — 95
Freeman, Bob (QB) Auburn — 57-58
Fullwood, Brent (RB) Auburn — 90
Fulton, Dan (WR) Nebraska-Omaha — 81-82
Furman, John (QB) UTEP — 62

Gain, Bob (DT) Kentucky — 52, 54-64
Gainer, Derrick (RB) Florida A&M — ##89, 90
Galbraith, Scott (TE) UCLA — 90-92
Garcia, Jim (DE) Purdue — 65
Garlington, John (LB) LSU — 68-77
Gartner, Chris (K) Indiana — 74
Gash, Thane (S) E. Tennessee State — 88-90
Gatski, Frank (C) Marshall — 46-56
Gaudio, Bob (G) Ohio State — 47-49, 51
Gault, Don (QB) Hofstra — 70
Gautt, Prentice (RB) Oklahoma — 60
George, Tim (WR) Carson-Newman — 74
Gibron, Abe (G) Purdue — 50-56
Gibson, Tom (DE) Northern Arizona — 89-90
Gillom, Horace (P-WR) Nevada — 47-56
Gilmore, Corey (RB) San Diego State — *87
Glass, Bill (DE) Baylor — 62-68
Glass, Chip (TE) Florida State — 69-73
Goad, Tim (DT) North Carolina — 95
Goebel, Brad (QB) Baylor — 92-94
Goins, Robert (SS) Grambling — *87
Golic, Bob (DT) Notre Dame — 82-88
Goode, Don (LB) Kansas — 80-81
Goosby, Tom (LB) Baldwin-Wallace — 63
Gorgal, Ken (DB) Purdue — 50, 53-54
Goss, Don (DT) SMU — 56
Gossett, Jeff (P) East Illinois — 83, 85-87
Graf, Dave (LB) Penn State — 75-79
Graham, Jeff (QB) Long Beach State — ##89
Graham, Otto (QB) Northwestern — 46-55
Grant, Wes (DE) UCLA — 72
Graybill, Mike (OL) Boston University — 89
Grayson, David (LB) Fresno State — *87-90

Green, Boyce (RB) Carson-Newman — 83-85
Green, David (RB) Edinboro State — 82
Green, Ernie (RB) Louisville — 62-68
Green, Ron (WR) North Dakota — 67-68
Green, Van (DB) Shaw — 73-76
Greenwood, Don (RB) Illinois — 46-47
Greer, Terry (WR) Alabama State — 86
Gregory, Jack (DE) Delta State — 67-71, 79
Griffin, Don (CB) Middle Tenn. State — 94
Grigg, Forrest (DT) Tulsa — 48-51
Griggs, Anthony (LB) Ohio State — 86-88
Gross, Al (S) Arizona — 83-87
Groves, George (G) Marquette — 46
Groza, Lou (T-K) Ohio State — 46-59, 61-67
Gruber, Bob (OT) Pittsburgh — 86
Guilbeau, Rusty (LB) McNeese State — *87

Hairston, Carl (DE) Md.-E. Shore — 84-89
Hairston, Stacey (DB) Ohio Northern — 93-94
Haley, Darryl (OL) Utah — *87-88
Hall, Charlie (LB) Houston — 71-80
Hall, Dana (S) Washington — 95
Hall, Dino (KR-RB) Glassboro State — 79-83
Haller, Alan (DB) Michigan State — 92

Hannemann, Cliff (LB) Fresno State — *87
Hansen, Brian (P) Sioux Falls — 91-93
Hanulak, Chet (RB) Maryland — 54, 57
Harper, Mark (CB) Alcorn State — 86-90
Harraway, Charley (RB) San Jose St. — 66-68
Harrington, John (DE) Marquette — 46
Harris, Duriel (WR) New Mexico State — 84
Harris, Marshall (DE) TCU — 80-82
Harris, Odie (DB) Sam Houston State — 91-92
Hartley, Frank (TE) Illinois — 94-95
Harvey, Frank (FB) Georgia — ##94
Haynes, Hayward (OL) Florida State — ##91
Hawkins, Ben (WR) Arizona State — 46-68
Helluin, Jerry (DT) Tulane — 52-53
Herring, Hal (LB) Auburn — 50-52
Hickerson, Gene (G) Miss. — 58-60, 62-73
Hilgenberg, Jay (C) Iowa — 92
Hill, Calvin (RB) Yale — 78-81
Hill, Jim (DB) Texas A&I — 75
Hill, Travis (LB) Nebraska — 94-95
Hill, Will (S) Bishop College — 88
Hilliard, Randy (CB) LSU — 90-93
Hoaglin, Fred (C) Pittsburgh — 66-72
Hoard, Leroy (RB) Michigan — 90-95

Hoggard, D.D. (CB) N.C. State — 85-87
Holden, Steve (WR) Arizona State — 73-76
Holland, Jamie (WR) Ohio State — 92
Holloway, Glen (G) North Texas State — 74
Holohan, Pete (TE) Notre Dame — 92
Holt, Harry (TE) Arizona — 83-86
Hooker, Fair (WR) Arizona State — 69-74
Hoover, Houston (G) Jackson State — 93
Hopkins, Thomas (T) Alabama A&M — 83
Horn, Alvin (DB) UNLV — *87
Horn, Don (QB) San Diego State — 73
Horvath, Les (RB) Ohio State — 49
Houston, Jim (DE-LB) Ohio State — 60-72
Houston, Lin (G) Ohio State — 46-53
Howard, Sherman (RB) Nevada — 52-53
Howell, Mike (DB) Grambling — 65-72
Howton, Bill (WR) Rice — 59
Humble, Weldon (LB) Rice — 47-50
Hunt, Bob (RB) Heidelberg — 74
Hunter, Art (C) Notre Dame — 56-59
Hunter, Earnest (RB) S.E. Oklahoma State — 95
Hutchinson, Tom (WR) Kentucky — 63-65
Hutchison, Chuck (G) Ohio State — 73-75
Huther, Bruce (LB) New Hampshire — 81
Hynoski, Henry (RB) Temple — 75

Ilgenfritz, Mark (DE) Vanderbilt — 74
Ingram, Darryl (TE) California — 91
Irons, Gerald (LB) Maryland-E. Shore — 76-79
Isaia, Sale (OL) UCLA — #95
Isbell, Joe Bob (G) Houston — 66

Jackson, Alfred (DB) San Diego State — 91-92
Jackson, Bill (S) North Carolina — 82
Jackson, Enis (CB) Memphis State — *87
Jackson, Michael (WR) Sou. Miss. — 91-95
Jackson, Rich (DE) Southern University — 72
Jackson, Robert E. (G) Duke — 75-85
Jackson, Robert L. (LB) Texas A&M — 78-81
Jacobs, Dave (K) Syracuse — 81
Jacobs, Tim (CB) Delaware — 93-95
Jaeger, Jeff (K) Washington — 87
Jagade, Harry (RB) Indiana — 51-53
James, Lynn (WR) Arizona State — 91
James, Nathaniel (DB) Florida A&M — 68
James, Tommy (DB) Ohio State — 48-55
Jefferson, Ben (T) Maryland — ##89, 90
Jefferson, John (WR) Arizona State — 85
Jenkins, Al (G) Tulsa — 69-70
Johnson, Bill (DL) Michigan State — 92-94
Johnson, Eddie (LB) Louisville — 81-90
Johnson, Lawrence (DB) Wisconsin — 79-84
Johnson, Lee (P) BYU — 87-88
Johnson, Mark (LB) Missouri — 77
Johnson, Mike (LB) Virginia Tech — 86-93
Johnson, Mitch (T) UCLA — 71
Johnson, Pepper (LB) Ohio State — 93-95
Johnson, Ron (RB) Michigan — 69
Johnson, Walter (DT) Cal State-L.A. — 65-76
Joines, Vernon (WR) Maryland — 89-90
Jones, Bobby (WR) No College — 83
Jones, Dave (WR) Kansas State — 69-71
Jones, Dub (WR) Tulane — 48-55

Jones, Edgar (RB) Pittsburgh — 46-49
Jones, Homer (WR) Texas Southern — 70
Jones, James (DL) Northern Iowa — 91-94
Jones, Jock (LB) Virginia Tech — 90-91
Jones, Joe (DE) Tenn. St. — 70-71, 73, 75-78
Jones, Keith (RB) Nebraska — 89
Jones, Kirk (RB) UNLV — *87
Jones, Marlon (DE) Central State — 87-89
Jones, Reginald (CB) Memphis State — #94
Jones, Ricky (CB) Tuskegee — 77-79
Jones, Ricky (WR) Alabama State — ##92
Jones, Selwyn (DB) Colorado State — 93-#94
Jones, Tony (OT) Western Carolina — 88-95
Jordan, Henry (DT) Virginia — 57-58
Jordan, Homer (QB) Clemson — *87
Junkin, Mike (LB) Duke — 87-88

Kafentzis, Mark (S) Hawaii — 82
Kanicki, Jim (DT) Michigan State — 63-69
Kapter, Alex (G) Northwestern — 46-47
Katolin, Mike (C) San Jose State — *87
Kauric, Jerry (K) Kennedy Collegiate — 90
Kellermann, Ernie (DB) Miami (Ohio) — 66-71
Kelley, Chris (TE) Akron — *87
Kelly, Leroy (RB) Morgan State — 64-73
Kemp, Perry (WR) California (Pa.) — *87
Killian, P.J. (LB) Virginia — ##94
Kinard, Billy (DB) Mississippi — 56
Kinchen, Brian (TE) LSU — 91-95
King, Don (T) Kentucky — 54
King, Ed (OL) Auburn — 91-93
King, Joe (DB) Oklahoma State — 91
Kingrea, Rick (LB) Tulane — 71-72
Kirk, Randy (LB) San Diego State — 91
Kissell, John (T) Boston Coll. — 50-52, 54-56
Kmet, Frank (NT) Purdue — ##92
Kolesar, Bob (G) Michigan — 46
Konz, Ken (DB) LSU — 53-59
Kosar, Bernie (QB) Miami (Fla.) — 85-93
Kosikowski, Frank (WR) Notre Dame — 48
Kovaleski, Mike (LB) Notre Dame — *87
Kramer, Kyle (S) Bowling Green — 89
Kreitling, Rich (WR) Illinois — 59-63
Krerowicz, Mark (G) Ohio State — *85
Kuechenberg, Rudy (LB) Purdue — *87

Lahr, Warren (DB) West. Reserve — 48-59
Landry, George (RB) Lamar — *87
Lane, Gary (QB) Missouri — 66-67
Langham, Antonio (CB) Alabama — 94-95
Langhorne, Reggie (WR) Eliz. City St. — 85-91
Lauter, Steve (S) San Diego State — *87
Lavelli, Dante (WR) Ohio State — 46-56
Lee, Barry (OC) Grambling — *87
Lee, Marcus (RB) Syracuse — 94
Lefear, Billy (WR) Henderson State — 72-75
Leigh, Charles (RB) No College — 68-69
Leomiti, Carlson (OL) San Diego State — ##94
LeVeck, Jack (LB) Ohio — 75
Lewis, Cliff (QB) Duke — 46-51
Lewis, Darryl (TE) Texas-Arlington — 84
Lewis, Leo (PR) Missouri — 90
Lewis, Stan (DE) Wayne-Nebraska — 75

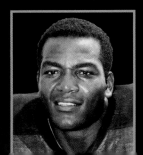

JIM BROWN

ENSHRINED, 1971

LOU GROZA

ENSHRINED, 1974

DANTE LAVELLI

ENSHRINED, 1975

LEN FORD

ENSHRINED, 1976

Lilja, George (G-T) Michigan	84-86
Linden, Errol (T) Houston	61
Lindsey, Dale (LB) Western Kentucky	65-72
Lingenfelter, Bob (T) Nebraska	77
Lingmerth, Goran (K) Northern Arizona	*87
Lloyd, Dave (LB) Georgia	59-61
Logan, Dave (WR) Colorado	76-83
Logan, Ernie (DL) East Carolina	91-93
London, Tom (DB) North Carolina State	78
Long, Mel (LB) Toledo	72-74
Loomis, Ace (RB) LaCrosse St. Teachers (Wis.)	52
Lucci, Mike (LB) Tennessee	62-64
Luck, Terry (QB) Nebraska	77
Luneberg, Chris (OL) West Chester	##93
Lund, Bill (RB) Case Tech	46-47
Lyle, Rick (DE) Missouri	94-95
Lyons, Damion (DB) UCLA	##94
Lyons, Robert (S) Akron	89
Maceau, Mel (C) Marquette	46-48
Macerelli, John (G) St. Vincent	56
Mack, Kevin (RB) Clemson	85-93
Majors, Bobby (DB) Tennessee	72
Malone, Ralph (DE) Georgia Tech	86
Manoa, Tim (FB) Penn State	87-89
Marangi, Gary (QB) Boston College	#77
Marshall, Dave (LB) Eastern Michigan	84
Marshall, Jim (DE) Ohio State	60
Martin, Jim (DT) Notre Dame	50
Mason, Larry (RB) Troy State	*87
Massey, Carlton (DE) Texas	54-56
Matheson, Bob (LB) Duke	67-70
Matthews, Clay (LB) USC	78-93
Mayne, Lewis (RB) Texas	47
Mays, Dave (QB) Texas Southern	76-77
McCardell, Keenan (WR) UNLV	92-95
McClung, Willie (DT) Florida A&M	58-59
McCollum, Andy (OL) Toledo	##94
McCormack, Mike (T) Kansas	54-62
McCusker, Jim (DE) Ohio State	63
McDade, Mike (WR) UNLV	*87
McDonald, Paul (QB) USC	80-85
McDonald, Tommy (WR) Oklahoma	68
McGonnigal, Bruce (TE) Virginia	91
McKay, Bob (T) Texas	70-75
McKenzie, Rich (DE) Penn State	95
McKinnis, Hugh (RB) Arizona State	73-75
McLemore, Tom (TE) Southern Univ.	93-94
McMillan, Erik (S) Missouri	93
McNeil, Clifton (WR) Grambling	64-67
McNeil, Gerald (WR/KR) Baylor	86-89
Memmelaar, Dale (G) Wyoming	64-65
Metcalf, Eric (RB) Texas	89-94
Meylan, Wayne (LB) Nebraska	68-69
Michaels, Walter (LB) Wash. & Lee	52-61
Middleton, Ron (TE) Auburn	89
Miller, Cleo (RB) Arkansas AM&N	75-82
Miller, Mark (QB) Bowling Green	78-79
Miller, Matt (T) Colorado	79-82
Miller, Nick (LB) Arkansas	87
Miller, Willie (WR) Colorado State	75-76
Milstead, Rod (G) Delaware State	#93
Minniear, Randy (RB) Purdue	70

Minnifield, Frank (CB) Louisville	84-92
Mitchell, Alvin (DB) Morgan State	68-69
Mitchell, Bobby (RB) Illinois	58-61
Mitchell, Mack (DE) Houston	75-78
Modzelewski, Dick (DT) Maryland	64-66
Modzelewski, Ed (RB) Maryland	55-59
Mohring, John (LB) C.W. Post	80
Montgomery, Cleotha (KR) Abil.Christian	81
Moog, Aaron (DE) UNLV	*87
Moore, Earnest (CB) Arkansas-Pine Bluff	*87
Moore, Stevon (DB) Mississippi	92-95
Moriarty, Pat (RB) Georgia Tech	79
Morin, Milt (TE) Massachusetts	66-75
Morris, Chris (T) Indiana	72-73
Morris, Joe (RB) Syracuse	91
Morris, Mike (C) N.E. Mississippi St.	90
Morrison, Fred (RB) Ohio State	54-56
Morrison, Reece (RB) S.W. Texas St.	68-72
Morrow, John (C) Michigan	60-66
Morze, Frank (C) Boston College	62-63
Moseley, Mark (K) Stephen Austin	86
Mosselle, Dom (RB) Wisconsin-Superior	50
Mostardo, Richard (DB) Kent State	60
Motley, Marion (RB) Nevada	46-53
Murphy, Fred (WR) Georgia Tech	60
Mustafaa, Najee (CB) Georgia Tech	93
Myslinski, Tom (OL) Tennessee	##92
Nagler, Gern (WR) Santa Clara	60-61
Nave, Stevan (LB) Kansas	*87

Nelsen, Bill (QB) USC	68-72
Neujahr, Quentin (OL) Kansas State	#95
Newman, Patrick (WR) San Diego State	94
Newsome, Ozzie (TE) Alabama	78-90
Newsome, Vince (DB) Washington	91-92
Nicolas, Scott (LB) Miami (Fla.)	82-86
Ninowski, Jim (QB) Mich. St.	58-59, 62-66
Noll, Chuck (G-LB) Dayton	53-59
Nugent, Terry (QB) Colorado State	#84
Nutting, Ed (DT) Georgia Tech	61
O'Brien, Francis (T) Michigan State	59
O'Connell, Tom (QB) Illinois	56-57
O'Connor, Bill (DE) Notre Dame	49
Oden, McDonald (TE) Tennessee St.	80-82
Odom, Clifton (LB) Texas-Arlington	80
Oliphant, Mike (RB) Puget Sound	89-91
Oliver, Bob (DE) Abilene Christian	69
Oristaglio, Bob (DE) Pennsylvania	51
Owens, Kerry (LB) Arkansas	##89
Pagel, Mike (QB) Arizona State	86-90
Palelei, Lonnie (OG) UNLV	#95
Palmer, Darrell (DT) TCU	49-53
Palumbo, Sam (LB) Notre Dame	55-56
Parilli, Vito (QB) Kentucky	56
Parker, Frank (DT) Okla. St.	62-64, 66-67
Parker, Jerry (LB) Central State	*87
Parris, Gary (TE) Florida State	75-78
Parrish, Bernie (DB) Florida	59-66

Parseghian, Ara (RB) Miami (Ohio)	48-49
Patten, Joel (T) Duke	80
Paul, Don (DB) Washington State	54-58
Payton, Eddie (KR) Jackson State	77
Peebles, Danny (WR) N.C. State	91
Pena, Bob (G) Massachusetts	72
Perini, Pete (RB) Ohio State	55
Perry, Michael Dean (DE) Clemson	88-94
Perry, Rod (CB) Colorado	83-84
Peters, Floyd (DT) San Francisco St.	59-62
Peters, Tony (DB) Oklahoma	75-78
Petersen, Ted (T) Eastern Illinois	84
Petitbon, John (DB) Notre Dame	55-56
Phelps, Don (RB) Kentucky	50-51
Philcox, Todd (QB) Syracuse	91-93
Phipps, Mike (QB) Purdue	70-76
Pierce, Calvin (FB) Eastern Illinois	*87
Pierce, Steve (WR) Illinois	*87
Pietrosante, Nick (RB) Notre Dame	66-67
Pike, Chris (DL) Tulsa	89-90
Piskor, Ray (T) Niagara	47
Pitts, Frank (WR) Southern University	71-73
Pitts, John (DB) Arizona State	75
Pizzo, Joe (QB) Mars Hill	*87
Pleasant, Anthony (DE) Tennessee St.	90-95
Plum, Milt (QB) Penn State	57-61
Polley, Tom (LB) UNLV	*87
Poole, Larry (RB) Kent State	75-77
Powell, Craig (LB) Ohio State	95
Powell, Preston (RB) Grambling	61

Powers, Ricky (RB) Michigan	95
Prestel, Jim (T) Idaho	60
Pritchett, Billy (RB) West Texas State	75
Pruitt, Greg (RB) Oklahoma	73-81
Pruitt, Mike (RB) Purdue	76-84
Ptacek, Bob (QB) Michigan	59
Pucci, Ben (DT) No College	48
Pupua, Tau (DT) Weber State	#95
Putnam, Duane (G) College of Pacific	61
Puzzuoli, Dave (NT) Pittsburgh	83-87
Quinlan, Bill (DE) Michigan State	57-58
Quinlan, Voiney (RB) San Diego State	56
Quinton, Dustin (OL) UNLV	##91
Raimey, Dave (DB) Michigan	64
Rakoczy, Gregg (OL) Miami (Fla.)	87-90
Ratterman, George (QB) Notre Dame	52-56
Rechichar, Bert (DB) Tennessee	52
Redden, Barry (RB) Richmond	89-90
Reeves, Ken (OL) Texas A&M	90
Reeves, Walter (TE) Auburn	94
Renfro, Ray (WR) North Texas State	52-63
Reynolds, Billy (RB) Pittsburgh	53-54, 57
Reynolds, Chuck (C) Tulsa	69-70
Rhome, Jerry (QB) Tulsa	69
Rich, Randy (DB) New Mexico	78-79
Richardson, Gloster (WR) Jack. St.	72-74
Riddick, Louis (DB) Pittsburgh	93-95
Rienstra, John (OL) Temple	91-92
Righetti, Joe (DT) Waynesburg	69-70
Risien, Cody (T) Texas A&M	79-83, 85-89
Rison, Andre (WR) Michigan State	95
Roan, Oscar (TE) SMU	75-78
Roane, Morgan (DE) Virginia State	*87
Robbins, Kevin (OT) Michigan St.	##89, 90
Roberts, Walter (WR) San Jose State	64-66
Robinson, Billy (DB) Arizona State	*87
Robinson, DeJuan (DB) No. Arizona	*87
Robinson, Fred (G) Washington	57
Robinson, Mike (DB) Arizona	81-82
Rockins, Chris (S) Oklahoma State	84-87
Rogers, Don (S) UCLA	84-85
Rokisky, John (DE) Duquesne	46
Roman, Nick (DE) Ohio State	72-74
Romaniszyn, Jim (LB) Edinboro State	73-74
Rose, Ken (LB) UNLV	90
Rouson, Lee (RB) Colorado	91
Rowe, Patrick (WR) San Diego State	93
Rowell, Eugene (WR) S. Mississippi	90
Rucker, Reggie (WR) Boston Univ.	75-81
Runager, Max (P) South Carolina	88
Rusinek, Mike (NT) California	*87
Ryan, Frank (QB) Rice	62-68
Rymkus, Lou (T) Notre Dame	46-51
Rypien, Mark (QB) Washington State	94
Saban, Lou (LB) Indiana	46-49
Sabatino, Bill (DT) Colorado	68
Sagapolutele, Pio (DL) Hawaii	91-95
St. Clair, Mike (DE) Grambling	76-79
Sandusky, John (T) Villanova	50-55
Sanford, Lucius (LB) Georgia Tech	87

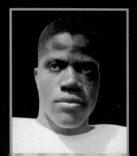

Scales, Charley (RB) Indiana — 62-65
Scarry, Mike (C) Waynesburg — 46-47
Schafrath, Dick (G-T) Ohio State — 59-71
Schoen, Tom (DB) Notre Dame — 70
Schultz, Randy (RB) Iowa St. Tchrs. — 66
Schwenk, Bud (QB) Washington Univ. — 46
Scott, Bo (RB) Ohio State — 69-74
Scott, Clarence (DB) Kansas State — 71-83
Sczurek, Stan (LB) Purdue — 63-65
Seifert, Mike (DE) Wisconsin — 74
Selawski, Gene (T) Purdue — 60
Sensanbaugher, Dean (RB) Ohio State — 48
Sharkey, Ed (G) Nevada — 53
Shavers, Tyrone (WR) Lamar — 91
Sheppard, Henry (G-T) SMU — 76-81
Sheriff, Stan (G) California Poly — 57
Sherk, Jerry (DT) Oklahoma State — 70-81
Shiner, Dick (QB) Maryland — 67
Shoals, Roger (T) Maryland — 63-64
Shofner, Jim (DB) TCU — 58-63
Shorter, Jim (DB) Detroit — 62-63
Shula, Don (DB) John Carroll — 51-52
Shurnas, Marshall (WR) Missouri — 47
Sikich, Mike (G) Northwestern — 71
Sikora, Robert (T) Indiana — #84
Simonetti, Len (DT) Tennessee — 46-48
Simons, Kevin (OT) Tennessee — ##89
Sims, Darryl (DE) Wisconsin — *87-88
Sims, Mickey (DT) South Carolina St. — 77-79
Sipe, Brian (QB) San Diego State — 74-83
Skibinski, Joe (G) Purdue — 52
Slaughter, Webster (WR) San Diego St. — 86-91
Slayden, Steve (QB) Duke — #88
Smith, Bob (LB) Nebraska — 55-56
Smith, Daryle (OT) Tennessee — 89
Smith, Gaylon (RB) Southwestern — 46
Smith, Jim Ray (G) Baylor — 56-62
Smith, John (WR) Tennessee State — 79
Smith, Ken (DB) New Mexico — 73
Smith, Leroy (LB) Iowa — ##92
Smith, Ralph (TE) Mississippi — 65-68
Smith, Rico (WR) Colorado — 92-95
Snidow, Ron (DE) Oregon — 68-72
Sparenberg, Dave (G) W. Ontario — *87
Speedie, Mac (WR) Utah — 46-52
Speer, Del (S) Florida — 93-94
Spencer, Joe (DT) Oklahoma State — 49
Stams, Frank (LB) Notre Dame — 92-94
Stanfield, Harold West Virginia Tech — *87
Staroba, Paul (WR) Michigan — 72
Steinbrunner, Don (DE) Washington St. — 53
Stephens, Larry (DT) Texas — 60-61
Steuber, Bob (RB) Missouri — 46
Stevenson, Ricky (CB) Arizona — 70
Stewart, Andrew (DE) Cincinnati — 89
Stienke, Jim (DB) S.W. Texas State — 73
Stover, Matt (K) LSU — 91-95
Stracka, Tim (TE) Wisconsin — 83-84
Strock, Don (QB) Virginia Tech — 88
Sullivan, Dave (WR) Virginia — 73-74
Sullivan, Gerry (T-C) Illinois — 74-81
Sullivan, Tom (RB) Miami (Fla.) — 78
Summers, Fred (DB) Wake Forest — 69-71

Sumner, Walt (DB) Florida State — 69-74
Sustersic, Ed (RB) Findlay — 49
Sutter, Ed (LB) Northwestern — ##92, 93-95
Swarn, George (RB) Miami (Ohio) — *87
Swilling, Ken (LB) Georgia Tech — ##92

Taffoni, Joe (T) Tennessee-Martin — 67-70
Talley, John (TE) West Virginia — ##89-91
Tamm, Ralph (G) W. Chester State — 90-91
Taseff, Carl (DB) John Carroll — 51
Taylor, Terry (CB) Southern Illinois — 92-93
Teets, Dick (LB) Wisconsin — *87
Teifke, Mike (C) Akron — *87

Tennell, Derek (TE) UCLA — *87-89
Terlep, George (QB) Notre Dame — 48
Terrell, Ray (RB) Mississippi — 46-47
Testaverde, Vinny (QB) Miami (Fla.) — 93-95
Thaxton, Jim (TE) Tennessee State — 74
Thomas, Johnny (CB) Baylor — 95
Thome, Chris (OL) Minnesota — 91-92
Thompson, Bennie (DB) Grambling — 94-95
Thompson, Tommy (C) Wm. & Mary — 49-53
Thornton, John (DL) Cincinnati — 91
Tidmore, Sam (LB) Ohio State — 62-63
Tierney, Leo (C) Georgia Tech — 78
Tillman, Lawyer (WR) Auburn — 89, 92-93

Browns Career Leaders

RUSHING YARDS

Player	Yards	Att.	Avg.	TDs
Jim Brown	12,312	2,359	5.2	106
Leroy Kelly	7,274	1,727	4.2	74
Mike Pruitt	6,540	1,593	4.1	47
Greg Pruitt	5,496	1,158	4.7	25
Kevin Mack	5,123	1,291	4.0	46

RECEIVING

Player	Rec.	Yards	Avg.	TDs
Ozzie Newsome	662	7,980	12.1	47
Gary Collins	331	5,299	16.0	70
Greg Pruitt	323	3,022	9.4	17
Brian Brennan	315	4,148	13.2	19
Reggie Rucker	310	4,953	16.0	32

PASSER RATING (minimum 1,000 attempts)

Player	Rate	Att.	Com.	Yards	TDs	INT
Milt Plum	89.9	1,083	627	8,914	66	39
Bernie Kosar	81.6	3,150	1,853	21,904	116	81
Frank Ryan	81.4	1,755	907	13,361	134	88
Otto Graham*	78.2	1,565	872	13,499	88	94
Brian Sipe	74.8	3,439	1,944	23,713	154	149

SCORING

Player	Pts.	XPM	XPA	FGM	FGA	TDs
Lou Groza*	1,349	641	658	234	405	1
Don Cockroft	1,080	432	457	216	328	0
Jim Brown	756	0	0	0	0	126
Matt Bahr	677	248	252	143	193	0
Leroy Kelly	540	0	0	0	0	90

*Does not include AAFC statistics

Tinsley, Keith (WR) Pittsburgh — *87
Tomczak, Mike (QB) Ohio State — 92
Trocano, Rick (DB-QB) Pittsburgh — 81-83
Trumbull, Rick (OL) Missouri — ##91
Tucker, Travis (TE) So. Conn. St. — 85-87
Tupa, Tom (QB-P) Ohio State — #93, 94-95
Turnbow, Jese (DT) Tennessee — 78
Turner, Eric (S) UCLA — 91-95
Turner, Kevin (LB) Pacific — 82

Ulinski, Ed (G) Marshall — 46-49
Upshaw, Marvin (DE) Trin.-San Ant. — 68-69

Van Dyke, Ralph (T) Southern Illinois — *87
Van Pelt, Brad (LB) Michigan State — 86
Vardell, Tommy (RB) Stanford — 92-95
Verser, David (WR) Kansas — *87

Wagner, Bryan (P) Cal. St. Northridge — 89-90
Waiters, Van (LB) Indiana — 88-91
Walker, Dwight (RB-WR) Nicholls St. — 82-84
Wallace, Calvin (DE) West Virginia Tech — *87
Walls, Everson (DB) Grambling — 92-93
Walters, Dale (P) Rice — *87
Ward, Carl (DB) Michigan — 67-68
Warfield, Paul (WR) Ohio St. — 64-69, 76-77
Washington, Brian (S) Nebraska — 88
Watkins, Tom (RB) Iowa State — 61
Watson, Karlton (QB) Winston-Salem — *87
Watson, Louis (WR) Miss. Valley State — *87
Watson, Remi (WR) Bethune-Cookman — *87
Weathers, Clarence (WR) Delaware St. — 85-88
Weathers, Curtis (TE-LB) Mississippi — 79-85

Webb, Ken (RB) Presbyterian — 63
Weber, Chuck (DE) W. Chester State — 55-56
Webster, Larry (DT) Maryland — 95
White, Bob (RB) Stanford — 55
White, Charles (RB) USC — 80-82, 84
White, James (DE) LSU — #85
White, Lorenzo (RB) Michigan State — 95
Whitlow, Bob (C) Arizona — 68
Whitwell, Mike (WR-S) Texas A&M — 82-83
Wiggin, Paul (DE) Stanford — 57-67
Wilburn, Barry (CB) Mississippi — 92
Wilkerson, Gary (DB) Penn State — ##89
Wilkinson, Jerry (DE) Oregon State — 80
Williams, A.D. (WR) Coll. of Pacific — 60
Williams, Arthur (WR) Abilene Christian — *87
Williams, Clarence (TE/RB) Wash. St. — 93
Williams, Gene (T-G) Iowa State — 93-94
Williams, Larry (G) Notre Dame — 86-88
Williams, Lawrence (KR) Texas Tech — 77
Williams, Ray (WR) Clemson — *87
Williams, Sidney (LB) Southern Univ. — 64-66
Williams, Stacy (DB) East Texas State — *87
Williams, Tony (T) Kansas State — 93
Williams, Wally (C) Florida A&M — 93-95
Willis, Bill (G-LB) Ohio State — 46-53
Wilson, Tom (RB) No College — 62
Wilson, Troy (CB) Notre Dame — *87
Wingle, Blake (G) UCLA — *87
Winslow, George (P) Villanova — 87
Winters, Frank (C) W. Illinois — 87-88
Wise, Mike (DL) California-Davis — 91
Wiska, Jeff (G) Michigan State — 86
Wolfley, Ron (RB) West Virginia — 92-93
Woods, Rob (OL) Arizona — 91
Woolsey, Rolly (DB) Boise State — 77
Wooten, John (G) Colorado — 59-67
Wren, Junior (DB) Missouri — 56-59
Wright, Alvin (NT) Jacksonville State — 92
Wright, Felix (S) Drake — 85-90
Wright, George (DT) Sam Houston — 72
Wright, Keith (WR-KR) Memphis St. — 78-80
Wycinsky, Craig (G) Michigan State — 72

Yanchar, Bill (DT) Purdue — 70
Yonaker, John (DE) Notre Dame — 46-49
Young, George (DE) Georgia — 46-53
Young, Glen (WR) Mississippi — 84-85, 87-88
Youngblood, George (DB) Cal. State-L.A. — 67
Youngelman, Sid (DT) Alabama — 59

Zeier, Eric (QB) Georgia — 95
Zeno, Lance (C) UCLA — 92-93

* Denotes replacement player during 1987 players strike
# On active roster, but did not play in a game
On practice squad, but did not play in a game

BROWNS ENSHRINED IN THE PRO FOOTBALL HALL OF FAME

FRANK GATSKI
ENSHRINED, 1985

LEROY KELLY
ENSHRINED, 1994

OZZIE NEWSOME
ENSHRINED, 1999

It's only fitting that the "Wizard of Oz," the 14th Browns Hall of Famer, was inducted on August 7, two days before the new Browns made their debut with a Hall of Fame game against the Dallas Cowboys at Canton.

In Search of the Browns

August 21, 1998
Tower City Center, Cleveland.

I'm here on a mission to find it.

You know, *it*—the reason the Browns have such loyal and passionate fans whose bond with the franchise has survived for more than a half-century—and three long years without football.

I am standing in the middle of a high school-style pep rally that officially begins the one-year countdown for the Browns' return to the field. Former players and thousands of fans are celebrating, ecstatic that the wait is almost over.

The players are introduced, their names cutting through the air amid deafening cheers. Otto Graham. Bobby Mitchell. Brian Brennan. The great Jim Brown. Barking greets Frank Minnifield and Hanford Dixon. Fans who weren't even alive when some of these players last took the field scream and welcome them like long, lost family. The enthusiasm and emotion is tough to describe.

Mike Baab, a former Browns offensive lineman, offers this theory about *it*.

"Remember, when the Browns first came into the NFL they kicked everybody's butt," he said. "And they didn't win the Super Bowl but they were very, very good for a long time. And it was easy to love a winner. You took to them just like that."

Baab snapped his finger for effect and added, "They were a winner coming in."

Yes, it's easy to love a winner. But It can't be that simple. There has to be more. For every one of Cleveland's eight league championships there has been a disappointment—Red Right 88, The Drive, The Fumble, the uprooting of the original team. For every Jim Brown there has been 10 Mike Junkins or Clifford Charltons.

No Super Bowl, lots of frustration, no team for three years, yet the fans continue to display a loyalty that goes beyond simple words.

Then, suddenly, I see *it*, standing right in front of me.

Derek Moore has been a Browns fan all 41 years of his life. He spent 24 of those years in the Air Force, which took him all over the world, from Germany to Korea. But he is here today with his two sons, Henry and Eugene.

"I retired from the Air Force just so I could be back home with my family and root for the Browns," Moore said.

He says his father took him to his first Browns game—in 1962.

"I was about 6 years old. I don't remember who they were playing, I just remember whenever they announced Frank Ryan or Gary Collins or Jim Brown you could barely hear their names because of the crowd. The stadium was rockin'. You know, at 6 years old, it's just the enthusiasm.

"That's why I brought my kids here, see. They didn't really understand what it was all about, you know, because they are only 8 and 6. But I wanted them to understand what the Browns meant."

What the Browns meant?

I ask myself that question and, having grown up in northeast Ohio as a Browns fan, several memories come to mind.

I recall Sunday afternoons brought to life by the radio voice of Gib Shanley describing the excitement of the Kardiac Kids. And the unforgettable call of Nev Chandler: *"5-4-3-2-1, touchdown Browns!"*

I remember cavernous Cleveland Stadium on cold, grey, winter afternoons. And I remember sharing the sights, sounds and experiences of game day with family and friends.

"What the Browns meant" drives much deeper than the men dressed in the orange and brown—the colors of autumn—playing football.

"It's a very family-oriented situation in Cleveland," said John "Big Dawg" Thompson, the nationally-known symbol of the Dawg Pound and a season-ticket holder since 1978.

"If you ask any fan how did they get turned on to the Browns, they're going to tell you that it was their father. Or their

Former Browns safety Felix Wright awaits his introduction to a lively crowd during a rally at the Tower City Center in downtown Cleveland.

grandfather. That's why I fought so hard to get football back. To keep the tradition alive for my daughters, to give them the same opportunity that we had."

Brad Richert grew up in the 1970s, a period in which the Browns did not win consistently. But he remembers the family attachment that hooked him as a Browns fan for life.

"Cleveland Stadium was one of the first places I really bonded with my Dad," Richert said. "Not just attending games, but watching games on TV with the whole family."

Baab has seen *it*, too.

"The biggest thing is that generations have been crazy about the Browns and they teach the younger generation," he explains.

Fair enough. Maybe *it* is not about just one moment or victory. It's about loyalty. It's about family and friends. It's about the ghosts and echos of the great games and players that built the foundation of this generational tradition, and the commitment of sticking with those players through championships as well as painful defeats.

Perhaps that same commitment will pay off with the expansion Browns. Or should I say resumption Browns? Fans like Moore don't act like the Browns ever left Cleveland, even though they did not cheer at a Browns game for three years.

"I love them, whether we win or lose," Moore said. "And that's what being a fan is all about. Rooting for your team."

Henry and Eugene, I hope you get *it*, too.

"Closing Thoughts" writer Michael Nyerges is a lifelong Browns fan, a Dawg Pound regular and associate art director for THE SPORTING NEWS.

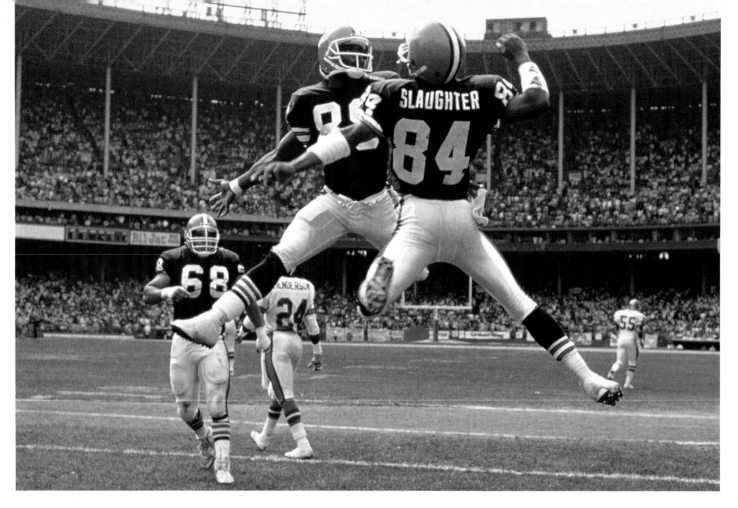

PHOTO CREDITS